TAMPERING WITH
CRICKET

DON OSLEAR
AND
JACK BANNISTER

CollinsWillow
An Imprint of HarperCollins*Publishers*

First published in 1996
by CollinsWillow
an imprint of HarperCollins*Publishers*
London

© Don Oslear and Jack Bannister 1996

1 3 5 7 9 8 6 4 2

A CIP catalogue record for this book is
available from the British Library

ISBN 0 00 218724 8

Printed in Great Britain by The Bath Press

The publishers would like to thank the following for
permission to reproduce photographs for this book:
Allsport, *The Cricketer*, Patrick Eagar, Chris Middleton,
Brendan Monks, Graham Morris, David Munden,
Don Oslear and Bill Smith

Contents

Preface

Cricket has undergone its biggest face-lift in living memory, and all because of an eroding of behavioural standards which has come close to destroying the game.

Since 1992, the controlling mechanism governing the way Test cricket is played has changed beyond recognition. Where two umpires were in sole charge of a match, there are now three, one of whom is from abroad; where the only overseer of that sole authority was the domestic governing board of each country, there is now a match referee appointed by the International Cricket Council; and the ICC itself was re-constituted following the biggest scandal ever to hit cricket in England.

The allegations of ball tampering by the Pakistan team in the fourth Texaco one-day international against England at Lord's on 23 August 1992 lifted the lid off a pressure-cooker scenario. An already controversial and acrimonious tour disintegrated further when, following complaints by England batsman Allan Lamb, umpires John Hampshire and Ken Palmer changed the ball being used by Pakistan during the England innings, an action carried out under Law 42.5 – Unfair Play, which stipulates what is legal and illegal in the maintenance of the state of the ball.

The match referee at Lord's, Deryck Murray, was present when the ball was changed during the lunch interval but refused to provide a precise explanation for why the ball was replaced. Speculation and suspicion followed in what was to become the first international incident involving an official report from umpires about alleged interference with a cricket ball. History was made, culminating in a High Court libel case fifteen months later.

This book delves deeply into the origins of ball tampering and its growing use in the modern game; its development for the purpose of reverse swinging an old ball is traced from clumsy beginnings to the present sophisticated methods which still call for a high degree of skill by the bowlers. Expanding the debate on the sinister diseases afflicting the modern game, we examine the evidence surrounding the allegations of betting and bribery levelled against Pakistan teams in Sharjah in recent years, and against then captain, Salim Malik, by Australians Shane Warne, Tim May and Mark Waugh in September 1994.

In virtually every case of alleged wrong-doing, the authorities took no action, which is why the unsavoury aspects of cricket were allowed to escalate – until two men were prepared to stand up and say 'Enough'.

Sir Colin Cowdrey became the first Chairman of the ICC to be given a four-year term of office, and he was largely responsible for introducing remedial measures, such as the match referee, and an international panel of umpires to implement his brainchild, the Code of Conduct. The other man, without whom such a book could never have been written, is Don Oslear, now compulsorily retired from the English list of first-class umpires after serving fearlessly and without favour from 1975 to 1993. One of the few umpires who never played first-class cricket, Oslear made such an impact in his initial years on the list that he stood in five Test matches between 1980 and 1984. He was the first umpire to report a case of suspected ball tampering when Imran Khan took six for 6 in 23 balls in a hitherto high-scoring match for Sussex against Warwickshire at Edgbaston in 1983. He subsequently reported Surrey bowlers, including the Pakistan player Waqar Younis, on three occasions in 1991 and warned the Test & County Cricket Board of the consequences of inaction.

Oslear was proved right, and his officially documented accounts of the most controversial events of the Pakistan tour of England in 1992 reveal, for the first time, the troubles and problems which faced umpires and match referees in three of the five Tests (at Lord's, Old Trafford and Headingley) before the now infamous one-day international at Lord's, where he was the third umpire.

Oslear broke the mould when he brought to a premature end the libel case between the retired Pakistan bowler, Sarfraz Nawaz and his former Northamptonshire teammate Allan Lamb, by confirming under oath that the ball was changed during the Lord's one-day international under Law 42.5.

Other issues undermining the game, such as dissent, verbal abuse and the deterioration in relationships between the modern player and umpire are detailed by Oslear, who served a period as Chairman of the First-Class Umpires Association. He is scathing about authority, and intolerant of anyone who does not use his powers to punish proven transgressors of cricket's laws and rules. All in all, Oslear filed five reports in eleven years concerning suspected illegal interfering with the ball, but not one report was used by the authorities to punish an individual player. The TCCB asked all umpires to uphold behavioural standards, yet fudged the issue time after time. Oslear believes that every strong umpire suffered for doing his duty, and lists John Holder, Alan Whitehead and himself as examples of men who disappeared off the Test panel once they caused ripples.

The modern game has changed dramatically in the last twenty years. Most of the changes have occurred since Kerry Packer's World Series – and these, together with the reasons for them, are recorded in a book which highlights the weakness of authorities, all of whom appear too easily guided away from trouble by their legal representatives.

One of the most revealing chapters in the book concerns Oslear's report of Worcestershire bowler Kenny Benjamin for allegedly making abusive remarks to him at Northampton in 1993, and the attitude towards that report by the TCCB. Correspondence, some of which is revealed, continued for several weeks and, so Oslear believes, led to his compulsory retirement by the Board on the grounds of age, an action which he vigorously disputes.

Oslear's brushes with authority were many, usually because his official reports were not acted upon. He was frank and outspoken in his views throughout his nineteen-year career in English cricket in which he dodged nothing. Nor does he in this book.

If the TCCB and the ICC do their duty, the public face of cricket should improve under the stronger control of umpires who, at international level at least, are encouraged by the support of match referees. Indeed, in my opinion the long list of ex-players who did duty in the early years has now been reduced to include only firm and strong officials. Interestingly, Deryck Murray, the match referee at the Lord's game in August 1992, is not on that list.

Jack Bannister
Pontypridd, Mid Glamorgan

Tampering with the Ball

CHAPTER 1

The festering sore

On 23 August 1992, the tip of an iceberg emerged from the muddy waters of weak and inept cricket administration by the game's authorities all over the world. Fittingly, with the International Cricket Council's offices at Lord's, the incident that was to blow away a smokescreen created by the authorities during the previous ten years, took place at the most famous cricket ground in the world. It was here that the festering sore of ball tampering finally erupted following years of whispers and mutterings about illegal interference with the ball by the bowling side, specifically with a view to accelerating the natural wear and tear which produces so-called 'reverse swing'.

The key to what is a modern phenomenon in cricket is that one side of the ball must be dry and rough in order to have an effect on its aerodynamics. Depending upon the nature of the pitch and outfield, the natural deterioration can take anything up to 50 or 60 overs before the wear and tear is sufficient for expert practitioners to swing the ball, sometimes by as much as two feet and, for the faster bowler, late in flight.

Whatever the methods used to prime the ball, either naturally or illegally by gouging and interfering with the quarter seam, great skill and natural pace is necessary, and the Pakistan pair of Wasim Akram and Waqar Younis have both. The two fast bowlers had dominated the last four Tests of the five-match summer series which was the most acrimonious in England for many years. Pakistan won that 1992 series 2–1, their victories at Lord's and the Oval owing much to 28 wickets from Wasim and Waqar.

In fact, throughout the series these two bowlers induced several spectacular collapses among England batsmen who had become increasingly suspicious of the methods used to obtain extravagant swing with a worn ball. Wasim and Waqar bowled 334.5 overs for

1019 runs in nine games between them in the series. They took 43 wickets out of 71 taken by Pakistan in the series, with the other 28 coming from 316.2 overs, with the difference in comparative strike rates a startling one. Wasim and Waqar struck every 46.7 deliveries, the rest of the bowlers every 67.7.

Part, but not all, of that difference is explained by the fact that the two fast bowlers were the side's most penetrative weapon and, like all great bowlers of the past, the most effective are those who hunt in pairs. Bowlers such as Fred Trueman and Brian Statham, Harold Larwood and Bill Voce, Dennis Lillee and Jeff Thomson, Bill O'Reilly and Clarrie Grimmett, Sonny Ramadhin and Alf Valentine, Jim Laker and Tony Lock, Ray Lindwall and Keith Miller and any two of Malcolm Marshall, Joel Garner, Andy Roberts, Michael Holding, Curtly Ambrose, Courtney Walsh, Wes Hall and Charlie Griffith.

The complaints from the England camp centred on the nature of the 43 dismissals – 26 were clean bowled or lbw and 14 caught in the arc from wicket-keeper to gully – and the stage in the life of the ball when the wickets started to tumble.

The dismissals first. High-quality fast bowlers rarely claim too many dismissals caught in the covers. The counter-argument to this is that Wasim and Waqar bowl a fuller length than most other bowlers of their pace and therefore the dismissals described above are to be expected. Moreover, in Pakistan's defence, they could justifiably point to the record of their third main pace bowler, Aqib Javed, whose nine wickets in five Tests cost 40.66. The disparity between his performances and those of Wasim and Waqar underline the considerable skill of the latter pair; after all, if it was just a matter of tampering with the ball until prodigious swing resulted, it could be reasoned that any above-average bowler would take wickets.

The series got off to a quiet start at Edgbaston in a drawn match ruined by rain. Wasim did not play in that match, but when he joined the Pakistan team at Lord's for the second Test, the result was an exciting win by two wickets for the tourists, with Wasim and Waqar taking 13 wickets, six of which were clean bowled and three lbw. Most of the damage was done with a worn ball when England seemed to be on course for a good score: in their first innings, the home side went from 197 for three to 255 all out and, in their second innings, from 108 for two to 175 all out.

The next Test at Old Trafford was overshadowed by an astonishing confrontation between umpire Roy Palmer and Pakistan captain

Javed Miandad accompanied by most of his team. This followed a warning given to Aqib Javed for intimidatory bowling. After that drawn match, the ball tampering issue surfaced again before the start of the fourth Test at Headingley, with the England management making comments to the match referee at his pre-match talk.

In the event, England collapsed from 270 for one to 320 all out in their first innings. Waqar took five wickets for 13 runs in 38 deliveries with all the damage done *after* the ball was 85 overs old. Raymond Illingworth, then pundit for BBC television, continually queried the decision not to take the second new ball with England going so well, but the 113 overs of the innings were bowled with the same ball. Waqar's five dismissals were unassisted – three clean bowled and two lbws – and included Alec Stewart, Graeme Hick and Chris Lewis. Before his blitz, his figures were 26.4–3–104–0.

England won that game, but another double collapse at the Oval further disturbed an England dressing room that now made little attempt to hide its views. The fifth Test finished exactly two weeks before the now infamous Texaco game at Lord's, with England losing the match by 10 wickets, and thus the series 2–1.

At the Oval, batting first and going well at 182 for three, England were rushed out for 207 – Wasim being the destroyer this time. His five wickets for 18 in 43 balls, as with Waqar at Headingley, were unassisted with three clean bowled and two lbws. Before this spell of carnage, his figures were 15–3–49–1. The first three batsmen to be swung out were Mark Ramprakash, Chris Lewis and Derek Pringle. The latter still effuses about the ball that bowled him in the first innings as the best he has ever received. 'He bowled to me from over the wicket and when I saw the ball going leg-side, I thought it was just a matter of getting bat on it and playing it anywhere for a single. It was full in length and just before it pitched it started to boomerang from leg to off. It opened me up like a can of beans and took my off stump. I could hardly believe it possible, to do so much from leg to off. When he swings it so much, he switches sides to increase the angle against which the swing occurs, rather like an off spinner going around the wicket on a turning pitch to increase his chances of bowling the batsman or getting him lbw, and he bowled me with one from around the wicket in the second innings. It was only when I got back into the dressing room and saw the replay that I fully understood what had happened. I don't really care how he did it. It was just great skill.'

The collapse in the second innings was just as swift, England going from 153 for five to 174 all out, although a tail of Neil Mallender, Phil Tufnell and Devon Malcolm was never likely to keep the scorers working overtime.

In the five Tests, England scored 2083 runs for the loss of 71 wickets. The itemised collapses, always when the ball was more than halfway through its scheduled minimum life of 85 overs, produced 36 of the 71 wickets while a paltry 221 runs were scored.

Figures can be interpreted in many ways, but this statistic explains the high-running feelings in the England dressing room, even if it does not prove them correct. The first part of the eight England innings in the five Tests produced 1862 runs for the loss of 35 wickets. *The remaining 36 wickets produced 221 runs.*

Allan Lamb, who ended up as one of the central characters in the ball tampering controversy, says: 'There had been a lot of media speculation about the method used by Wasim and Waqar – and by Aqib Javed, the other Pakistan fast bowler – to obtain their considerable swing when the ball was well worn, when other international fast bowlers were unable to do so. I remember that in early August, our team manager, Micky Stewart, had stated publicly that he knew the method they used, but would not say what it was. I knew what it was, and became so frustrated by what I regarded as a conspiracy of silence by cricket officials that I decided to make it public.

'I played in the Lord's Test and I saw Pakistan players tampering with the ball during England's first innings of the second Test match shortly after lunch. A wicket fell and I was non-striker. A group of Pakistan players gathered together and I could see some of them scratching at the ball. I complained to umpire Barry Dudleston about what they were doing and he replied: "My job is hard enough without worrying what they are doing with the ball." He added that he could not see any of their players scratching the ball. We then lost our last seven wickets for 83 and the last six for 58. Out of nowhere the ball swung all over the place and Waqar bowled me, Ian Botham and had Chris Lewis lbw.

'At the end of play we complained to Micky Stewart, and one of the players I heard have a go was his son Alec. Micky told us: "I will have a word with the umpires, but there is nothing else I can do."'

Micky Stewart had this to say of the summer of discontent: 'Before the start of the Texaco series in May, the match referee, Bob Cowper, met both captains and managers, as is customary. He was referee for the first two one-day games and the first two Tests, then he would hand over to Clyde Walcott. I put it in such a way as not to give offence and asked him to instruct all the umpires concerned to make regular, but inconsistent inspections of the ball. I said there was no point in doing it at the end of every over, because the players would be expecting it and could dampen down any obvious interference. Also, I expected it to be done for both sides and Cowper agreed he would do this.

'There was no problem in the first two Texaco games and the first Test at Edgbaston, and I took particular note of the umpires and how often they inspected. But at Lord's on the first day, I had not seen them inspect and I asked Bob Cowper to mention it to them. All I can say is that we collapsed to Waqar after the break. The ball did swing a lot, but there were one or two poor strokes played.'

Lamb did not play in the subsequent Tests but he has this to say: 'I saw Pakistan players tamper with the ball during the games at Headingley and the Oval while I was watching on television. I know about the method of tampering with the ball because it was first shown to me by Sarfraz Nawaz, the former Northamptonshire and Pakistan bowler. I remember I played in a Test in Karachi in 1984 when Sarfraz was bowling and got me out caught at forward short-leg from a big inswinger with the old ball. Normally it is the new ball which swings more, and after the close of play, I said to Sarfraz, with reference to what he had told me at Northampton about how he achieved swing with the old ball, something like, "Saf, you're still using that same method you showed me." Sarfraz just laughed and said, "Yes Lambie, I am the best." Sarfraz also told me many times that he had shown Imran the method.

'I remember the lunch time on the Wednesday before the start of the Lord's Test: I was sitting on a pavement table outside a wine bar in St John's Wood with Robin Smith. Imran was walking past and joined us for a chat. He asked Robin how Aqib Javed, now playing for Hampshire, was getting on. Robin replied: "Very well – he was doing a good job for us but then got warned on numerous occasions for tampering with the ball." Imran replied, "Yes, I've told him to be more discreet when he does it."

The issue bedevilled the Test series, with the England players so convinced that illegal practices were being used that they decided to force the issue at the first available opportunity, which happened to be at Lord's for the fourth of the five one-day Texaco internationals.

With England having won the first three games before the Tests, the final two games at Lord's and Old Trafford were expected to be of academic interest only.

That is the background for the fateful Sunday in late August 1992. The situation came to a head when Allan Lamb walked in to bat with England on 72 for three in response to Pakistan's total of 204. He and his colleagues believed that, because the match was 50 overs per side and the pitch and surrounds were damp from the previous day's rain, there was insufficient time for natural wear and tear to assist the bowlers.

The match was the fourth one-day international between England and Pakistan, and the scene was set for the next confrontation between two sides who were now almost in open warfare. The cast for a production which was to run for the 452 days it took a High Court case to penetrate the cover-up – which, so it is said in justification by those concerned, was put in place at the instigation of the lawyers advising the ICC and the TCCB – included Lamb, brought back for the one-day games, umpires John Hampshire and Ken Palmer who had each stood in one Test that summer, and Don Oslear. The Lincolnshire-born third umpire was to become the biggest player in a game which brought shame to cricket. Oslear was first appointed to the umpires' list in 1975, one of only a handful who never played first-class cricket. A fearless man – some would say abrasive – he never shirked what he saw as his duty, despite many brushes with his employers at Lord's.

The authorities surely regretted the hand of fate which dealt Oslear the Lord's game, but history will be grateful that it was his refusal to be diverted from what he saw as the truth, that finally forced into the public domain the first recorded instance, explained under oath in court, that the ball at Lord's was changed under Law 42.5 – which states that: 'No-one shall rub the ball on the ground, or use any artificial substance, *or take any other action to alter the condition of the ball.*'

The game was scheduled to begin and end on Saturday 22 August, but rain meant that most of England's reply to Pakistan's 204 for five in a match now reduced to 50 overs per side, took place on Sunday.

Where better than Lord's on a sunny Sunday to watch the second half of a one-day international? Except that by mid-afternoon, the peaceful pocket of St John's Wood became a breeding place for rumour and counter-rumour involving the three umpires, the match referee Deryck Murray, the managements of both teams, TCCB senior officials – and Allan Lamb.

Lamb says: 'In the Lord's one-day international in August, I saw a lot of illegal interference with the ball by Wasim and Waqar. I scored 55 runs and batted long enough to see what was going on. Normally, it happened more after 50 overs or so, but this time it was earlier, because it was a 50 overs game. Just before lunch the ball started to swing in exceptional fashion. I reported to umpires Ken Palmer and John Hampshire the state of the ball where the scuff marks had got bigger and bigger. They took note of what I was saying, and I remember saying to them as we walked off for lunch, "You boys have got to do something about the ball, it's now got out of hand."

'Graeme Hick got out just before lunch and I had said to the umpires, "Look at them, they are scratching the ball there." The players were huddled together, and as soon as I had the chance, I picked the ball up and showed it to both umpires. One side had three big scuff marks on it which had grown considerably since the start of the day – much more than would have been the case in the normal wear and tear of 26 overs on the lush outfield. When I got back to our dressing room, I told Micky Stewart about what had happened and he went to see the umpires.'

The England manager says: 'I had seen Allan Lamb talking to the umpires, obviously about the ball, so I went to their room to see what had happened. I opened the door and saw a meeting taking place so did not go in.'

Oslear, the third umpire for the match, followed Stewart into one of the small rooms opposite the umpires' room. 'I told Micky that I would keep him fully informed of any action taken and that was the only time I left the umpires' room throughout the entire discussions – I was away for no more than 90 seconds.'

Oslear, of whom it is difficult to imagine there has even been a more meticulous taker of notes or committer to paper of every detail of matters likely to have repercussions, says: 'My father told me at an early stage to "get it down in writing" and I always have.' Thanks to that parental advice being followed to the ultimate, Oslear is able to describe that Sabbath day, which was soon to become Sunday Bloody Sunday, in detail and was to embarrass the cricket authorities and their legal advisers who, so it is claimed by many, for the umpteenth time advised a screen of silence.

It was to be a screen which only a man of Oslear's persistence and refusal to be dissuaded from toeing the establishment's party line could have penetrated.

CHAPTER 2

The Oslear dossier

'Immediately prior to lunch at 1 pm,' says Don Oslear, 'I went to the umpires' room to prepare drinks for Ken Palmer and John Hampshire. When they came in, John turned to Ken and said: "I think we had better get the match referee in." John then asked me if I could find him. The MCC Secretary John Stephenson told me he was probably in the dining room. I found him there and asked him if he would come to the umpires' room.

'John passed the ball to match referee Deryck Murray and told him they wanted the ball to be changed because of clear and obvious tampering. Murray had a look and said he fully supported the proposed action. He then asked me to find the Pakistan team manager, Intikhab Alam, who was immediately told that the ball had been illegally interfered with and would be changed.

'The correct procedure is that the ball must be replaced by one of inferior condition, but it was difficult to pick one from the box of six spare balls available. Two were hardly used and very good, two others had been used for a similar number of overs but were still in much better condition than the match ball after its scuffing, which left a choice of two.

'It was left to Intikhab to choose, which he did. During the process, he asked: "Who is interfering with the ball?" and was told that the umpires could not identify a player or players, but the state of the ball showed that the interference was blatant. Intikhab was also told that the damage could not have been done by contact of the ball with the pitch, as it certainly was not a dry hard one, and the outfield was very lush because of the recent rain. Also, the ball had not suffered damage from impact onto wooden seats or concrete terraces, and so the damage must have been inflicted from and by another agency.

'The umpires and I then went to eat what we could in the short time left, and I put the ball out of the way and locked the umpires' room. After dining, Ken left the table before John and I, and on returning to the room he found Intikhab and his captain, Javed Miandad, trying to open the door. They told Ken they wanted to inspect the ball, but Ken could not find it and assumed I had it.

'When Ken told me what had happened, I again found Deryck Murray and asked him to come to the umpires' room. He asked me to find the Pakistan manager and captain which I did. The subsequent conversation was aimed at having the decision to change the ball rescinded, and Javed even got the ball in question and rubbed the damaged side on the cycle shorts that he was wearing. The reason for him taking this action escapes me; it could be that he was trying to obliterate the damage or put some shine on one side of the ball – yet the ball had already been changed.

'They then wanted the umpires to take the ball out onto the field and change it after one delivery. At first I wondered what the sense was in that, because everyone would know about the change, and it was originally felt that it would be best to keep the matter as quiet as possible, at least until the end of the match. It was only much later that I followed their thinking. If it was seen that the ball was changed on the field, they would then have claimed it was only because it had gone out of shape. If that was later challenged, they could claim that had it been changed under Law 42.5 the replacement ball would have to be of inferior quality – and the umpires do not carry such a ball.'

In making that valid point, Oslear pinpoints a weakness in the procedure laid down by the authorities.

'All the balls I have seen that have sustained illegal damage have made it virtually impossible when necessary to find one in a worse condition – unless a dog chewed it for a few weeks.'

The TCCB acknowledged this point, and at an umpires' meeting in September 1991 with the Board at Edgbaston, chaired by the Chairman of Cricket, Ossie Wheatley, the following discussion was minuted in the presence of the umpires, Alan Smith, Tony Brown and Tim Lamb.

Item (g). Condition of the ball. Law 42.5: The umpires confirmed that the problem of interfering with the ball was definitely on the increase, with more bowlers now trying to pick and raise the quarter-seam. Umpires were reminded that the law required them to change the ball 'for one of a much inferior condition in such instances'. The umpires replied that in some cases that was what the bowler wanted because a very old 'doctored' ball could be made to swing much more.

It was suggested that the umpires could each be issued with a 'really ropey old ball' by the Board, for use as necessary as a way of solving the problem.

Oslear is understandably cynical about the lack of any follow-up of an idea which must have been worth trying. That meeting took place eleven months *before* the Lord's fiasco; Palmer and Hampshire would have been able to change the ball on the field before lunch had that minuted discussion been implemented. Yet they were not, and the fact that the only way they could have acted promptly was to suspend play while a ball 'of much inferior quality' was found – if this was possible – does not reflect any credit on the TCCB.

Oslear comments: 'It is no surprise to me that nothing happened. Not from an authority which pays lip service to stamping out ball tampering and yet, in my time certainly, have only ever acted on official reports with the greatest reluctance, and even then only dealt out insignificant penalties.

'While Intikhab and Javed were asking for the decision to be changed, Micky Stewart came to find out what action would be taken and I told him I would inform him as soon as possible. We agreed that Intikhab would tell his players that the ball had been changed, the umpires would tell the two batsmen prior to the start of the session, and I would go along to the England dressing room to tell the manager.

'I then suggested to Deryck Murray that I should show the ball to the Chief Executive of the TCCB, Alan Smith, and he agreed. Mr Smith could not see me for about 30 minutes. We met in his office behind the pavilion. I showed him the ball and related the events of the lunch interval. He did not say much, but I remember one remark. "I never thought they would be so foolish as to try such tricks in a one-day match."

'He also expressed the wish that the tour could already have ended and that the Pakistanis had left England, and then perhaps the time might have been right to have disclosed the various misdemeanours committed by the players.

'He drafted a statement which said that as the condition of the ball had been altered, the umpires had changed it during the lunch interval. I felt it did not go far enough, but it covered the facts and so I made no comment. We then went to see the TCCB's Press Officer, Ken Lawrence, and Mr Murray, both of whom were watching the game in the committee room.

'In fairness to the referee, it had been agreed by all during the meeting that had taken place previously in the umpires' room, that the matter should be kept as quiet as possible until the end of the game. Now in the committee room, Ken Lawrence and myself told Mr Murray we thought this would be foolish, because both teams knew the facts. If the press picked up the story, his own credibility would be questioned. Therefore he should issue a statement.'

Oslear's fears were well founded. I was alternating between the BBC television commentary box and the adjoining press box, and soon found that a call had been received from the England dressing room, giving chapter and verse of the change and the reason of it. The cat was now out of the bag, although it would be correct to say that it was never in there in the first place. Calls were made from the press box to the Committee room and, after the match, it was pandemonium.

Oslear recalls: 'Reporters were everywhere wanting to know what had taken place. The cover-up by the match referee was already beginning to cause huge problems, simply because the truth was not being told. When the match ended, a brief meeting took place in the umpires' room, but because it was such a small room, I was asked to organize a meeting in the ICC office of John Stephenson.

'This was attended by Khalid Mahmoud, the manager of the Pakistan tour party, Intikhab Alam, Javed Miandad, Micky Stewart, Deryck Murray and Ken Lawrence, while I there representing the two umpires. It was at this meeting that the text of the first statement, prepared by A C Smith, was changed. Intikhab objected to the mention of Law 42.5, significantly saying to the match referee "but we agreed at lunchtime", suggesting that he and Murray had agreed that no mention of ball tampering be included in the statement.'

It is worth emphasizing that Murray, as the ICC representative, was in sole charge. The ground authority was the MCC, in the form of John Stephenson, and the TCCB could not become involved until they received the umpires' reports. That tenuous chain of command is crucial to establish, exonerating Alan Smith from any blame on that day. He had done his best by writing a brief statement of the facts which were only two in number.

The umpires had changed the ball, because of a clear breach of playing conditions. When the rider was left out of the statement, Smith was powerless to argue, because of the overriding power of the ICC representative, Murray. Had the latter held his nerve – and remember he was not under any of the legal pressures that were to mount in the next few days – justice would have been done, and seen to be done.

Oslear says: 'The original statement said that "as the condition of the ball had been altered, the umpires changed it during the lunch interval". At Deryck Murray's insistence, it now read that "the match ball had been changed during the lunch interval, and that Mr Murray would be making no further statement on the matter". Worse than that, Khalid Mahmoud wanted the statement to be amended further to read that "the ball had been changed because it had gone out of shape".

Oslear's reaction to this was immediate and forthright. 'This was the first time that this idea had been put forward and I objected in the strongest terms on behalf of my colleagues. Knowing all that had gone on during the lunch break, I could never agree to a statement like that. It was obvious that the Pakistanis were not going to accept the decision and at the meeting they tried to have any press release include an excuse as well as a lie for the reason the ball was changed.'

Micky Stewart has this to say: 'When I attended the meeting, it was the first I knew of any proposed statement. I heard all the arguments, but I was mainly concerned that whatever statement was issued did not include a lie. I had been told by Don Oslear that the ball had been changed because of illegal tampering, so any reference to the ball going out of shape was unacceptable. I made this point before I left the meeting to go to Old Trafford for the final Texaco game the next day.'

Stewart's point was met, although the final statement made no reference to the reason for the changing of the ball. The public were left to make their own judgement on the reverse premise that, if the statement did not say that the ball had gone out of shape, there was only one alternative deduction to be made.

Weak? Undoubtedly, because the lawyers had not entered the fray. And fray it was, with the already strained relations between the two countries' authorities now close to breaking point.

As for the press, I was present at the reading of the statement by Ken Lawrence who, being a former journalist, gave an off-the-record briefing about the reason missing from the statement. This briefing was not done out of mischief, but simply to ensure that unnecessary speculation was avoided in what was bound to be a highly coloured reporting of what had now become a sensational day's play.

Oslear makes one further point: 'In my opinion, the reason the damage to the ball was so easily spotted by the umpires was that the scuffed side usually had dust rubbed onto it, not only to keep it dry but also to hide the damage. On this occasion, no dust could be found because of the previous day's rain, and the bare pitch ends, usually a ready source of dry dust and dirt, were still damp on Sunday.'

The sequence of events provided the media with sufficient material to start a long-running saga which was exactly what the authorities did not want, but the press did. Once the *Daily Mirror* signed up Allan Lamb, and he agreed to go public, the problem would not go away.

It was a classic case of a decision to withhold the truth spawning a web of intrigue and cover-up. The lawyers wasted no time. They gagged the ICC senior officers, Chairman Sir Colin Cowdrey and Secretary John Stephenson, and only allowed them to make ineffectual statements which, far from damping down the fires of controversy, served only to add fuel to the flames. In the meantime, the Pakistan party were threatening legal action against all and sundry. The *Mirror* mounted a campaign to uncover the truth which lasted for weeks, although the rest of the national press pursued the issue with noticeably less zeal once the obvious follow-ups were carried out by the end of the month.

To deal with such an incident, involving three umpires, two teams, and a match referee representing one of three authorities with some sort of jurisdiction over the match, the predictable buck-passing becomes a high speed game of musical chairs – except this time, the music never stopped.

A popular view, initially, was that had the umpires changed the ball at 12.30 pm when they were aware of the tampering, the immediate storm would have blown itself out quickly. Hampshire and Palmer would argue that, because they had no ball of inferior quality with them, the delay in sending for a box and choosing one in the middle of the pitch would have caused an inordinate stoppage in play. The counterpoint to that is they had no such ball because of the TCCB's failure to implement the minute of 26 September 1991 which proposed that each umpire in every first-class match be issued with such a ball.

Another view, perhaps cynical, perhaps not, is that bowlers who are found guilty of illegally tampering with the ball would profit more by being given an even older ball. A better ball would be a more fitting penalty, because it would delay further the natural wear and tear which is the basis of reverse swing.

Umpires Hampshire and Palmer acted properly once they had left the field. They told Murray that they would change the ball. It was their decision, not his. It is ironic that, having pioneered the system of match referees, ICC Chairman Colin Cowdrey should be eventually gagged by that system and the lawyers. He was out of the country on the day of the match, and it must have rankled with him that the ICC Code of Conduct, which was his brainchild, was used for the suppression of the truth by omission.*

With the officials John Stephenson and Alan Smith blame-free, the buck must stop with Murray. His action negated the main thrust of Smith's statement. He decided that the statement would contain no explanation for the change of ball, thus fuelling the publicity he, personally, successfully shunned in a traumatic aftermath which was to lead to the High Court.

Two questions remain unanswered, because only Murray can answer them. Why did he bow to the wishes of Intikhab to cover-up the clear breaking of Law 42.5? What did he think would be the benefits of such tampering with the truth, and to whom? Possibly the Pakistan team, although the transgression by their players was now compounded by the cover-up.

As to why he backed off, it could not have been because of any legal ramifications, not on the same day as the incident. Even the lawyers are not sitting by their telephones on Sunday waiting for a chance to earn large fees from the cricket authorities.

The simple answer might be that Murray, not notably the strongest match referee ever appointed, opted for the quiet life, not realising that his weakness in not publicly supporting the umpires would create the biggest cricket scandal in many years.

The truth would have prevented all the problems his economy with it precipitated. It is inescapable and ironic that the man appointed to ensure that the game was played to the highest standards of behaviour and conduct should be the one who, on all the available evidence, did most to exascerbate the problems caused by the incident.

The verdict on Murray? In my opinion, guilty.

* The Code calls for the statement to be made by the Chief Executive or his nominee, in this case Ken Lawrence. It also says that 'The Referee must not discuss or comment upon his decision at any time'.

CHAPTER 3

From Lord's to the High Court

Late on Sunday 23 August 1992 the Pakistan and England teams, along with the media brigade, travelled to Manchester for the fifth and final Texaco one-day international. Meanwhile, Don Oslear was on his way home to Grimsby for a 36-hour stop-over, prior to travelling to Worcester for their four-day match against Nottinghamshire, followed by five days against Warwickshire.

It is somewhat ironic that without the TCCB's experiment to extend the number of Texaco games from two or three per season to five, the forthcoming crisis would not have arisen. England had up until that time steadfastly refused pleas to increase the number of games played and, prior to the 1992 Pakistan tour, the matches were always contested as a curtain-raiser to the Test series. But for the 1992 series, the TCCB decided there would be five matches, with the final two coming after the Test series. It is doubtful if Lamb, or any England player, would have taken the same action and complained about an interfered ball in a Test match – simply because the ball would have had a longer lifespan than 50 overs in which to develop wear and tear.

As Oslear drove from St John's Wood to Humberside, he wrestled with a problem. 'I thought of what I knew and what I could prove. I also thought about my contractual position with the TCCB and the fact that I was Chairman of the First-Class Umpires representative body.

'I knew that, as reserve umpire, I would be required to write a report of the day's happenings, but I decided to delay that because I did not know how Jack Hampshire and Ken Palmer would handle their reports. It was their duty to include the change of ball and the reason for it.

'I was due to drive to Worcester on Tuesday 25th when I was

contacted by Chris Lander from the *Daily Mirror* asking for my comments. I said "No comment" and then decided that I had to write a full account of Sunday's events as quickly as possible, while the sequence was fresh in my mind. I also realized that Jack and Ken might not be able to recollect accurately what had taken place and when, because they had a match to umpire and would not know about what happened during the afternoon while they were in the middle.

'I stood in for them then – in fact, I was the only one present at every meeting. I tried to contact both of them before I left, because Chris Lander had told me that the following morning, Wednesday 26 August, his paper was running an article on the changing of the ball. I couldn't speak to Jack, but did to Ken as well as to the TCCB's Assistant Secretary of Cricket, Tony Brown , when I got to Worcester that evening.

'That call had an amazing effect. I had gone to New Road the next morning, the first day of the match, and I was in the umpires' room writing my account of the Lord's game, when Tony Brown came in. He told me that no umpires' reports had been received and asked me if I could contact Jack and Ken and ask them to send in their reports. I knew that the Board were trying to hush things up, because the same thing had happened before with Alan Smith when earlier reports of ball tampering had appeared in the press. They needn't have worried in my case, because nobody got a word in public from me until I appeared in the witness box in High Court in November 1993.

'Tony's visit to see me was the start of a concentrated effort on the Board's part to muzzle everyone. Why, I don't know, especially as Alan Smith had been so keen to explain the reason for changing the ball at Lord's in his original statement which Deryck Murray later overruled. I suppose the lawyers had started to nibble away, because the TCCB became involved as soon as the reports were received from the umpires, who were their contracted employees.

'Next morning, on the second day of the match, I was asked by the Worcestershire Secretary, Michael Vockins, to ring Tony Brown on his mobile phone. Talk about mystery. He handed me a sealed envelope which contained the number. Tony Brown was travelling by rail to Scotland and he instructed me that none of the three of us was to speak to the press, and I need not contact Jack and Ken, as he would be speaking to them.

'I wonder if his intention was to influence them, because I was assured that the umpires' reports for that match had not been changed. I also wonder if it was pure coincidence that the TCCB had Tony Brown in attendance at Worcester, a match in which I was umpiring, immediately after there had been publicity concerning abuse of Law 42.5?

'All this because of the *Daily Mirror* who were now digging deeper. I had featured in the article by Allan Lamb on the 26 August, and I knew that the Board officials were terrified in case I said anything. So much so that they also faxed me and my colleague at Worcester, David Constant, to repeat the instruction of silence. I was insulted that, despite our contracts which were specific about what we could say, to whom and when, it was felt necessary to remind us of what we already knew.

'It rained all Thursday, so it was a case of putting up the barricades against the press, and I was pleased we had a full day's play on Friday to get away from them all. That weekend I had a message asking me to ring Sir Colin Cowdrey on his return from India on 1 September.

'He asked me to fax him my version of events, and I tried but it turned out that his phone and fax were out of order, so it would have to wait. Things were hotting up even though we were now nine days down the road. John Stephenson, clearly under legal instructions, had announced that "no further statements would be issued".

'I found that particularly interesting as earlier that day Sir Colin had already told me that both umpires confirmed that the ball had been changed under Law 42.5. Chris Lander was very persistent but, in front of witnesses, I refused to answer his question as to which law the ball had been changed under.

'The last day of my stint at New Road was on Thursday 3 September, and Tony Brown rang me in the umpires' room. The call was on the speaker system in the TCCB office, and both he and Tim Lamb suggested that I had been speaking to the press about the ball changing. I took the greatest possible exception to that. They then suggested that I fax my account to them and they would pass it on to Sir Colin later that day.

'I did this, but now believe I was foolish to do so. As I understand it, they took a copy before passing the document to Sir Colin, and that was locked away with the ball. I went straight away to the Worcestershire office to get confirmation that the fax had gone through. Remember, it was a private and confidential document, but it did not stop someone at Lord's telling Brian Scovell of the *Daily Mail* that it was on the way. He rang me in the Worcester office, and I immediately phoned Tony Brown who said he would try to find out the source of the leak.

'Mr Brown said he would ring me back in the umpires' room, which he did to the astonishment of David Constant and myself – not because he had rung, but because for around 90 seconds it seemed that nobody at the other end of the line, which was again hooked to the speaker system, was aware that the call had been put through. I heard three voices, Tony Brown, Tim Lamb and Ken Lawrence, all cobbling together a story which I relayed to Constant until, for the first time, someone realized I was on the line.

'Tony Brown put Ken Lawrence on, and he said that he was surprised that I had only had a call from one reporter. He then said he believed I was not telling the truth about speaking to the press. I now knew for certain the authorities were running scared and it sickened me how one cover-up led to another and another. Was it really the lawyers who had shackled them, or was it just instinct to run for cover when something unpleasant needed to be done?

'I got a much better call on Friday 4 September from Sir Colin. He said he had read my account and could we meet as soon as possible? I told him that I was umpiring for three days in Horsham the following week and he kindly invited me to stay at his residence in Angmering on the night of the 8th. I had a pleasant dinner with Sir Colin and Lady Ann before he and I spent a few hours discussing the whole matter.

'We talked about all the implications, and it was clear to me that he was deeply troubled by knowing the facts as presented to him, and yet being advised by the lawyers of the legal dangers of speaking out.

'He told me that he was determined to avoid concealing the facts if possible, and he would seek my assistance to help him do this. He asked me if I would contact a number of my colleagues for their support and I felt that at last I was talking to someone as keen as I was to resolve the matter properly. In the open, with no lies. It would not only put the blame squarely on the right people, but a public announcement would surely be a step in the right direction to eradicate what was now a serious problem in cricket.

'Sir Colin told me that the Pakistan management was even saying now that the ball I had taken to Alan Smith was not the match ball, and it was then that I made the first of two promises which I am proud to say I have kept.

'I knew what an invidious position Sir Colin was in. He loved the game. He wanted to restore old-fashioned values, but the lawyers were inhibiting him. It was a terrible dilemma and so without any soliciting, I volunteered the following: "Sir Colin, my account is there to be used by you in any way you wish and I will never divulge its contents while you remain in your position as Chairman of the ICC."

'I kept that promise until the moment I spoke to him during the first week of November 1993, fourteen months later, and before handing the document to the TCCB's lawyer, Francis Neate, in the Board's offices on 9 November.

'I left Angmering at 9 am on the morning of 9 September and drove to Horsham for the 2nd XI game between Sussex and Middlesex. Throughout the first day and a half, I was pestered by the press, particularly Chris Lander who was desperate to know about the contents of my document. He could hardly have chosen a worse time to try to get me to reveal everything. After all, I had only just given my promise to Sir Colin that my document was his, to do whatsoever he wanted with it, while he remained in office.

'On the second morning of the match, Sir Colin rang me at 10 am to tell me that he had spoken to most of the full members of the ICC and he was particularly heartened by the response of South Africa's Dr Ali Bacher. He asked me about the likely response of my umpiring colleagues because he hoped the next day, 11 September, to make his statement.

'He said he would telephone me at 10am and said that if he made a statement, it would include the crucial phrase "that the ball was changed on 23 August under Law 42.5". The next morning I told him that I had spoken with Barry Meyer, Mervyn Kitchen, Ken Palmer and Nigel Plews, all of whom were in solid support of his decision to make such a statement. The slightly worrying thing was that he told me that he was pleased to receive such support, but thought that it still might be a few days before the statement would be issued.

'He asked me where Jack Hampshire was, and I told him that he was standing at the Oval in a 2nd XI match between Surrey and Lancashire. I drove up to Leicestershire where I was standing in the game against Northamptonshire. I guessed that Allan Lamb would want to talk to me, for by then he had been told he would face disciplinary charges for his quoted comments in the *Daily Mirror* on 26 August. I told Allan that I agreed with everything he wrote, but that he was unwise to say anything because he was clearly in breach of his contract, both with his county and the Board.

'He asked me if he could see my account of events and if he could have a copy. I refused because of my promise to Sir Colin, and felt sorry I had to do so. Allan is such a straight bloke and I felt sorry for him, but a contract is a contract and we are all bound by them. However, I then made the second of my three promises.

'I told Lamb that if he was ever in serious trouble because he had spoken the truth, and my account would help him, then I would reveal the necessary information. He thanked me for that, and the matter was not referred to again in the next four days. I had to admire how he played in that match, despite the mounting pressure on him. Northamptonshire were set 290 in 73 overs with third and fourth place in the table up for grabs. Allan hit a marvellous unbeaten 122 and Northants won with 19 balls to spare, and it was one of the most aggressive innings I have ever seen. As I was also under pressure from all quarters, I could honestly say I appreciated what a true professional he was to play an innings like that.'

If Oslear thought that the end of the 1992 season would bring peace and quiet, it did not take long to disabuse him. In fact, just as long as it took for him to drive from Leicester to the Birmingham hotel where he was staying prior to the annual meeting of the First-Class Umpires body, of which he had been Chairman for two years. But not, as it turns out, for a third. Let Oslear take up the story.

'I was shocked to learn that I would not be proposed for re-election by any of my colleagues. Dickie Bird had proposed me in September 1990, but now he was going to put forward somebody else. I was grateful to find that at least one of my colleagues had the decency to tell me that night, and not let it be sprung on me at the next day's meeting. Nigel Plews gave me the full story and when I asked him for the reason, he told me that the TCCB felt it would be better if I did not hold such a prominent position.

'The knives were out, and there they stayed until my enforced retirement eighteen months later, before the start of the 1994 season. I now knew that my part in the Lord's ball-changing episode had put me on a collision course with the TCCB. A course not of my choosing, because all I had done was to record all that had taken place, and then keep my pledge that I would not divulge it, except to Sir Colin Cowdrey.

'To stick to the truth and keep a promise may be a problem to some people, but not to me. I know I have ruffled a few feathers in my life –

no, make that a lot – but only because I cannot tolerate people who either tell me one thing, then do another, or make a promise and then break it because it suits them.

'I think carefully before I commit myself, but once I have done so, that is that. I realise that politicians and people holding office in sport often have to be all things to all men. I know they have to balance the general good, and I also know that they cannot keep everyone happy. But, when an issue of clear principle is at stake, I never budge, and I lose respect for those who do. It was one thing for the TCCB to stay silent at the insistence of the lawyers, but quite another for them to try to influence matters which are only the concern of the umpires.'

Oslear might also have added that his removal from the chair highlighted the fear factor among the membership. Too many first-class umpires, mostly ex-players, settle for the quiet life, rather than risk upsetting their employers. It is almost an unsolvable chicken-and-egg situation. The umpires maintain they rarely receive full support if they report players for disciplinary transgressions. The Board insist that, if umpires do their duty, they will always receive backing. The more pliable section of the panel will relate instances of reports not being acted upon, but will never go on the record in case it prejudices future contracts.

It is an extension of the resentment they feel about the umpire marking system, done by captains, which they claim is often a reflection of vested playing interests.

Oslear knows he has sometimes been regarded with suspicion by those colleagues who feel that, occasionally, he enjoys making waves. Sometimes, they say, he appears to be officious, and sometimes he seems to enjoy making his role one of enforcing the law, rather than interpreting it.

Whatever his perceived faults – and what human being does not have them – the question of who holds office on behalf of the first-class umpires should be a matter for those men and nobody else.

The meeting on 16 September did two things. Nobody proposed Oslear, mainly because an internal lobby had produced a candidate for the chair who, for the first time, was not an umpire. The chairman represents the interests of his members on matters of finance and working conditions. The perennial problem was that the man charged with conducting the negotiations with the Board representatives had always been an umpire, and therefore disadvantaged when it came to an impasse. He would always be negotiating for improved terms which would benefit, among others, himself, and it was felt that a complete neutral, such as Roy Kerslake who was also a solicitor, would carry more clout.

Sound thinking? The idea came from the strong South-west section of the panel – 10 out of 26 in 1995 played either for Somerset or Gloucestershire – and as there was no other nomination, the election of Kerslake was a formality. But Tony Brown, Assistant Secretary of Cricket, objected on behalf of the TCCB.

Kerslake recalls: 'It seems that they did not want an outsider sitting on various sub-committees on which the umpires had representation. The point was put to me that on committees such as the Appointment of Umpires and the Pitches Committee, it would not make sense to have someone who was not at the sharp end of things.

'I could understand that, but agreed to stand as Chairman, with vice-Chairman John Harris representing his colleagues on those committees. It was hardly a satisfactory situation, either for the umpires or myself, but I stayed on as Chairman throughout the 1993 season.

'I was able to help them in various ways. For instance, their body was only an informal one, so I drew up a workable constitution for them, including their present title, the First-Class Cricket Umpires' Association. I stepped down from the chair before the 1994 season, but still advise them when necessary about contracts and working conditions.'

Oslear drove home, reflecting on the 24 days, beginning on 23 August, which had more twists and turns – mostly behind the scenes – than in his whole umpiring career of 18 seasons. He asked himself three things. Had he done the right thing by writing up the events of 23 August? Was he right in promising Sir Colin Cowdrey that what he, Oslear, considered to be the definitive account of the day, would never be made public until Cowdrey was out of office? And, if he could reverse Omar Khayyam's moving finger would he have done things in exactly the same way again?

The answer was an affirmative 'yes' to all these questions. He had done his duty as he saw it. Besides, there was the Cowdrey statement to come ... or was there?

Hard though Sir Colin Cowdrey tried, he was never able to obtain the encouragement he needed from the lawyers to say what, by now, the whole cricketing world knew by implication. The fact that the original statements from the ICC did not bow to the repeated requests of the Pakistan management and say that the ball was changed because it had gone out of shape, indicated by omission the fact that the umpires had ordered it to be replaced because of what they saw as a clear breach of Law 42.5.

Cowdrey's predicament was that Deryck Murray's unilateral backtracking on the day in question gave ammunition to the Pakistan management that, otherwise, they would not have had. Had Alan Smith's original statement been issued, Ken Lawrence would not have offered his unofficial briefing to the media.

The sequence of events would have been straightforward.

1. The umpires change the ball, informing but not requesting permission from the match referee.
2. Both team managers are informed of the change and the reason for it.
3. The match referee's after-match statement would have recorded the facts.

Who would the Pakistan management and players sue? The umpires for taking a decision well within their rights as sole arbiters of fair play? Or Murray, for following the procedure regarding making a public statement in accordance with the ICC Code of Conduct?

The answer has to be 'no' to both questions, as proved by empty threats to sue Allan Lamb for stating the same facts in the *Daily Mirror* article of 26 August, which was to bring disciplinary action from the TCCB because of an admitted breach of his contract with them.

Cowdrey only became involved a few days later, following his return from India and Sri Lanka. He learned from ICC Secretary, John Stephenson, of how the latter had been pressured on the day to issue a statement saying that the ball had been changed because it had gone out of shape. Stephenson was quoted in the *Sunday Times* of 2 January 1994 as saying: 'After that game but before I left my office, the president of the Pakistan cricket board telephoned me and instructed me to say there had been no ball tampering. He told me that I must make that statement. I refused to do so. About half an hour later, the manager of the Pakistan tour party, Khalid Mahmoud, came into my office and apologised for the unpleasantness of the call.'

The lawyers might not have gone as far as preventing the issue of a full, proper statement, but they did outline the possible consequences if this was done. Even though the umpires would confirm why they had changed the ball, a court of law would require proof. For instance, how would the production of the ball have proved anything? Oslear's understandable action in locking the ball away during the lunch interval had already prompted the suggestion that the ball handed to Alan Smith was not the ball used in the middle.

Cowdrey has this to say: 'John Stephenson and I faced a dilemma. Our natural instinct was to make a public statement giving a full explanation of the facts as we saw them. Our difficulty was that we were faced with too many uncertainties and loose ends. The lawyers explained the possible consequences of speaking out without sufficient evidence, should our views have been challenged. I would have needed the authority of the MCC as well as all the other Test match playing countries, and it would have been irresponsible for me to go ahead without it. John Stephenson and I decided that not to say anything was the wisest counsel, and this proved to be sensible advice.'

Cowdrey was made aware that legal proceedings could involve the MCC with possible costs of over £200,000 added to the annual £200,000 the MCC contributed towards the costs of running the ICC. (Now it is different, with a reconstituted ICC fully incorporated and insured against legal costs involved in a case of one member country suing the parent body, or any of its officers.) It is more than likely that the Pakistan government would have funded any legal action, but who would provide the finance for the defence?

Cowdrey was clearly in a vulnerable position. How could he speak without provoking the Pakistan players and management? He first took office in 1989 and, when his term was extended to four years, he set about re-organizing a world body which had little or no executive power. It is a pity that the 23 August 1992 came three years after his induction, and not four. Then there would have been no problems about making a statement, and the threat of legal action would not have extinguished the oxygen of publicity.

More a case in 1992 of an opportunity being denied by circumstances, rather than wasted.

CHAPTER 4

The hearing

The issue was now closed as far as the ICC and TCCB were concerned, but Oslear's chance to put the facts into the public domain came from an unexpected quarter. Lawyers acting on behalf of the Pakistan management and players had issued threats of legal action against Lamb, the *Daily Mirror* and anyone who repeated charges about ball tampering, past and present.

The threats were never backed up with action, but the one writ to be served against Lamb for libel came from a former player of both Pakistan and Northamptonshire, Sarfraz Nawaz. He sued because of the following sentence attributed to Lamb: *'I know about the method of tampering with the ball because it was first shown to me by Sarfraz Nawaz.'* Sarfraz and his advisers believed they now had a chance to win a libel case and, with it, substantial damages.

Fifteen months had elapsed since the 1992 Lord's game. The link between the Lamb case and that match was a tenuous one, but strong enough for the employment of two law firms for the High Court case which took place on 15 November 1993. Oslear was to become the unscheduled final witness called on the fourth day, after three days of technical explanation about reverse swing, video evidence of alleged ball tampering, and a succession of former and current first-class cricketers who had played with and against both plaintiff and defendant.

Let Oslear recount his part in the final act of the short play: 'During the month of September 1993 as the Sarfraz Nawaz/Allan Lamb hearing moved towards the venue of the High Court, I was contacted by Deryck Murray on the 8 September. Mr Murray appeared to be most concerned by certain approaches which had been made to him and questions which were being asked. He wanted to know whether I would be attending court as a witness in the case, to which I explained, as I'm sure he was aware, that I had already received a subpoena earlier in the year.

'He asked if we could meet at his office to discuss certain matters regarding the incident which took place at Lord's in August the previous year. He suggested we meet at his office, but as I had a four-day match coming up at Old Trafford I told him it would be better if he came up to Chesterfield on the 15 and 16 September, when I would be standing in what turned out to be my last match as a member of the first-class panel of umpires. Unfortunately, he failed to contact me but rang a week later and we made arrangements for him to visit my home on 19 October.

'Many matters were discussed at our meeting, including a financial investment with the company who employs Mr Murray; this, I felt, was a front for what was the main thrust of our discussions, namely the hearing. He appeared worried about what might happen, what he might be asked, and what he might have to say. He asked me what he should do. "Tell the truth," was my instant response.

'As it turned out, Mr Murray did not attend the hearing and the truth was not revealed. However, some months later on a programme televised by London Weekend Television entitled *The Devil's Advocate*, in which I was a member of the audience, Mr Murray admitted when quizzed by interviewer Darcus Howe about the state of the ball in the Lord's match:

'"Yes, I agree with Don [Oslear]. There were scuff marks on the ball."'

Oslear continues: 'The week before the hearing, on Tuesday 9 November, I had to attend a function in London, and that afternoon I went to Lord's to discuss various things about the 1994 season. I learned that the Appointment of Umpires Sub-Committee had not yet met. That surprised me because it usually is convened earlier than that, but my guess was that they were waiting for the hearing to see how it turned out, and who agreed to give evidence.

'I know the TCCB had tried to dissuade several people from taking part, and I wondered what they would say to me. I met their legal adviser, Francis Neate, and thought it was then appropriate for him to see my account of 23 August 1992, although I find it hard to believe he had not seen it in the previous 14 months, when I faxed it to the TCCB to pass on to Sir Colin Cowdrey.

'I asked Mr Neate one question. "Will it cause problems for me?" He replied, "No, but it may for the TCCB." I was not bothered about that, because I was now keeping my second promise to Allan Lamb, and was free to do so because Sir Colin had since stepped down from the ICC chair.

'I know there had been arguments between the lawyers about whether the Board should produce the ball and the umpires' reports from the one-day international, with Mr Neate apparently arguing that neither was relevant, and anyway, according to precedent, the Board could not be subpoenaed to produce an object, such as the ball.

'I had to turn up at 9 am at the offices of Lamb's lawyers, Vallance Lickfolds, with my copy of my report. Only then, nearly 15 months after I wrote it, did it go out of my hands so that copies could be made for the Court. The Northamptonshire Chairman, Mr Lyn Wilson, was also there, and I was pleased to see a club supporting its player.

'In court, the press section was overflowing. I sat with David Capel and Robin Smith who had also agreed to testify. So had Ian Botham, but his plane was delayed. However, the legal system was not going to grind to a halt because of him.

'David and Robin were questioned mostly about the behaviour of the ball in matches they had played against Pakistan in 1992, but I was asked about my duties as third umpire in the Lord's game, with particular reference to the lunch interval.

'Finally came the question from Mr Eady QC which led to the sudden end of the case. *"Are we correct in thinking that the ball was changed under Law 42.5, Mr Oslear?"*

'At last, 452 days after the event, I could establish the facts. All that time. All that concealment, stemming from fear of the legal repercussions, yet I was now free to say what I had wanted said for 15 months. Now I was under oath anyway, so I could not be guilty of breaking my contract with the TCCB. They had done their best to persuade me it was in the best interests of cricket if I did not give evidence, but I did not share that view. It was clearly not in their best interests, as Francis Neate seemed to have hinted to me nine days earlier, but now the truth had to be told.

'"*Most certainly sir,*" I replied. What an impact that made. The previous day, Sir Colin's son, Christopher, had presented video evidence of 53 instances of interfering with the ball as a bowler was walking back to bowl and that, in my view, should have been the major factor in Lamb's defence. Especially the comments of Richie Benaud on one particular clip of Pakistan bowler Aqib Javed scratching the ball.

'Benaud wrote this to Lamb's solicitors on 8 September 1993. "On the final day of the last Test between England and Pakistan at the Oval in 1992, I was the commentator when there was an incident concerning the Pakistan pace bowler Aqib Javed and the ball being used in the match. My comment which went to air at the time was 'Awww ... steady on', and regrettably I added, off microphone, 'Jeesuz', something that was fortunately lowered in volume when played back on air later in the week on Friday night's *Nine o'clock News* on BBC 1.

'"It was an involuntary remark made as the picture flashed on to the screen, and it was followed by Ray Illingworth asking the producer on the lazy mike, 'Could we see that again?'

'"I am satisfied that what I said on television at the time provides an accurate summing up of my feelings over the incident and various other matters which took place in the summer. It is my opinion that if any player tampers illegally with a ball being used in a match, it may provide an unfair advantage to bowlers on his side. If such a practice exists then, in my opinion, it is against the spirit of the game of cricket."'

Oslear says, 'I suppose that strength of evidence from the world's best cricket commentator would have eventually won the case for Lamb, but the next three hours following my three-word answer brought a flurry of behind-the-scenes activity. His Lordship sent out the jury while legal submissions were put to him.

'He then adjourned until 3 pm. I was told that, as I was still in the witness box, I must not speak to anyone about the case, so I wandered over the road for a bite to eat and a drink. There were plenty of press about, but they knew the score and I was left alone with my thoughts.

'I had mixed feelings. I felt glad that, at long last, the public would now know what they should have learned at the time. I felt angry that it had been necessary to involve the legal system to settle something the cricket authorities should have had the guts to do. And I hoped that I had helped Allan Lamb, whose case really depended upon support from other people concerning the validity or otherwise of his statement linking Sarfraz with ball tampering.

'Court 13 was packed when I got back at 2.45 pm, with Ian Botham present, but now it was his turn to be kept waiting. Three o'clock came and went and still no sign of a resumption. Ian said to me: "I don't sit padded up for as long as this – at least I don't when I'm playing for England."

'Then he said at about 3.30pm, "I reckon something has happened.

Either the case has been dismissed or they've pulled out." Sure enough, he was right. His Lordship re-entered the Court at 4.15pm and announced that counsel for Sarfraz had agreed to drop the case. Both sides made statements claiming victory, with Sarfraz saying he dropped the case "because I achieved my motive – Lamb admitted he had never seen me cheat on a cricket field...my honour was upheld".

'How on earth Sarfraz could say that is beyond me. He had been thumped in public to the equivalent of being hit for 36 in one over. No argument. Not when he gave up as soon as I told the world that the Pakistan players had been found guilty of breaking the cricket law about interfering with the ball.

'Counsel for Sarfraz decided not even to cross-examine me once I had given my answer before lunch. I suppose he had worked out that if he did, I would give several other instances known to me about Pakistan transgressions. I dodged the photographers outside and met Allan Lamb and Ian Botham in a nearby wine bar. Typical "Both", he greeted me with "Don, you've often ended an innings of mine, but you've never stopped me playing one before."

'As far as I was concerned, it was a day that never should have been, but at least justice had been done. At what cost I was shortly to find out. Even after the case was over, the TCCB refused to make any comment, saying that the case between Allan Lamb and Sarfraz Nawaz was nothing to do with them. In which case, why did they have legal representatives heavily involved in the previous months? Why did they have representatives at court during the case? And why did they interfere with the requirements of my original subpoena?

'Part of it was to do with the Leeds Test, umpired by Ken Palmer and Mervyn Kitchen, with me as third umpire again, and part to do with the Lord's one-day game. I was ordered to bring to court my report of that game, together with two balls used at Headingley, which I had presented to the match referee, Sir Clyde Walcott. The TCCB solicitors blocked this. I still had the balls despite requests from Alan Smith for me to return them. If I had done this, they would have gone the same way as all the others I had sent, together with reports.

'The subpoena was presented to me at Chelmsford on 9 July 1993, following correspondence from Allan Lamb's solicitor, Alan Herd. I referred this to Tony Brown, whose reply contained this paragraph: "The simplest way to deal with Alan Herd's letter is to say that any reports you have made when umpiring cricket matches for the Board since 1975 have been sent to the Secretary of the TCCB in private and confidential form. You have nothing you can help them with. Therefore, the best advice to you is to say as little as possible, however hard you are pushed."

'As for my reports and their confidential nature, it seems they have a cricketing Bermuda Triangle at Lord's, into which certain things disappear, never to be seen or heard of again.'

Could the TCCB have hoped that the same thing might happen to Oslear once they had decided to stop him umpiring in 1994? The facts are these: Oslear would have been 65 on 3 March 1994, and therefore the Board's decision was that, having passed official retirement age before the start of that season, he would not be offered a contract.

Oslear, however, is quick to make these counterpoints.

1. 'The precise rule which applied at the time was that, if the applicant's 65th birthday fell after 1 January, he would be available for selection for that year, but if it fell before, then he would have been retired. There are many instances in the past of umpires continuing to be on the first-class list after the age of 65, and the usual practice was to allow a man to stand in his 65th year, whatever the date of his birthday. For instance, Bill Alley, Lloyd Budd, Jack Crapp, Arthur Jepson, John Langridge, Eddie Phillipson and Tom Spencer were all allowed to umpire after their 65th birthday on the grounds of ability and fitness.'

2. 'I [Oslear] also believe that at the Appointment of Umpires sub-Committee meeting on 5 October 1992, it was decided to give me a two-year contract, but this was subsequently amended to one year within hours by Board officials. I put this point in a letter to Alan Smith dated 24 January 1993. His reply, dated 7 April, ignored it but I think it crucial, because I know it is fact as told me by a couple of the county captains involved.'

The Board's answer to the first point is contained in a letter to Oslear dated 30 March 1993. It says that, regardless of the practice he says was followed by TCCB Secretary Donald Carr and his assistant Brian Langley prior to 1986, 'The Executive Committee of the Board discussed the principle and arrived at the decision which now affects you and any other umpire who reaches retirement age before the cricket season starts. Remember that you start drawing a pension before the start of the season.'

The letter also points out that a material factor in considering appointments for the 1994 season will be 'the age, experience, potential etc of other candidates'. The same points were made in other letters, all of them written before the pending trial.

As for the second point, it seems that the captains did go in to bat for Oslear to get a two-year contract. They made the point that he was one of the better umpires, but by then the Board's officers had decided to play it by the book, or rather their version of what the book said. Oslear maintains he was told that he was awarded a two-year contract at that meeting. Captains I have spoken to agree they wanted him to have one, but say that the Board's immediate reaction was to invoke the 65-year retirement rule.

Put simply, they wanted him off the list and his birth certificate gave them the opportunity. Oslear contacted both Donald Carr and Brian Langley, who both confirmed what was accepted practice before 1986 when Alan Smith became the Board's first Chief Executive.

Oslear remains unconvinced that he was treated properly, or fairly. The arguments on both sides are persuasive, though a former member of the International Panel of Referees, Nigel Plews, says, 'I think the goalposts were moved.'

The conspiracy theory is an easy one to float on a matter as contentious as this. Oslear says: 'The first notification I had that I was not guaranteed a contract for 1994 came in a letter from Tony Brown dated 24 November 1992. It said that there were precedents for the best umpires to be kept on after their 65th birthday, if the Board considered there were no adequate replacements to maintain the highest standards of umpiring. My marks (out of 5) were given as 3.95 for championship matches and 3.88 for one-day games.

'The marking system causes so many problems. In 1988, I and several colleagues persuaded the Board to send us duplicates of our markings, and they did this for one year. That helped us to work out our total and average markings, but it did not suit the Board, because I maintain they want a bit of leeway to juggle things around at the end of a season. Many umpires are not in favour of captains marking them, because they believe that some captains mark them down if the match has gone against them. I do not share that view, and think it a fair system, with one or two exceptions.

'The markings are out of five, so I was happy with 4.17, 3.95 and 3.97 for the 1991, '92 and '93 seasons.'

Oslear's last year on the first-class list in 1993 was not a happy one, once it became obvious that he was unlikely to be re-appointed for

1994. At times like this, it is difficult to maintain an objective view of events and, understandably, Oslear is adamant he was the victim of a Board conspiracy to get him off the list because he often found himself at odds with his employers.

He says he only ever did his duty. The Board maintain that, occasionally, he was unnecessarily officious and fussy. Their rapidly fraying relationship was encapsulated by an incident at Northampton on 3 June 1993.

CHAPTER 5

A problem at Northampton

'**I**t is my misfortune to have to report a case of foul and abusive language by one of the Worcestershire bowlers, K Benjamin. Also, the fact that my request to the Worcestershire captain for himself, together with the said bowler, to attend the umpires' room 10 minutes after the close of play was not complied with.'

These were the words contained in a fax sent by Don Oslear, one of the umpires standing at the four-day match between Northamptonshire and Worcestershire on 3 June 1993, to Tony Brown at Lord's, the Reverend Michael Vockins, Secretary of Worcester, and a copy to Steve Coverdale, the Northamptonshire Chief Executive, concerning an incident which rumbled on for ten weeks, and which was to cause a further deterioration in the strained relationship between Oslear and his employers, the TCCB.

As usual in a matter of on-field discipline, there is more than one version of the facts but, in this case, only one fact was in dispute – the actual abusive words allegedly uttered by the player, Worcestershire fast bowler Kenny Benjamin.

Oslear's action was swift, that fax going at 9.31 am on 4 June. Let him set the scene: 'On the first day of the four-day match between Northamptonshire and Worcestershire in June 1993, I indicated more than once to Ken Benjamin between 5.15 pm and 5.35 pm that he had bowled the allowance of one short-pitched ball to a batsman in an over, and twice I told him he had bowled such a delivery to each batsman in the same over.

'After another such delivery, I called and signalled to the scorers "no ball", only to see the bowler glare at me and ask the reason for the call. I told him that he had exceeded his ration as it was the second in the over.

'He then told me in what I thought was an arrogant manner that the other short ball had been bowled to the other batsman, who was now non-striker.'

The playing conditions in 1993 allowed only one short delivery per over per batsman, but that was later amended to two per over to either batsman, thus restoring the element of surprise missing in the former rule. What also needs saying is that one man's opinion of what constitutes arrogance must be subjective, and this is where the incident became uncontrollably magnified.

Oslear's official report continued: 'I said that if that was so, I am sorry, but please continue the game. He [Benjamin] refused to do so. My intention was that it should not be seen by all and sundry that the bowler was making an objection. The fielding captain, Tim Curtis, then became involved, stating that I was incorrect. I apologised to him, admitted my mistake and asked that the game continue, and I would make the necessary adjustments to the score and bowler's analysis at the close of play.

'The bowler then started to walk past me to his mark, but looked straight at me and said: "That was crap umpiring."'

Oslear could have done one of two things. Ignore a comment made in the heat of the moment by a bowler he had wronged, or pursue the matter with Curtis.

'I immediately called over the Worcestershire captain and informed him of what was said. Instead of fulfilling his responsibilities under Law 42.1 ("The captains are responsible at all times for ensuring that play is conducted within the spirit of the game as well as within the laws"), Curtis replied, "Well, he is frustrated, he has had a couple of catches put down."

'The game continued and at 6.08 pm we went off for bad light. I asked the captain and his bowler to come to the umpires' room ten minutes after the scheduled close of play. They failed to do this. Meanwhile, I asked the scorers to delete the no ball from their book; it was the fourth ball of the 92nd over, and they also deducted the two-run penalty from the bowler's analysis and the two runs from the score.

'At 7.05 pm Tim Curtis came to me in the pavilion and said he would see me at 10.30 am the following day. I informed him this would not suffice, hence my report.'

Curtis says: 'I was fielding in the gully and when I spotted a problem between the umpire and my bowler, I went over to help resolve it. I don't think that the umpire realised he had made a mistake until I told him. I thought he could and should have settled everything there and then, but he said he would do it at the close of play. I was bothered that the home crowd would think that Ken Benjamin was causing trouble, but he wasn't. I went back to gully, and then was called over by Don Oslear who told me that Kenny had abused him. I told Oslear that Kenny had had a couple of catches put down and, in this case, he had been wrongly penalised.

'When we went off for light, I went to the umpires' room because Don asked me to do so ten minutes after close of play. He wasn't there – I think he was in the middle checking the light – but I saw him an hour later in the pavilion and told him that we would see him at 10.30am next morning. He said that would not do and that was that. It was a pretty fraught match, because I felt bound to ask about the last over dismissal of Phil Newport in the Sunday match. He was given out by Nigel Plews, caught off a shoulder-high delivery, and I think I was entitled to query it, even though I was not playing. Also on that last day of the four-day match, when Northants wanted 108 from 24 overs, I bowled Richard Illingworth over the wicket, and the umpire called wides which I thought were harsh and were based upon one-day criteria.'

Could Oslear have handled things any differently? Of course he could, but the nature of the man has to be considered. Firstly he had been caught out in a mistake. He could have defused Benjamin by throwing up his hands and admitting his error. He could have done what his colleague over the next troubled five days, Nigel Plews, did in a similar situation involving the Yorkshire bowler Paul Jarvis. It seems that the bowler turned round and laughed, 'Wrong batsman, Nigel,' which prompted Plews to signal dead ball with no damage done to scorebook or pride.

Oslear chose a different path, and what a long and winding road it became. The temperaments of the Worcestershire captain and his bowler also have to be taken into account. Curtis was Chairman of the Cricketers' Association and a school teacher as well as captain. Normally a quiet, almost introspective man, he still has a fuse, albeit a long one. This time, it burned brightly and quickly. As for Benjamin, he is like many fast bowlers. He reacts quickly to situations, especially when, as in this instance, right was on his side. If his attitude towards Oslear had been similar to that shown by Jarvis to Nigel Plews, perhaps Oslear may have viewed the matter in a different light.

The ingredients were all there and they proved too combustible for both sides to handle. Curtis could have apologised for his bowler and Oslear could have delayed his first fax. Neither happened, and so the collision course was set for all parties plus, as far as Oslear was concerned, the TCCB.

The central figure in the matter says: 'In spite of my initial fax to Worcestershire CCC and the TCCB, I received no acknowledgement that day or Saturday. The Sunday League match, in which Tim Curtis did not play, was a tie. During the final over Phil Newport was caught off a ball which he thought was a beamer. Nigel Plews, at the bowler's end, did not call it, and when we left the field, Tim Curtis immediately followed us into our room to ask why it had not been called.

'Both Nigel and I were treated to a display of arrogance which I do not think I have seen equalled in any of the many sports I have been associated with. My report read: "It would be desirable if the non-playing captain of Worcestershire CCC did not accost the umpires in their dressing room within two minutes of them entering it."'

Plews agrees that Curtis was worked up and, later, both men agreed it would have been better to have waited a while. The strengths of a man sometimes become a weakness. Oslear's unwillingness to duck anything he sees as an issue can make him inflexible, but take that away and you have a different animal.

Hostilities – and that was what they now were – resumed on the final day of the four-day game.

Oslear says: 'I found it surprising that neither Tim Lamb nor Michael Vockins, who were both on the ground for a meeting that day, approached me regarding my fax. As for the match, in the final stages I found the attitude, conduct and objections to my decisions from the Worcestershire captain Tim Curtis, his vice-captain Steve Rhodes, and one of their bowlers disgraceful and deplorable. It would seem by collusion, that from the outset of the match hostility was to be directed towards me throughout the game.

'For instance, the captain accused me of being officious when I asked one of his batsmen, who was injured and standing at square leg, to pick up his gloves from the ground. In fact, I was merely trying to prevent another incident. Had the ball struck his gloves from a shot by the other batsman and there been an appeal, the injured batsman would have been given out under Law 37 for obstructing the field. The obstruction would have been ruled deliberate because gloves are supposed to be worn and not placed on the ground whilst the ball is in play.'

A fraught final day culminated with Oslear calling the odd wide in the last 20 overs, and that brought more reaction from the Worcestershire players. Oslear's report contained this phrase: 'The Worcestershire captain disputes too many of the umpires' decisions while upon the field of play.'

There it was. Dissent, abuse and general dissatisfaction with the conduct of a captain, at least one bowler and other players. Small wonder that Oslear expanded on his original fax with a fuller account of the incident which sparked everything off.

Tony Brown acknowledged the receipt of the reports in a letter dated 16 June — surely too long a gap after such a strong report – but, before then, Oslear's impatience with the slow-grinding wheels of authority had taken the matter an important step further.

'I had been appointed to umpire the second round of the NatWest Bank Trophy match at New Road against Derbyshire on 7 July, so I rang Lord's to tell them on 9 June that, effectively, under no consideration would I stand in matches involving Worcestershire CCC.

'My call was made early that morning and I asked Tony Brown to ring me back before I left for my next match at Basingstoke. He did not do so, nor did he contact me at the ground, although he did speak to my colleague John Harris during the match. That call was about the photographs of the two cricket balls which had appeared in the *Daily Mirror* on 28 May, and the article that appeared with them. In fact, that day, I was actually umpiring at Lord's, but nobody from the TCCB had the guts to come and discuss the matter with me. I suppose the reason was that they had sanctioned the content of my book, *The Wisden Book of Cricket Laws* in correspondence with the publishers in March 1993.

'The letter acknowledging my reports also said "they will be passed on to Alan Smith and Peter Bromage [Chairman of the TCCB Discipline Sub-Committee], together with my request not to officiate in any future games involving Worcestershire".

'I soon told them it was not a request, but a message of intent and called in to Lord's on 29 June, when I was told of the changes to my fixtures. That was all right, but what was not was that I was also told that Alan Smith and Peter Bromage had met and were of the opinion that no further action would be taken in regard to my report, and I would receive a letter to that effect.

'I was informed that Mr Vockins had spoken to Kenny Benjamin, who had denied using those words. Benjamin also claimed that I questioned him about what he said. Untrue. I heard perfectly well what he said from two paces as he looked straight at me.

'It seemed to me it was all part of a plot to get me off the list with as little trouble as possible. At Basingstoke, I spoke to Mark Nicholas who was present at that Appointment Sub-Committee meeting in October 1992, and as I remember he confirmed I had been offered a two-year contract, subsequently amended and reduced to one year.

'I now wondered why my reports were not accepted. I told John Harris that I would be writing to the Chairman of the Board once I received the letter telling me the matter was closed. I finally received it in Durham on 19 July, nearly seven weeks after the start of the match in question.'

The already cloudy waters were now muddied. An article in the *News of the World* stated that Oslear was not standing in Worcestershire matches at the insistence of the county. Oslear later learned that 'the reports of the Worcestershire captain for the game at Northampton were adverse and stated that "their confidence in me taking charge of their matches had plummeted". Nowhere near as much as mine in them.'

Now it was open warfare, with Brown's explanatory letter infuriating Oslear. It relayed the decision of Alan Smith and Peter Bromage, with Brown writing thus:

'Regarding the incident, it was decided that from the evidence available, there were errors made by both you and Benjamin. Those by you were that you did not properly follow the Laws of Cricket and that you did not handle the incident in a way which would have remedied the situation with the minimum of fuss. As to the latter, surely you should have realised that the minute your error had been identified, you should have notified the scorers accordingly and also apologised to the bowler and the fielding captain. All this would have been with a light touch and everything would have passed off in the spirit that should be the hallmark of the way cricket ought to be played.'

As Nigel Plews had done with Yorkshire and Jarvis. Oslear's reply to that part of the letter was full of acid, from a man who now had had a bellyful of what he saw as cant.

'In my opinion, your letter is a pathetic attempt to excuse the non-

action of both Worcestershire CCC and the TCCB in what should have been a matter of great importance to the Discipline Committee. Your letter certainly contained an inaccuracy from yourself and lies from the Worcestershire captain.

'You say that I did not follow the Laws of Cricket. It was because I followed the Law to the letter and will continue to do so that is getting up the noses of those who have no comprehension of the Laws.'

An objective view might say that Brown was correct, because Oslear incorrectly interpreted the Law on no-balls, although undoubtedly he followed the procedure correctly for dealing with dissent, as set out in Law 42.13.

Oslear's reply gathered pace.

'In my report, which you do not appear to have read, I agree that mistakes were made by both myself and the Worcestershire player. Mine was simply in the identification of one player from another, because they were both of similar height, wearing helmets and carrying the same name of bat. His was to use foul and abusive language to an official of the TCCB.'

Another impartial view might be that, had the player chosen really to let rip, his Leeward Islands upbringing would surely have offered him a wider choice of words than 'crap'.

Back to the Brown letter which, far from pouring oil on the proverbial, only fuelled Oslear's belief that he was being given a dressing down.

'As far as Benjamin is concerned, Mike Vockins is convinced that he was frustrated and he did say something, but not the words you thought you heard him say. He has been warned of the danger of any frustration shown by him being misconstrued by umpires, players and the public. He has also been reminded of the need at all times to comply with the Board's regulations and directives.

'Tim Curtis is adamant that he tried to make contact with you that evening and the next morning.

'The conclusion is the Board would not be justified in taking this matter any further (as in appointing a Panel under the Discipline regulations), since it is clear that the weight of evidence of what happened does not call for any greater penalty than the warning which has already been given to Benjamin.

'Don, the sad part about all this is that it need not have turned out the way it did. I hope you will see that had you dealt with the initial error simply by indicating your "slip" to the scorers in the usual way, that would have been the end of it.'

The letter also referred to newspaper articles which referred to Oslear's change of fixtures and requested an explanation.

Oslear replied that the only article he had read was written by a journalist he had never spoken to. As for his accusation against Curtis, he wrote:

'It is a lie for the Worcestershire captain to state that he made efforts to see me. That can be borne out by my colleague Nigel Plews.'

A tightly wound up Oslear finished in this damning way.

'As I am not believed by officials of the TCCB, not even in regard to the content of my official reports, there is no point in dispensing further information to you, because it would only receive a similar lack of consideration.

'At times like this, I am reminded of lines from Rudyard Kipling's poem "If".

'"If you can bear to hear the truth you have spoken, twisted by knaves to make a trap for fools."

'All I can say is that I have spoken the truth, it has been twisted by knaves and it most certainly has trapped any number of fools.'

The case for the defence and the prosecution was apparently complete, although it is uncertain which role Oslear believed was his. Surely now, it was the end of the saga and Oslear could finish the season in peace and quiet.

Not a chance. There were to be four further letters from the Board, one from Tony Brown and three from Alan Smith, the last one of which dated 24 August ended thus: 'In all the circumstances, it is not appropriate to comment any further on your letters.'

Namely, the end of the line, but what precipitated the crash into the Board's buffers?

It was a letter to all umpires from the Board, dated 27 July. It said that the Discipline Committee believed that standards of conduct and sportsmanship left a lot to be desired, and reminded umpires of their duty 'firmly to apply the Laws of Cricket as required – *not* in an officious, heavy-handed way, but simply, clearly and quietly explaining to the cricketer what you expect of him. You may be assured that if you act in this way the Board will support you unequivocally.'

If that paragraph did not reduce Oslear to near-apoplexy, this one did the trick: 'Neither should you shirk your responsibility for fear of being "marked down" by the captain on his report. The Board will most certainly not allow captains to mark any umpire down for properly applying the Laws of Cricket.'

Oslear's reply was not only predictable but understandable. He referred to Tony Brown's letter dated eleven days earlier.

'In that letter Mr Brown criticised, condemned and crucified me for taking the very action which you advocate in your letter to me.'

Smith had also written that the Board's stance was supported by the Cricketers' Association. Oslear pointed out:

'I must make the point that the Chairman of the Association and the Worcestershire captain are one and the same person, who not only told lies about me in his report, but also refused to take action to remedy the situation which existed.'

Several other paragraphs of protest hammered home his message which ended with:

'This letter will be of no help in my efforts to secure at least one further season's contract, but I do have to be able to live with what I believe in – truth and loyalty and never to bow to hypocrisy.'

Honest words from an honest man, but still the fire smouldered, following his next match in early August which was at, where else, but Northampton.

Oslear says: 'Rob Bailey asked me what had happened regarding the Worcestershire match, and when I told him nothing, he volunteered that Alan Fordham, the non-striker at the time, had heard every word. Alan confirmed this that evening, and even repeated everything I had said to try to keep the game going. I decided to write once more to Alan Smith.'

Oslear felt so incensed that he even invoked Clause 13 of his TCCB contract, dealing with his rights if he had a grievance in relation to his employment. Should he be unable to resolve it with the Chief Executive, then he could raise the matter in writing with the Chairman of the Board.

On 9 August he wrote to Alan Smith with a supporting statement from the Northamptonshire captain, Allan Lamb, and requested a re-opening of the case, especially in the light of the recent Board directive to umpires. He closed the letter with a reminder of his rights under Clause 13.

Smith's acknowledgement, dated three days later – the Board can move swiftly when necessary – said that Oslear's letter, together with his previous two letters, would be passed to the Chairman of the Discipline Committee, and Tony Brown wrote the same day to say 'All I wish to say to you personally on the matter at this stage, is how surprised and disappointed I am at the tone and content of your letters.'

And so to the final curtain-fall. On 24 August, 366 days after the ball-tampering affair at Lord's, Oslear saw Brown at Lord's.

'I asked him [Brown] one straight question. "Has it been proved I told the truth?" I could tell from his manner that he knew I was right, but all he did was to try to carry the attack to me by stressing that I had not observed the letter of the law when I adopted the procedure of bringing the matter to the attention of the bowler, the captain and my colleague. Also, why did I not erase the matter there and then? I explained the siting of the scorers and the pitch, but he carried on, citing many of the remarks Nigel Plews had made to me at the time, and I was not sure what he had put in his report.

'I was then handed a letter from Alan Smith in which he said that the incident would not be re-opened. Also further enquiries had been made at Northampton and from Allan Lamb in particular. As it happened I spoke to Allan that evening and he read out his reply to the letter from Tony Brown. He had written that the non-striker, Alan Fordham, confirmed the use of the words "crap umpiring" and said that the reason he had put nothing in his original match report was that the incidents concerned Worcestershire players only.

'Yet, at no time in my meeting with Tony Brown did he concede I was being unfairly treated. He then finished with a lie. He told me that, while others on the field of play, including the non-striker, heard the remark and it was a derogatory remark, the phrase used was not what I said I heard. Lamb's letter to Brown proves that is a lie.'

Alan Smith's final words were written thus:

'In correspondence and public remarks you make much of being a "strong" umpire, of being prepared "to stand up and be counted" and "upholding the dignity of the game". In Tony's letter to you about the game in question, he expressed the view that "if you had handled everything with a light touch, no incident would have taken place". It is widely recognised that sensitive umpiring is the key to the application of proper standards and I urge you to reconsider your approach in this light. A slavish adherence to the approach can be counter-productive. By contrast, sensitive handling of potential problems can resolve them before they blow up into incidents.

'In all the circumstances, it is not appropriate for me to comment any further on your letters.'

The incident is a typical consequence of entrenched positions. Oslear undoubtedly deals only in black and white, and is intolerant of lighter shades of argument whenever he thinks a principle is at stake. He also believes that the truth is incontrovertible. What the series of letters reveals is that, either there was insufficient corroborating evidence from other players to back up Oslear's statement of events, or the authorities soft-pedalled because of what they believed to be an over-officious approach on his part. Even so, that does not excuse a refusal to acknowledge that he did his duty as he saw it.

In most disputes, the truth lies somewhere in between the arguments of both parties. In this instance, it appears to lie much nearer Oslear than the TCCB.

So Oslear's wish to complete 20 years as a first-class umpire was not fulfilled. Appointed in 1975 at the age of 46, he rose to the Test panel within six years having established his reputation as a good umpire, with a temperament well suited to the growing difficulties of controlling first-class cricket in England. Not short of self-confidence and self-belief, he commanded respect, if not affection, among colleagues and players alike.

As for the authorities, his play-it-exactly-by-the-book approach was one they had rarely encountered before, with their tolerance level changing when the TCCB Secretariat underwent its biggest change in the mid-1980s.

Once Donald Carr retired and Alan Smith was appointed as the Board's first Chief Executive in October 1986, the winds of change blew a gale. With Smith came Tony Brown and Tim Lamb and a new administrative structure. It was one which Oslear found frustrating, but nothing deflected him from whichever course of action he believed to be the correct one.

It is an unusual and meticulous man who keeps a record of his career, but Oslear has both characteristics, plus others. The difference in his outlook on life, compared with many other people, is considerable. So much so that, as Alan Smith's final letter to him on 24 August 1993 indicated, the Board's senior officer felt bound to put in writing that he would put nothing else in writing.

I have known 'AC' for 40 years and Oslear about a quarter of that time. No useful purpose is gained by apportioning blame for such an impasse. In fact, such apportionment is impossible, but the sad thing is that two men with a similar objective in their jobs – to serve cricket in the best way they know – found it impossible to agree on certain subjects.

Oslear's final year in 1993 was the stormiest possible – most of the squalls coming from the Headingley Test and the Lord's Texaco one-day match in 1992, other alleged ball tampering incidents in the same year and, of course, the High Court case. His suspicion, that what he saw as early retirement was the result of his actions in those events, is unprovable. What a pity that, if the events were inevitable, they could not have happened earlier in his career. There is no doubt that he would have followed his instincts and done exactly the same, but would the TCCB have given him more support than they did?

Oslear thus left the first-class game in a way which reflected little credit on anyone. But he left it as he entered it 19 years earlier – his own man.

CHAPTER 6

Sultans of swing

Throughout the 1980s and the first half of the next decade, interfering with the condition of a cricket ball has been on the increase, and so has the assistance obtained by such interference. Oslear was one of the first umpires to report, officially, an instance of alleged illegal interference with the ball (Sussex in 1983, a game in which Imran Khan took six for 6 in 23 balls) and in the next 11 seasons he filed four other reports (all but one of which had been co-signed by the other umpire standing at the time) naming teams who had illegally treated the ball, as well as several other verbal reports of matches in which he was dissatisfied about the methods used to maintain the ball.

Oslear: 'Of the four reports, two were counter-signed by Bob White and one by Barry Dudleston. The one regarding the India game against the Board Under-25 team was not counter-signed, because my colleague, Mike Harris, was only a member of the reserve panel, but he endorsed my views.'

'It is well known that certain methods have been used by bowlers to improve their wicket-taking chances. Although 1983 was the first time I reported such an incident, I can think of at least two others before that in my early years on the list. One concerned the picking of the seam to make it more prominent and therefore more likely to seam off the pitch, and the other one concerned a new ball being scrubbed on the ground.'

The latter instance is interesting because, although Oslear is correct in saying it was illegal then, it was not always so. I played for Warwickshire from 1950 to 1969 and we were allowed to rub a new ball on the ground if we wanted the spinners on early. Such action was allowed until 1980, since when most changes in playing conditions have not favoured the spinners, especially the covering of pitches.

I would allow bowlers to rub the ball on the ground, because the umpires are able to control any over-enthusiastic action. The administrators have made many decisions in the last thirty years regarding the ball. To encourage spinners and prevent time-wasting when fielders polish the ball instead of returning it immediately to the bowler, they even experimented with a playing condition which allowed only the bowler to shine the ball.

It is worth looking at the current Laws 42.4 and 42.5.

42.4 A player shall not lift the seam for any reason. Should this be done the umpire shall change the ball for one of similar condition to that in use prior to the contravention.

42.5 Any member of the fielding side may polish the ball provided that such polishing wastes no time and that no artificial substance is used. No-one shall rub the ball on the ground or use any artificial substance or take any other action to alter the condition of the ball.

In the event of a contravention of this Law, the umpires, after consultation, shall change the ball for one of similar condition to that in use prior to the contravention.

The Test and County Cricket Board have introduced an amendment to Law 42.5 in which they stipulate that the ball shall be changed for one of inferior condition. They did this in order to impose a further penalty on the fielding side but, as the aim of scuffing and gouging a ball is to worsen its condition to promote reverse swing, the amendment could nullify what they are trying to achieve.

The whole concept of tampering with the ball was anathema to Oslear: 'Actions like those are foreign to the game of cricket and I cannot tolerate anything like that.'

An explanation of the aims of such ball tampering makes interesting analysis. Between leaving the bowler's hand and hitting or missing the bat, a cricket ball can move in the air or off the pitch in three ways only: (a) The ball can swing or swerve in the air; (b) When bowled by the faster bowlers, it can land on the seam and alter direction off the pitch; (c) When bowled by slow bowlers, and therefore spun from the hand, the rotating spin can make the ball deviate off the pitch.

The first two are dependent upon many factors, including the surface of the pitch and overhead weather conditions, while the third depends upon the surface of the pitch being such that the ball will grip and then spin one way or the other, dependent upon which way it is rotating. The simplest illustration of this is to roll a billiard or snooker ball along the table with the fingers imparting sideways spin on release. The ball will then rebound off the cushion at an angle.

Ball tampering, as it is now known, is rarely done to help spinners, because they only need a ball they can grip. A newer ball is of more use to them, providing it is not too shiny to grip, because it will bounce more, thus making the turn more difficult to counter. A prominent seam is a help to gripping the ball, but a ball with a gouged surface is not.

It is the quicker bowlers who derive most benefit from interfering with the seam, or the surface of one side of the ball. Consider the picking of the seam. Since time immemorial, bowlers have tried to retain the original prominence of the seam, because of its crucial part in movement off the pitch and also the rudder-like part it plays in orthodox swing. Oslear remembers the first time he came across a picked seam: 'It was in my first season on the list in 1975. The match was between Kent and Leicestershire at Tunbridge Wells and when the ball was rolled to me, I picked it up and it felt as though a sharp piece of metal had rubbed against my hand. Being my first season I said nothing, but later in August I found myself umpiring at the Oval with David Constant.

'I mentioned the incident to David and he picked a ball out of the box of spares and ran a nail around the stitches. He threw it to me and asked, "Is that what you mean?" Again I felt a tingle in the palm of my hand as David smiled and said: "I can't do it very well, but when you stand with Ken Palmer, ask him to show you how it's done."

'I did just that. I watched Ken pick up a ball and holding it with one hand, and never touching it with the other, he rotated the ball with his fingers while the thumb was embedded into the ball and against the stitching of the seam. It didn't take him more than five seconds but what came out of the hand was unbelievable. The seam had been brought up in astonishing fashion. I realised, then, that a bowler could do that without being seen when he walked back to bowl, although nowadays the cameras can pick up all sorts of things.'

Palmer was a hard-bitten county all-rounder who never missed a trick – which is why ex-players generally make good umpires. Poacher turned gamekeeper, so to speak.

Oslear says: 'In those days we rarely used to look at the ball, but in recent times we have been instructed to inspect it regularly, at least once an over'.

The Law allows bowlers to polish the ball, although not with any artificial substance. Tell that to Keith Miller who, in 1945 in the 'Victory' Tests, sought advice from the former Derbyshire all-rounder, George Pope, on how to swing the ball.

'I never go on the field bare-headed,' said George.

'Why not?' asked Keith.

George simply showed Keith the heavily greased peak inside his cap. Hair oil was the answer, hence Miller's use of his great friend Denis Compton's well advertised commodity, Brylcreem.

Vaseline, which John Lever was accused by the Indians of using in Delhi in 1976, and lip salve are other substances from which quite a gloss can be obtained and maintained. The same applies to a wax spray applied to flannels in the dressing room, with the ball then rubbed on that area – all illegal and all old-fashioned methods, now as out of date as national service and a batsman walking when he knows he is out. More effective methods of ball-priming were needed, especially on unhelpful pitches, and instances of inexplicable swing with an old ball began to surface from the subcontinent around the turn of the Eighties.

Oslear was in his ninth season as an umpire when he felt obliged to report officially, for the first time, the illegal treatment of a ball.

'It was in August 1983 at Edgbaston, Warwickshire v Sussex, and I sent my report to Lord's shortly after the match. It was the first of five such reports in the next nine years, but there is a bit of a mystery about this one. When I wrote on 5 September 1992 asking for copies of my reports, they sent four but said that they had no trace of a file record on the Warwickshire match.'

The Lord's Bermuda Triangle again.

'This was the first time I had seen one side of the ball scratched and torn, with pieces of leather ripped out. The quarter-seam had been opened up at a point where it meets the stitched seam and it appeared that some of the stitches had been cut. This allowed a triangle of leather to be pulled up from the surface of the ball; it was a piece large enough to be gripped between forefinger and thumb, and by which the ball could be suspended.

'The match situation was interesting when Imran came on to bowl his four overs. In two days and one session 756 runs had been scored and 14 wickets taken, with the game going nowhere on a flat pitch.

'Imran bowled the 45th, 47th, 49th and 51st overs of the innings and three balls of the 53rd, which was all that was necessary to finish the innings. He took six for 6 in 23 balls, including the hat-trick. He clean bowled five batsmen – Geoff Humpage, David Thorne, Chris Old, Norman Gifford and Willie Hogg – and I gave Paul Smith out plumb lbw. All six wickets fell to one of the most amazing spells of swing bowling I have ever seen.'

Oslear's report on that match went missing as did his accompanying letter; fortunately he had retained a copy of the latter in which he outlined the damage to the ball, and made the following comment.

'*Further to my report which I submitted after the recent match, I write so as to bring certain other matters to your attention.*

'*The Warwickshire second innings finished quite suddenly with Imran Khan taking the last six wickets in a very short space of time with some very accurate bowling. As my colleague and I left the field, I noticed that a piece of the ball was sticking up, and upon a closer examination it could be seen that this piece was the triangle of leather which joins the cross-seam and quarter-seam. The stitching did not appear to be frayed, BUT MORE AS IF IT HAD BEEN CUT, and the piece which was proud of the ball was large enough by which to hold the ball.*

'*Upon the same side of the ball as this piece of leather were a number of small cuts...None of the fielding side had made any complaint as to its [the ball's] condition, so I can only assume that it happened towards the latter part of the innings.*

'*At the end of the day, my colleague and I brought the matter to the attention of Norman Gifford, the Warwickshire captain, when he came to our dressing room to examine the ball. He will no doubt be bringing this matter to your attention in his report.*'

Gifford had this to say about one of the most devastating spells of swing bowling he had ever seen in over twenty years as a first-class cricketer. 'I looked at the ball, but did not really know what I was looking for. The most common form of tampering in my career was the picking of the seam, but we had never heard of anything else. Since that game in 1983, I learned a lot more, especially during my time as coach with Sussex, when players who had played with Imran told me of different methods he used to swing the old ball.

'With hindsight, I suppose that ball at Edgbaston could have been doctored, but it was still skill of the highest order to do what they did.'

Another one of Imran's victims that day, Chris Old, was more certain of things. Even some eleven years after the event, he was able to recall the state of the ball in an article for the *Daily Mirror*. According to the former England Test bowler: 'I saw the ball he [Imran] tampered with, and it looked like a dog had chewed it...I was annoyed and saddened to think that he'd ruined what appeared to be a great bowling performance by cheating.'

Geoff Humpage says: 'I have never seen anything like it. For two and a half days the ball had gone straight. Imran had hardly bowled because of his stress fracture, and then trotted in off about a six yard run. I know I was looking to get on with it, but the ball he bowled me swung a huge amount, just as did the balls which got Paul Smith, David Thorne and the rest out. Back in the dressing room, we almost regarded it as a joke. None of us knew anything about interfering with the ball then. I haven't got a clue if anything illegal was done to the ball, but I have to say it was the most astonishing spell of swing bowling, out of nowhere so to speak, that I ever saw.'

The non-striker throughout the 27-ball spell of pure mayhem was Alvin Kallicharran, who completed his second hundred of the match, with the last 35 runs hit while wickets tumbled at the other end. Like Humpage, the thing that astonished him most was the pace which Imran swung the ball off such a short run. 'He was really quick. I remember him hitting David Thorne on the helmet and saying something like "So you think you're quick, do you?"

'The funny thing was that he'd got the wrong man, because he thought it was Paul Smith who had bounced one or two of their players. In the context of the conditions and in view of the fact he had hardly bowled that year, for Imran to do what he did was exceptional.

'I knew nothing about ball tampering then, at least not about the use of bottle tops, although I had heard about vaseline, lip ice and the like to polish the ball. In all the time I played for the West Indies, I can honestly say that I never saw one of our bowlers scuff the ball.

'I do remember how surprised we were during the series at home against Pakistan in 1977 (which we won 2–1) that their bowlers rarely bothered to take the second new ball when it was available. In fact, Imran and Sarfraz bowled better with the old ball than the new.

'How Imran did what he did in that spell of six for 6, I will never know. It was easily the most astonishing spell of bowling I have ever seen in my entire career.'

Quite a testimony from a man who played 834 first class innings and scored 87 hundreds.

A final set of statistics to show the bizarre nature of the Imran intervention. His championship figures for the 1983 season, in which he played in thirteen matches for Sussex, were: 46.2-12-86-12. Or, put another way, in the other twelve matches that season, he took six for 80 in 41.5 overs. Good figures. Even outstanding ones, but nothing to compare with his nuclear effort at Edgbaston.

The Sussex wicketkeeper in the game was Ian Gould. He remembers vividly that game and another one against Derbyshire at Eastbourne in mid-August 1981. 'Imran came back for a second spell in the Derbyshire second innings, and his first ball started outside off stump and swung about ten feet down leg side for byes. That was the start of a great spell in which he took five wickets, including good batsmen like Barry Wood and David Steele. Don't ask me how, but he suddenly started swinging the ball miles, just as he did in that Edgbaston game.'

Imran's five wickets were, as is typical in such devastating spells, unassisted, with one clean bowled and four lbws. As a result, Derbyshire slumped from 193 for three to 227 all out. Then Imran blasted a magnificent hundred to win the match for Sussex and show that the pitch was trustworthy.

Oslear has this to say, more than a dozen years after the match at Edgbaston. 'Neither my colleague, Bill Alley, nor myself had a look at the ball in the forty minutes it took Imran to demolish the Warwickshire innings. We certainly would nowadays but, in those days, nobody had heard of ball tampering other than picking the seam.'

That point is underlined by the remarks of the players quoted – Kallicharran, Gifford and Gould. They all said that despite the phenomenal amount of swing obtained by Imran, they had no clue as to why the ball behaved in such an extraordinary fashion, so suddenly, after two and a half days of not moving much either off the seam or in the air.

Oslear makes two further important points. 'I honestly thought at the time that the cuts on the side of the ball were not the sort that fingernails alone could achieve, but the most curious thing to me was that the ball changed condition so suddenly. Had it been normal wear and tear, fair enough. But remember, this happened during the first session of the third and final day. The ball was only 22 overs old when we gave it to the Sussex captain, John Barclay, at the start of play, and it was in the good condition you would expect from a ball of such little usage. By the time Imran came on, another 22 overs had been bowled making 44 in all. By the time Imran took his sixth and Warwickshire's tenth wicket in that 53rd over of the innings *the ball, as described in my letter to Donald Carr, looked as if its stitching had been cut.*'

Oslear adds: 'In my opinion, the ball had been interfered with to a considerable degree. There is no other logical explanation. And is it just coincidence that Imran's sensational spell came in the same period as the condition of the ball changing so much? I think not.

'Imran later made the point on LWT's *The Devil's Advocate* that it was usual for him to be able to swing the ball a lot after 70 or 80 overs. But this ball was only 45 overs old when he had his first bowl of the innings…'

So the facts as presented by Oslear to the TCCB in writing – together with a spell of bowling from Imran that, despite him bowling from a short run-up, was classed by players of both sides as the best exposition of swing at pace that they had ever seen – only point to one thing. The six wickets fell because of the condition of the ball which, in the opinion of Oslear, had been interfered with illegally, including cuts which he did not believe were caused by fingernails alone.

Orthodox swing of a cricket ball evolved throughout the 20th century as the ball changed in appearance and durability. Swerve came before swing for the faster bowler, who would cut the ball with side-spin which would move the ball in flight. Much as the off-spinner's 'arm ball' leaves the right-hander, so out-swerve was achieved by off-cut, with the leg-cutter the basis of in-swerve.

Swing is different, because the ball must travel through its flight path in an upright position, compared with the sideways rotation of swerve. A ball tends to swing more when a few overs old, and when one side is more highly polished than the other. Dealing only with a right-hand bowler bowling to a right-handed batsman – reverse everything for left-handers – the outswinger is released with the smoother, shiny side facing leg-side. With less resistance through the air on the shiny side, the slightly angled seam causes a flow of turbulent air and the ball is pushed the other way, from leg to off and leaves the right-hander.

Conversely, the shiny side faces the off side for the inswinger, with the ball then pushed from off to leg. The fuller the length and the quicker the ball is bowled, the later in flight it will swing.

That is the only common denominator with reverse swing – full length and an optimum speed of between 75 and 85 mph. In fact, the term 'reverse swing' is an apt description because every necessary factor involving the condition of the ball is reversed. Shine is irrelevant, with one rough side and one smooth side the key to swing. The rudder role of the seam in orthodox swing is also unnecessary, with the ball held with more of a baseball grip than the traditional two fingers and a thumb of the seam bowler. I remember Richie Benaud studying Waqar Younis in action at the Oval in the 1992 Test with binoculars. Benaud played top baseball and said, 'He's using more of a baseball grip, with the ball wedged firmly into the hand.'

There are two theories about reverse swing. The first is that, by roughening one side and wetting the other, an imbalance of weight occurs, and the ball behaves rather like a crown green bowl which contains a manufactured bias. That bias only takes effect towards the end of the bowl's track when it is slowing down.

Subscribers to that theory say the proof is the extravagant swing achieved when, as with the Imran ball in 1983 at Edgbaston, it is scratched and gouged. That reduces the weight of the roughened side, while the wetting of the other half of the ball makes that heavier. The first time Warwickshire's Director of Coaching, Phil Neale, was aware of what was, to him, a phenomenon, was when he was captain of Worcestershire in 1987.

'Graham Dilley did it because nothing much was happening. He really soaked one side and the ball started to swing a lot. I had heard a bit about it, but had never really seen it happen to that extent. Stuart Lampitt soon learned the lesson, and he became a real expert at it.'

The second theory discounts the effect of weighting a ball. Several scientific experiments involving reverse swing have been conducted in the last 15 years* with the following deductions made.

1. There is a maximum speed beyond which conventional swing cannot be obtained.
2. Beyond this speed there is a reversal in the direction of the side

---

* *Swerve or the Flight of the Ball* by P A Valle (1905)
  The Boundary Layer and Seam Bowling by J C Cooke (1955)
  The Swing of the Cricket Ball by J C Cooke (1957)
  The Physics of Ball Games by C B Daish (1972)
  Swing of the Cricket Ball by J H Hurlock (1973)
  'Aerodynamics of the Cricket Ball' by R Mehta and D Wood, *New Scientist* (1980)
  'An Empirical Investigation into the Aerodynamic Theory Associated with the Swing of a Cricket Ball', Roehampton Institute (1989)

force produced throughout the ball's flight, and this produces reverse swing.

3. Such force reversal only occurs with balls possessing a quarter-seam.
4. For a new ball, force reversal only occurs at high speeds around 80–85 mph.
5. For an 80-over old ball, reverse swing was possible at lower speeds 65–70 mph.
6. The amount of reverse swing is less than that of conventional swing, and so the bowler should bowl a very full length to maximise the effect.
7. A naturally worn ball 30–50 overs old would swing one foot towards the end of a full length 19 yards journey at speeds in excess of 80 mph.
8. The degree of reverse swing depends upon the amount of contrast between the rough and smooth halves of the ball.
9. If one side of the ball was well protected after 40 overs, and the other excessively tampered with, the amount of reverse swing could be greater than on a similar ball protected on one side and naturally worn on the other.
10. Any tampering would hasten the wearing process and enable reverse swing to be obtained earlier in an innings than if the ball was allowed to wear naturally.

These are the 'Ten Commandments' of reverse swing, with number 10 of particular relevance to the games at Edgbaston in 1983 involving Imran and the Lord's Texaco game in 1992 involving Pakistan. In the former, Imran started to bowl in the 44th over, while Lamb's complaints to umpires Hampshire and Palmer in the Lord's game came before the ball was 30 overs old in what was a 50-overs match.

Leading English bowlers of the last 15 years agree that only in the mid-1980s did they first hear about reverse swing. Former England and Essex bowler Derek Pringle says this: 'Sarfraz is generally credited with discovering the affect of saturating one side of a worn ball with sweat and saliva. This was legal, creating an imbalance of weight, and the ball swung, but inconsistently. Then came the picking of the quarter-seam. I tried it in practice but found it unreliable.

'The driving force behind the refined evolvement of reverse swing was the lifeless, dry pitches in Pakistan. The bowler looks for every help he can get, and so other methods of priming the ball developed.

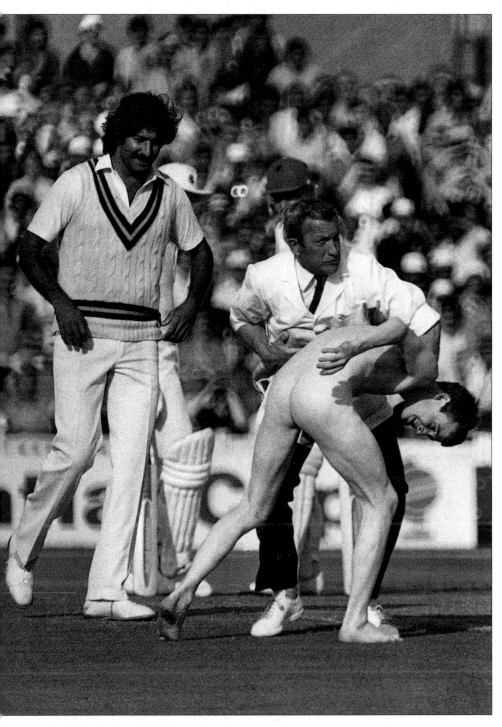

Umpire Don Oslear gets his man at Old Trafford in June 1983 as Sarfraz Nawaz looks on.
The English official and the Pakistan player would meet again in the High Court in November 1993
in an altogether more serious setting.

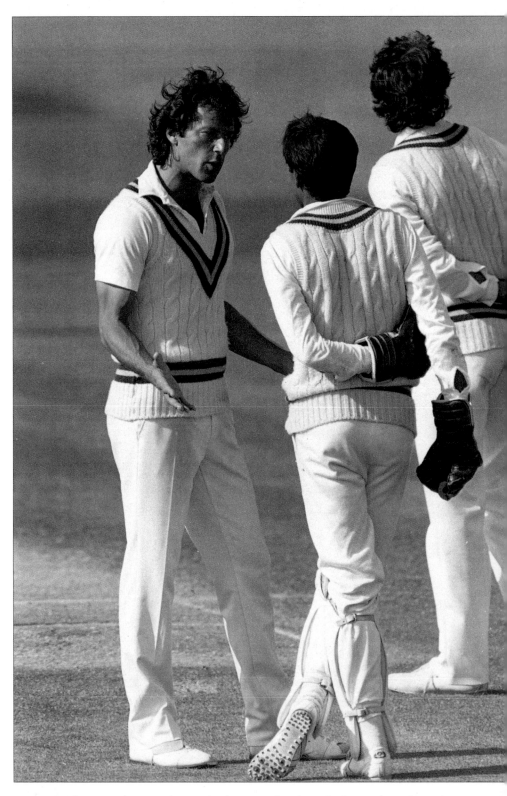

Imran Khan lectures Salim Yousef at Headingley 1987 after the wicketkeeper claimed a catch against Ian Botham which television replays showed had clearly bounced first.

Above: The ball used by the Surrey bowlers in the first innings of their match against Gloucestershire at Guildford, July 1991. The damage to the ball is clearly visible, with the opening of the cross-seam pronounced not only at the centre but also at the junction of the quarter-seam. Note the almost suede-like surface. Of the nine wickets to fall with this ball, seven were taken by Waqar Younis.

Left: The most famous eyeball-to-eyeball confrontation of them all between Mike Gatting and Shakoor Rana in Faisalabad, 1987. Play did not resume for two days, including the rest day, until the England captain, on instructions from the TCCB, apologised.

Below: The 1992 First-Class Umpires panel, custodians of the Laws of Cricket. (Back, l to r): R White, Dudleston, M Kitchen, D Shepherd, G Sharp, R Tolchard, G Stickley, J Bond; (Middle, l to r): Burgess, J Holder, J Balderstone, V Holder, A Jones, N Plews, R Palmer, B Leadbeater, J Hampshire, Harris. (Front, l to r): A Whitehead, R Julian, D Constant, P Wight, H Bird, K Palmer, B Meyer, D Oslear.

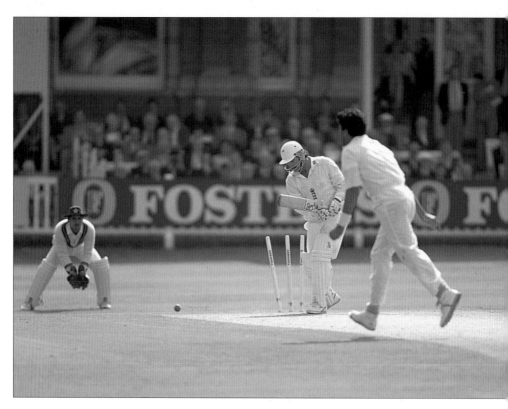

England v Pakistan, Second Test, Lord's 1992 and Allan Lamb (above) bowled by a typically big inswinging yorker from Waqar in the first innings. Eight runs later and Ian Botham (below) loses his wicket to a similar delivery from the same bowler. 'I knew what was coming,' said Botham, 'but I could do nothing about it.'

ENGLAND v PAKISTAN (Second Test)

Played at Lord's on June 18, 19, 20, 21, 1992. Pakistan won by 2 wickets.
Toss: England. Man of the Match: Wasim Akram. Debut: I.D.K. Salisbury.

ENGLAND

Batsman	Dismissal	Runs	Balls	Mins	4s	6s	Dismissal	Runs	Balls	Mins	4s	6s
G.A. Gooch*	b Wasim	69	98	132	13	0	lbw b Aqib	13	40	55	1	0
A.J. Stewart	c Miandad b Mujtaba	74	173	240	12	0	not out	69	138	249	9	0
G.A. Hick	c Miandad b Waqar	13	21	39	1	0	(4) c Moin b Mushtaq	11	20	31	2	0
R.A. Smith	c sub (Rashid) b Wasim	9	19	23	2	0	(5) b Mushtaq	8	5	8	2	0
A.J. Lamb	b Waqar	30	69	74	5	0	(6) lbw b Mushtaq	12	25	22	2	0
I.T. Botham	b Waqar	2	8	14	0	0	(7) lbw b Waqar	6	31	32	0	0
C.C. Lewis	lbw b Waqar	2	12	9	0	0	(8) b Waqar	15	18	19	2	0
R.C. Russell†	not out	22	38	55	3	0	(9) b Wasim	1	2	3	0	0
P.A.J. DeFreitas	c Inzamam b Waqar	3	22	28	0	0	(10) c Inzamam b Wasim	0	2	2	0	0
I.D.K. Salisbury	hit wkt. b Mushtaq	4	5	4	1	0	(3) lbw b Wasim	12	51	58	1	0
D.E. Malcolm	lbw b Mushtaq	0	3	7	0	0	b Wasim	0	1	1	0	0
Extras	(b6, .lb12, nb9)	27					(b5, lb8, nb15)	28				
TOTAL	(76.1 overs: 14.2 ph)	255					(52.4 overs: 12.7ph)	175				

PAKISTAN

Batsman	Dismissal	Runs	Balls	Mins	4s	6s	Dismissal	Runs	Balls	Mins	4s	6s
Aamir Sohail	c Russell b DeFreitas	73	108	156	11	0	b Salisbury	39	74	108	3	0
Ramiz Raja	b Lewis	24	36	53	5	0	c Hick b Lewis	0	1	8	0	0
Asif Mujtaba	c Smith b Malcolm	59	172	237	8	0	c Russell b Lewis	0	5	7	0	0
Javed Miandad*	c Botham b Salisbury	9	27	29	1	0	c Russell b Lewis	0	8	10	0	0
Salim Malik	c Smith b Malcolm	55	82	126	8	0	c Lewis b Salisbury	12	22	32	1	0
Inzamam-ul-Haq	c and b Malcolm	0	2	2	0	0	run out (Lewis/Russell)	8	24	35	1	0
Wasim Akram	b Salisbury	24	42	66	2	0	not out	45	64	124	4	0
Moin Khan†	c Botham b DeFreitas	12	52	63	1	0	c Smith b Salisbury	3	25	31	0	0
Mushtaq Ahmed	c Russell b DeFreitas	4	25	30	0	0	c Hick b Malcolm	5	16	21	0	0
Waqar Younis	b Malcolm	14	34	48	0	0	not out	20	33	58	2	0
Aqib Javed	not out	5	23	32	1	0	did not bat					
Extras	(b4, lb3, nb7)	14					(b2, lb5, w1, nb1)	9				
TOTAL	(98.5 overs: 13.8ph)	293					(45.1 overs: 12ph)	141 (8 wkts)				

Bowling

PAKISTAN	O	M	R	W	O	M	R	W
Wasim Akram	19	5	49	2	17.4	2	66	4
Aqib Javed	14	3	40	0	12	3	23	1
Waqar Younis	21	4	91	5	13	3	40	2
Mushtaq Ahmed	19.1	5	57	2	9	1	32	3
Asif Mujtaba	3	3	0	1	1	0	1	0

ENGLAND	O	M	R	W	O	M	R	W
DeFreitas	26	8	58	3				
Malcolm	15.5	1	70	4	15	2	42	1
Lewis	29	7	76	1	16	3	43	3
Salisbury	23	3	73	2	14.1	0	49	3
Botham	5	2	9	0				

Overall over rate: 13.2 ph

FALL OF WICKETS

	E	P	E	P
1st	123	43	40	6
2nd	153	123	73	10
3rd	172	143	108	18
4th	197	228	120	41
5th	213	228	137	62
6th	221	235	148	68
7th	232	263	174	81
8th	242	271	175	95
9th	247	276	175	–
10th	255	293	175	–

Umpires: B Dudleston and J. H. Hampshire

Above: With 13 of the 20 wickets to fall in the England innings, 9 of which were either bowled or lbw, Wasim and Waqar demolished the England batting line-up at Lord's.

Right: Salim Malik intervenes to try and restrain Aqib Javed at Old Trafford in the Third Test.

Above: The ball used by Pakistan (left) in the England first innings at Headingley in the 1992 Fourth Test, when England collapsed from 270 for 1 to 320 all out and the second new ball was never claimed. Note the scuff marks and obvious signs of damage, especially when compared with the ball used by England (right), a similar number of overs old.

Below: More carnage followed at the Oval Fifth Test – here, Derek Pringle is bowled by Wasim for 1 in the England second innings.

ENGLAND v PAKISTAN (Fifth Test)

Played at The Oval on August 6, 7, 8, 9, 1992. Pakistan won by 10 wickets.
Toss: England. Man of the Match: Wasim Akram. Debut: Rashid Latif.

ENGLAND

Batsman	Dismissal	R	Balls	Mins	4s	Dismissal	R	Balls	Mins	4s
G. A. Gooch*	c Mujtaba b Aqib	20	40	49	2	c Sohail b Waqar	24	71	87	3
A. J. Stewart†	c Ramiz b Wasim	31	42	65	4	lbw b Waqar	8	25	49	2
M. A. Atherton	c Rashid b Waqar	60	190	262	5	c Rashid b Waqar	4	9	15	1
R. A. Smith	b Mushtaq	33	122	149	3	not out	84	179	239	8
D. I. Gower	b Aqib	27	54	63	4	b Waqar	1	6	7	–
M. R. Ramprakash	lbw b Wasim	2	3	6	–	c Mujtaba b Mushtaq	17	39	44	33
C. C. Lewis	lbw b Wasim	4	7	12	–	st Rashid b Mushtaq	14	82	114	1
D. R. Pringle	b Wasim	1	3	3	–	b Wasim	1	10	11	–
N. A. Mallender	b Wasim	4	8	10	–	c Mushtaq b Wasim	3	10	17	–
P. C. R. Tufnell	not out	0	8	13	–	b Wasim	0	1	1	–
D. E. Malcolm	b Wasim	2	4	7	–	b Waqar	0	10	16	–
Extras	(b4, lb8, w1, nb10)	23				(b1, lb8, nb9)	18			
TOTAL	(78.1 overs: 14.2ph)	207				(72 overs: 14ph)	174			

PAKISTAN

Batsman	Dismissal	R	Balls	Mins	4s	Dismissal	R	Balls	Mins	4s
Aamir Sohail	c Stewart b Malcolm	49	86	126	10	not out	4	1	2	1
Ramiz Raja	b Malcolm	19	66	92	1	not out	0	–	2	–
Shoaib Mohammad	c and b Tufnell	55	155	200	5					
Javed Miandad*	c and b Lewis	59	101	141	9					
Salim Malik	b Malcolm	40	94	132	5					
Asif Mujtaba	run out (Smith)	50	165	196	5					
Wasim Akram	c Stewart b Malcolm	7	9	21	1					
Rashid Latif †	c Smith b Mallender	50	87	114	6					
Waqar Younis	c Gooch b Malcolm	6	3	6	1					
Mushtaq Ahmed	c Lewis b Mallender	9	22	27	2					
Aqib Javed	not out	0	4	12	–					
Extras	(b2, lb6, w4, nb24)	36				(w1)	1			
TOTAL	(127.5 overs: 14.2ph)	380				(0 wkt): (0.1 overs)	5			

PAKISTAN	O	M	R	W	O	M	R	W
Wasim Akram	22 .1	3	67	6	21	6	36	3
Waqar Younis	16	4	37	1	18	5	52	5
Aqib Javed	16	6	44	2	9	2	25	0
Mushtaq Ahmed	24	7	47	1	23	6	46	2
Aamir Sohail					1	0	6	0
ENGLAND								
Mallender	28.5	6	93	2				
Malcolm	29	6	94	5				
Lewis	30	8	70	1				
Tufnell	34	9	87	1				
Pringle	6	0	28	0				
Ramprakash					0.1	0	5	0

Overall over-rate: 14.13ph

FALL OF WICKETS

	E	P	E	P
1st	39	64	29	–
2nd	57	86	47	–
3rd	138	197	55	–
4th	182	214	59	–
5th	190	278	92	–
6th	196	292	153	–
7th	199	332	159	–
8th	203	342	173	–
9th	205	359	173	–
10th	207	380	174	–

Umpires: H. D. Bird and D. R. Shepherd.

Above: At the Oval Test, once again the Wasim-Waqar combination proved too much for England, this time 15 of the 20 wickets falling to the Pakistan bowling duo. In their first innings England lost their last seven wickets for 25 runs, all either bowled or lbw. Their second innings brought little improvement, with the last five falling for 21 runs.

Right: The ball used by Pakistan in the same match during the England second innings, with gouging marks near the quarter-seam.

Left: Aqib Javed celebrating the fall of Jack Russell for 4 during the Third Test at Old Trafford.

Below: Former West Indies wicketkeeper Deryck Murray, whose last match as an ICC appointed referee was the controversial Texaco one-day international between England and Pakistan at Lord's, 1992.

The one-day international between England and Pakistan at Lord's in August 1992 heralded the start of the great ball tampering debate. Here Waqar and Ramiz look for support from umpire Ken Palmer.

One side is polished to a medium sheen with sweat. Then, as the lacquer comes off the new ball, the unpolished side is gradually roughened by fingernails and kept dry by careful handling and lightly applying a bit of dirt and dust. After about 40 overs, the ball is smooth and damp with a slight sheen on one side, while the other is pitted and dry.

'It is a long way down the road from the discoveries made by Sarfraz, as was apparent particularly at the Oval in 1992. Pakistan defended with the new ball until it started to reverse swing. The methods by which they achieve this are against the rules, yet while it was obvious after the end of the innings that the ball had been tampered with – I happened to have a good look at it – it is virtually impossible for the umpires to detect the process as it is under way.

'I did it playing for Essex against Australia in 1985, about ninety minutes before the close of play, but was clumsy with it and John Hampshire changed the ball, which was swinging a lot. I was not nailed for it, and I remember Graham Gooch in the dressing room asking who had done it, and we all kept quiet. Some English bowlers who try it are usually doing it for themselves only, but Pakistan's entire match strategy is based upon getting the ball to reverse swing at some point during the match.

'One bowler who confessed to taking them on at their own game was Chris Pringle, the New Zealand seamer in Faisalabad in 1990-91. He admitted doctoring the ball and took 11 wickets in the match, including a career best seven for 52, after taking two for 180 in two earlier Tests.'

Of this instance described by Pringle, *Wisden* says: 'The New Zealand manager, Ian Taylor, on the team's return home, accused the Pakistan bowlers of doctoring the ball by lifting the seam or damaging the surface in order to obtain extra swing. The New Zealand manager even admitted that Chris Pringle had experimented with such tactics during the third Test in Faisalabad, in which he took seven for 52 in the first innings and Pakistan were bowled out for 102, their lowest total against New Zealand. The claim was strongly denied by the Pakistan Board and their players, while Intikhab Alam, the manager of the Pakistan side, described it as "rubbish".'

Warwickshire's Tim Munton first became aware of reverse swing around 1988. 'I had heard a lot about it,' Munton says, 'and at Edgbaston we started to try it. I find that you need a dry pitch and I don't wet the ball too much. It tends to swing more in than out. But I have also found over the years that no two cricket balls are exactly alike, even out of the same manufacturer's box. I usually bowl a couple of deliveries at the start of an innings to mid-off to see if I can detect if there is any bias in the ball. You only need a bit and it affects its performance.'

Former England, Middlesex and Glamorgan bowler Mike Selvey also subscribes to the baseball theory. 'When I was at Glamorgan, Javed Miandad showed us what he knew and it did make a difference. Also, we found that you can polish a ball better on flannel and cotton trousers than on artificial material.'

Paul Allott, formerly of England and Lancashire and a playing colleague of Wasim Akram, describes how a ball is primed legitimately for reverse swing. 'There is no need to gouge it. One side must be bone dry and never touched by sweaty hands. Sweat is best for the smooth side, because it is oilier than saliva. The dry side must get pitted, almost like the dimples on a golf ball, because it is that which makes the ball go.'

Like Munton, he found that the ball swung in more than out, but he also said he found it of little use because he had nothing like the pace of Wasim or Waqar which made it a devastating tactic.

Former England team manager Micky Stewart agrees about the speed factor. 'I rigged a couple of balls for practice before the Old Trafford Test against Pakistan in 1992. I knew how deadly reverse swing was from Waqar at Surrey, but I must emphasize I admire the skills involved in being able to exploit it at great pace and with control. Phillip DeFreitas and I bowled in the nets with the rigged balls, and he found he could swing it later than I could because of his extra pace. I am just sorry that the authorities have not got to grips with the problem and regularised it in some way.'

It is interesting to hear David Gower's thoughts on the phenomenon from a batsman's perspective. 'I remember the first time I was introduced to the mystery of reverse swing. It was 1982 at Lord's against Pakistan when I was standing in for Bob Willis as captain. I asked for the ball to be looked at by the umpires because I could not understand why it swung so much. Nothing was done about it, and I know that Imran has said since that he then knew how to take advantage of a naturally roughened ball by reverse swinging it.

'At county level, it was never really an item until 1990 when I joined Hampshire. We had Aqib Javed and he knew the theory. It still comes down to skill, and the authorities will have to face up to it because it is not going to go away. It needs a high-quality bowler to use it properly, and personally I would support a liberalisation of the Law. I would not go all the way and allow bottle tops and such like, but a reversion to the pre-1980 change of law to allow rubbing the ball into the ground is more easily controllable by umpires.

'I believe it would take a lot of suspicion out of the game. At Old Trafford in 1992, the two balls used by England and Pakistan were considerably different in appearance, and only the Roy Palmer incident deflected attention away from the way the ball swung a lot.

'What is noticeable is that while Waqar swings it more "in" then "out", Wasim can make it go both ways. He bent it a mile at Leicester in a knockout game, just as he did when he came back to get Allan Lamb and Chris Lewis in the 1992 World Cup final.'

Mark Nicholas led Hampshire for eleven years and has his own theories. 'The only new aspect of ball tampering is the scuffing. Andy Roberts could reverse swing in the mid Seventies but it was generally unheard of in county cricket until about 1990. The seam used to be picked and various agents such as lip ice would be used to enhance the shine. Skill was needed to maximise the benefits of extra swing, just as it is paramount now.

'If any bowler suddenly became a world beater only because of ball tampering, I would feel more strongly about it, but that is not the case. Only a handful of bowlers in world cricket have the ability to bowl fast at controlled yorker length. A naturally roughened old ball is more lethal in their hands than other bowlers in the same side.

'Expediting the wearing process is a fascinating exercise. I think it is brilliant – and is so easy to do that I have done it in the nets and made the ball go all over the place – but at such a gentle pace it would not bother any decent batsman.

'When Aqib Javed came to Hampshire in 1991, I remember a game against Somerset at Southampton. Jimmy Cook was over 150 not out when Aqib came back and the ball went sideways. Umpire David Shepherd looked at it and said "that's not legal". Cook said, "Let it go", but Shepherd told me to stop Aqib doing it, which is what I did.

'I still think that swing is good for the game. The ball has to be pitched up, so there is less of the short stuff. Of the current England bowlers, Peter Martin is one of the best at swinging the ball.'

According to former England captain Bob Willis: 'No bowler in any side I captained interfered with the ball. I would support a change of law to allow fingernails to help roughen one side. But I would not allow artificial aids such as a bottle top.'

Ian Botham is familiar with the phenomenon of reverse swing. 'We called it "Irish" at Somerset, and Graham Burgess and I knew about it. Sometimes it would happen without us trying it, but I was familiar with the principle of one roughened side. It seemed that reverse swing would happen naturally between 50 and 80 overs.'

Cricketers throughout the game admire the skill, but not the breaking of the current Law which is necessary if the natural deterioration of the ball is to be expedited. There appears to be a chain of shared communication in the art of reverse swing, beginning with Sarfraz who, many believe, passed the baton to Imran who, in turn, shared the recipe with Wasim and then Waqar.

Imran is a stout defender of the faith. 'Ball tampering, one way or another, has gone on since cricket has been played. The most common form was to lift the seam. This is illegal, but in my 21 years of cricket, I have never seen a bowler reprimanded by an umpire. In fact, seam lifting had almost become accepted in the game. Another form of tampering is by applying substances to the ball to enhance the shine.

'The third method is the act of scuffing the ball. In Pakistan the pitches are dry, so picking the seam or shining the ball is not effective. In these conditions we have this phenomenon that was, until recently, unheard of in England. Reverse swing – namely the ball swings towards the smooth side rather than away from it as with orthodox fashion. Because of our rough outfields and grassless pitches, the leather gets scuffed up. By using sweat and shine on one side and leaving the other rough, the ball swings towards the shining side.

'It is nonsense to say reverse swing can only be obtained by ball tampering. On dry pitches and rough outfields, it will often happen when a fast bowler comes back for his second spell. Sometimes in Australia, the pitches become so rock hard by the fourth and fifth days that the ball will take reverse swing in a bowler's first spell. I saw Dennis Lillee reverse swing it at Melbourne against Pakistan, and Max Walker did so four years earlier in Guyana. Fred Trueman also found that occasionally the ball would go with the shine, but never knew why.

'Had the TCCB not standardized the balls in 1981, reverse swing would have been unknown in this country. Before then it was impossible to reverse swing in England, as the ball had bigger seams and the wickets were never as bare or hard as in Pakistan or Australia. Also, the lush green outfields preserved the ball even when it was 100 overs old. Only in August, during dry spells, could I reverse swing.

'After 1981, due to the altered ball, I found I could reverse swing it after 40 to 50 overs from mid-July onwards. The thing about reverse swing is that not everyone can do it. Firstly, a bowler must be able to swing the ball anyway. Secondly, it takes a while to perfect the delivery, as the ball is gripped and released differently.

'In 1990 in England the seam was further reduced by the TCCB and since then reverse swing has become quite common in county cricket.'

Imran then queries Oslear's evidence presented in the High Court case. 'How come, despite repeated anti-Pakistan pressure from the press and a whispering campaign from the England dressing room, it was only after five Tests and during a one-day international that a ball used by Pakistan was changed? Were the English umpires so incompetent that, despite frequent ball inspections, they were unable to detect any ball tampering? I suspect that, because the pitches at Lord's, Headingley and the Oval were grassless, the balls were getting roughed up by the bare surfaces.'

Imran could be right, but that point destroys most of his criticism of the umpires in the Lord's one-day international. The game was held over to a second day because of rain, and the pitch, its surrounds and the outfield were damp and lush, *and the ball was not 30 overs old.*

As he says, 'Had England produced green pitches, it would have been impossible for Pakistan bowlers to use reverse swing, no matter how much scratching they did. The moisture from the grass would have smoothed the ball again. Moreover an umpire would easily have detected a scratch made by the bowler's nails.' *As umpires Hampshire and Palmer did, as confirmed in court by Oslear.*

Imran poses the crucial question and answers it in a revealing manner. 'Did the Pakistani bowlers tamper with the ball? My answer is, in one way or another, I feel every seam bowler has done it. It is only the degree of tampering that varies from bowler to bowler.'

In court, former Northamptonshire colleagues of Sarfraz Nawaz, Alan Hodgson and Wayne Larkins, both testified, under oath, of previous conversations in which Sarfraz had told them how best to tamper with the ball. Lamb's England colleague, Robin Smith, also gave evidence. He played in every international match in 1992 against Pakistan and said that the ball was doctored throughout the summer. 'In all the matches I played, I saw something going on.'

The difficulty facing umpires was that, if done carefully by a fielding side, gentle scratching is difficult to spot, because the bowler will dampen the ball at the end of an over, thus covering up the damage.

An instance of such handling of the ball came from an unexpected quarter during the Headingley Test in 1992. The umpires, Ken Palmer and Mervyn Kitchen, had a look at the ball during an interval, but could see little to which they could take exception. Palmer, unthinkingly, gave the ball a rub with sweaty hands before he put it into his coat pocket. As they walked out on to the field, the Pakistan captain, Javed Miandad, asked for the ball. When it was thrown to him, still slightly damp from the Palmer touch, he asked accusingly, 'Who's done this?'

That proved to be a non-event, unlike an incident in the third Test between Zimbabwe and Pakistan in Harare in mid-February 1995, when Aamir Sohail and Salim Malik accused home umpire Ian Robinson of ball tampering, by wetting it during an inspection. The players were given a severe reprimand from match referee Jackie Hendriks.

The responsibility for reverse swing and ball tampering becoming inextricably interwoven rests with the TCCB, according to former cricket correspondent of the *Sunday Times*, Robin Marlar, himself a past captain of Sussex.

'The fact is that the issue was tabled and discussed at the captains' meeting at Lord's in 1991, the year before Pakistan toured England. A damaged ball was passed around. David Hughes of Lancashire thought he recognized it as one which Wasim Akram had used. David passed it on and eventually the ball reached Ian Greig, then captain of Surrey. He told his colleagues that he recognized it as one used by Waqar Younis.

'Officials who deny the issue was the subject of lively debate in 1991, especially because Pakistan were the following year's tourists, behaved like the three wise monkeys. They had the opportunity to pronounce on ball tampering, a grey area in the laws, but waited until the damage was done before issuing edicts at the beginning of 1993.'

In military terms, the TCCB officials were guilty of desertion from the front line, as Oslear had already found out in 1990 and 1991, and would again in 1992 and 1993.

Oslear's record of his match reports details many instances when he felt obliged to reveal what he saw as illegal interference with the ball to the TCCB. The central figure in Oslear's first such report, the former Pakistan captain Imran Khan, went on the record to admit that, on at least one occasion, he had tampered with the ball, against Hampshire at Hove in early September 1981.

Imran says: 'I believe scratching was no more a crime than lifting the seam and you can only scratch a ball when it is well marked [Lord's 1992?]. I have occasionally scratched the side and lifted the seam. Only once did I use an object. The ball was not deviating at all, so I got the 12th man to bring on a bottle top and it started to move around a lot.'

Oslear's comments are these. 'Before Imran admitted he had broken the law in 1981, he wrote several articles on the matter, including one in May 1992. The headline was "Cheats Tag Rooted in Colonial Attitudes". He accused the British press and players of bias. He said, "They accuse us of doctoring cricket balls, with one side of the ball apparently scratched by the bowlers. Why should it be such a crime to do that?"'

Oslear's reply to that is clear. 'Because it is against the Laws of Cricket, and thank God for colonial attitudes if they make efforts to punish those who cheat in sporting contests. How can anyone be such a hypocrite as to write what he [Imran] did, knowing he had cheated with a cricket ball to gain an unfair advantage?

'In my remarks to Lord's about Imran in 1983, I did not accuse him of cheating, although the weight of evidence pointed that way and is now endorsed by his own admission. As for his questions, aimed at me, about the 1992 series and why no ball was changed before the Lord's one-day game, I would say this: There were complaints made during and after the third Test at Old Trafford, and repeated during the meeting prior to the Headingley Test. The ball used during the England first innings (England collapsed from 270 for one to 320 all out) was taken to the match referee, Clyde Walcott, because, in the opinion of the three officials, it had been tampered with. This was shown to him during the innings and not at the end of it.

'That is fact, because I was the third umpire who took it for inspection and photographed it. It was also photographed by others, and I still know where that ball is, although the TCCB do not.

'The state to which the ball had been reduced was unbelievable, and tampering had clearly taken place. The same thing happened at Lord's a month later, and I wish I had also taken photos of that ball.

'The only way Imran would have a defence is if the Laws of Cricket allowed what he admits he did, and the Pakistan team of 1992 did, at Lord's. Until they are changed, I only have contempt for anyone who, knowingly, flouts the law and then almost boasts about it.

'I deplore the fact that the authorities all over the world shuffled their feet and did nothing, especially as they were given reported chapter and verse twice within the ten-week period in 1990 when New Zealand and the West Indies toured Pakistan. Both touring sides sent official reports from captains and management about ball tampering. The Chris Pringle incident is well documented, and the West Indies also objected to what they saw as unfair practice.'

Wisden had this to say: 'As after the New Zealand series, there were complaints from the visiting team's management that the Pakistanis were tampering with the ball to help it swing. The charge was promptly denied by Imran Khan and the Pakistan Board.'

Imran said, 'It is a ridiculous charge. The Pakistan bowlers play in county cricket and have never been accused by any player or umpire. [Oslear will disprove that.] They played under the close scrutiny of John Hampshire and John Holder in the series against India, and not a finger was raised. I am surprised at the allegations.'

The West Indies manager, Lance Gibbs, was shown balls used by both teams in the first Test and apparently agreed that the ball used by the West Indies was in worse condition than the one used by Pakistan. Plenty of smoke again, but no visible fire.

Oslear switches his attack on the authorities to nearer home. 'The following season, 1991 in England, reports were received by the TCCB from a number of their contracted umpires about illegal interference with the ball by two or three sides, all of which contained a Pakistan Test fast bowler.'

It needs neither an Einstein nor a Sherlock Holmes to pin Lancashire, Surrey and Hampshire, for whom, respectively, Wasim Akram, Waqar Younis and Aqib Javed played. By 22 July 1991, four reports had been filed and a further two by 19 August.

Oslear: 'Despite the Board officers assuring us umpires that they would take strong action against offenders, nothing happened, except a slap-on-the-wrist type letter to Surrey, but more of that later.

'What annoyed me is that I made repeated approaches to Tony Brown and Alan Smith about the problem in 1991, and warned them about the possible consequences in 1992 when Pakistan would tour England.

'I had actually filed a report in 1990 following a three-day game at Edgbaston in August between a TCCB Under-25 side and India, and this was the first clear instance I had seen of scratching, gouging, slicing, peeling, call it what you like. Checking notes and reports, I found that other umpires had reported the Indians for ball tampering, two of them in the Tests at Lord's and the Oval. Nigel Plews stood in both games with Dickie Bird and David Shepherd, and was removed from the Test panel for 1991. Coincidence, I suppose.

'The Edgbaston game came before the Oval Test match, and the trouble started in the Board XI's second innings when they were chasing 200 in 56 overs. In the first nine overs of their reply they were 19 for three, with Nadeem Shahid, Graham Thorpe and Paul Johnson all lbw to deliveries which swung miles and late. Off the fifth ball of the tenth over, the ball was played slowly back down the pitch and I thought I was seeing things. I saw red, white, red, white, just as though it was one of those two-piece practice balls.

'After the next ball, I called "over" and demanded the ball. It was given to me reluctantly, and I can only say I had not seen a ball in such condition since the Imran one on the same ground seven years earlier. I showed it to my colleague, Mike Harris, who said, "They've destroyed it". Perhaps they had, but only half of it. The two bowlers were Sharma and Prabhakar, and I decided to approach the captain. Mohammad Azharuddin was not playing, and the acting captain, Ravi Shastri, was off the field, so I went to Dillip Vengsarkar, whom I had a high regard for as a cricketer and a person. I told him, the bowlers and the two batsmen, John Stephenson and Richard Blakey, that if the tampering did not stop, I would stop the game and inform the Indian management why.

'I told Vengsarkar to tell the rest of the side, and we had no more trouble. The Under-25s finished with 110 for three, with the ball now behaving normally. I spent some time after the match writing my report as I was obliged to do, but I may as well have gone to the bar instead, because no notice was taken of it at all – just like all the other reports filed that year.

'My report contained my explanation of the incident which I could not fit into the section on umpires' reports dealing with breaches of playing conditions. It said: *'The two umpires had to bring to the attention of the fielding captain [India] the fact that there was illegal interference with the ball. He was told that it must cease and if any individual was caught he would be reported to the management of his side immediately. The inspection of the ball was after 10 overs' play.'*

'I saw Vengsarkar five years later when I went with MCC to India and umpired in a game against Bombay Gymkhana. We spoke about the Edgbaston incident and he told me that we frightened his players out of their skin.'

CHAPTER 7

The Surrey factor

Oslear filed three reports about ball tampering in the month between 19 July and 19 August 1991, all of which had been co-signed by his umpiring colleague at the matches concerned and, significantly, all concerned Surrey. In that period, they played five three-day championship matches, winning two, drawing two and losing one. Waqar Younis was now in his second season at the Oval. In his first in 1990, he had taken 57 championship wickets in 14 matches at an average of 23.90, with three hauls of five wickets in an innings; in stark contrast to 1991, when he took 113 wickets in 17 matches at an average of 14.36, with 13 returns of five wickets in an innings and three of 10 wickets in a match.

The comparisons are not necessarily significant or sinister, because a 20-year-old, as he was in 1991, could be expected to progress rapidly. *Wisden* paid this tribute. 'It is doubtful whether anyone has bowled faster or straighter in an English season than Waqar Younis did for Surrey in 1991. The bouncer had a minimal place in his armoury; stumps were hit and pads thumped regularly to earn the young Pakistani a rich harvest of 151 wickets in all competitions, *with an astonishing two thirds of his victims either bowled or lbw.*'

Surrey's coach, Geoff Arnold, could think of no fast bowler in the world he rated more highly. 'He's unique. He has greater ability to swing the ball late and at a faster pace – not to mention landing it in the blockhole – than anyone I've seen.'

The first match reported by Oslear was against Gloucestershire at Guildford, with Oslear and the other umpire, Bob White, uneasy about the condition of the balls used when Surrey were in the field. The following game was on the same ground against Yorkshire, and this is Oslear's letter to the Board, which accompanied the match reports and was counter-signed by White.

'In the previous match there were certain thoughts that there had been tampering with the ball, but after talking with the captain, Ian Greig, the benefit of the doubt was given. At the end of the innings, we noticed that the cross-seam had been opened up, and we then knew that our initial thoughts were correct.

'In the Yorkshire match, I examined the ball at the end of the 47th over and found that the cross-seam had been pulled apart. My colleague and I called over the Surrey captain, Alec Stewart, and told him the practice must cease immediately. He looked at the ball with us, reprimanded Waqar Younis, and stopped him from bowling. The only ball we had of inferior quality was the one from the previous match against Gloucestershire and, as the seam of that one had also been opened up, we felt it would have been playing into the hands of the fielding side to have given them that ball to use.

'I therefore pressed the quarter-seam together and we carried on with the original ball, inspecting it at the end of every other over. Needless to say, the seam remained tightly closed, despite Waqar being brought back to bowl.'

In the second innings of that match, when the alleged transgression took place, Waqar transformed things with five wickets for eight runs in 27 balls, with three clean bowled and one lbw.

Such skill is remarkable and to be admired, almost regardless of the methods used to maximize it. That said, Oslear is correct in applying the Law as it is written. Breaking a bad law is no defence, because the remedy is to change that law in proper fashion.

Oslear's opinion of Waqar is also interesting. 'Waqar has always been polite and courteous in our dealings, although I find it disconcerting he always called me Mr Oslear.'

And so to New Road, Worcester, for the three-day game starting 16 August, only 25 days after Oslear had spoken to the Surrey captain, Alec Stewart. Again, Oslear felt obliged to send an accompanying letter to the Board, and again it was counter-signed by his colleague, Barry Dudleston.

'Unfortunately, I have to report again the lifting of the quarter-seam while Surrey were fielding. I first brought it to the attention of Alec Stewart after 40 overs, who was the Surrey captain when I reported the matter previously. This time Surrey were captained by

Ian Greig, but I asked Mr Stewart to remedy the situation before we, the umpires, had to take action.

'The penultimate over before lunch was bowled and I noticed that the ball was again tampered with. At the end of the over Mr Stewart took the ball again and tried to press the seam together, but he failed. When we left the field for lunch, my colleague noticed the interference with the ball, and during the break, I obtained from the Worcestershire coach the oldest ball he could find.

'We then informed Ian Greig that, should the action not cease, his bowlers would have to bowl with the very old one. He called his four bowlers together (Waqar, Martin Bicknell, Tony Murphy and Keith Medlycott) and asked us to tell them what we proposed to do. Both my fellow umpire and myself have observed this sort of action previously and I, if not both of us, have reported it. I do intend that this form of cheating is eradicated from the game and will take all steps to ensure I succeed.

'The only reason we issued a warning instead of changing the ball was, simply, it may have played into the hands of Surrey as the score was 281 for three.'

Worcestershire lost their last seven wickets for 98, but that often happened in three-day cricket when fewer scores of over 400 were recorded than in four-day cricket. Also, Waqar finished with four wickets, two of which were taken when Graeme Hick (145) and Tim Curtis (98) were well on top.

What would the TCCB do, with three reports from the same umpire about the same side, and all within a month? Surely they would be seen to take strong action, especially as Surrey had also been reported in 1990 for the same offence at Cheltenham against Gloucestershire. That meant three official reports, plus the equivalent of a fourth, also against Gloucestershire at Guildford in 1991.

Oslear was disappointed, but not surprised, at the response of authority. 'When I refer to the humbug and hypocrisy of officers of the TCCB, some may think I have an axe to grind. Not so. I simply want to see all incidents of unfair play eradicated from cricket. In my efforts to do just that, I have received no support whatsoever from those who have preached to the umpires that they will be supported to the hilt in any action they take to uphold the standards and dignity of the game.

'I thought that three reported offences in a month about the same side, following a previous report in 1990, would have brought some of the strong action the Board keep bleating about. Strong action? It's a joke, as this letter, signed on behalf of Tony Brown, shows.

'It was dated 23 August, exactly the same date, 12 months later, when the roof fell in on the same men who dodged any hint of firm action involving a bowler who had, by then, been involved in five matches in which the umpires reported ball tampering, and two series in Pakistan against New Zealand and West Indies, whose managements had complained about the same practice.

'This was what Tony Brown's letter to Surrey said. It was addressed to the Secretary of Surrey, David Seward.

'"*Following two reported incidents by umpires of deliberate tampering with the ball by Surrey players, and one bowler in particular, Alan Smith has asked me to tell you that the Board takes a very serious view of this breach of the regulations.*

'"*Would you please make it clear to your captain and players that it is possible for the Board to take action under the Discipline Regulation Appendix C Paragraph 2.3.5 and this the Board will do if there is any further umpire's report referring to the deliberate damage to the ball. If the allegations are proved it is possible for a variety of penalties to be considered and these are clearly listed under paragraphs 4.3.1 and 4.3.2. Please take all necessary action to prevent any such discipline procedures being necessary.*"'

The letter made no reference to the 1990 game at Cheltenham, nor the suspected third offence at Guildford.

The written time-bomb was to tick away at the Oval for a year, but then explode with the fall-out apparently costing the Surrey Secretary his job when, it was reported, the senior committee officers first became aware of its existence. Seward said that his departure from the Oval was only coincidental with the revelation that he had not informed his committee of the 1991 letter.

More important than how, procedurally, the letter was treated at the Oval, was a warning letter detailing the right way to deal with offences and offenders which could only be described as persistent. Why did the Board not tackle, head-on, the players concerned? Why did they, by confining action to a written warning, deny the umpires the sort of strong action support they needed, if they were to follow the edicts of the Board to clamp down firmly upon such serious cricketing crimes?

No wonder Oslear's frustration grew. 'I had done everything required of me, but the support could not even be termed "weak-kneed", it was non-existent. Why was not the warning a public one? Was it because the matter was never discussed at disciplinary level, and our reports never got further than Alan Smith and Tony Brown?'

Oslear's persistence on the subject could not even be considered by the Board as an obsession, because the three reports were counter-signed by two different umpires – Bob White at Guildford and Barry Dudleston at Worcester. The 1990 report was made by Chris Balderstone who, like Oslear, does his duty unflinchingly, and is not deterred by the possibility of unpleasant consequences. The three reports in 1991 now increased to five the number filed by Oslear since 1983, and no punishment was meted out to any of the players or the sides involved.

By their inaction, the TCCB forfeits any sympathy it might otherwise have been afforded 12 months later in the Lord's one-day international. A possible defence would be a reported approach to the TCCB from the Foreign Office. This pointed out that, should action be taken against the Pakistan side, the possible consequences could include a deterioration in relationships between the two countries at levels other than cricket.

Such a theory – and that is all it is – would explain some, but not all, of the alleged cover-up which is at the heart of Oslear's belief that the Board abrogated its responsibility to the good name of cricket, by refusing, consistently, to respond to any adverse reports from umpires. But surely any governmental approach would not also ask for immunity from punishment for individual cricketers in county cricket, if those cricketers happened to come from overseas and from one country in particular?

In the period from 1983 onwards, Oslear now feels bound to attack the Board on two fronts. Lack of support and a refusal to penalize the players concerned was one, but the other was more serious.

'It is untrue, as the Board claim, that no reports were received during the 1993 season of ball tampering. The real cheek of that is they have said that the improved situation was because of strong action they took. One letter, that was the total of the so-called strong action. The blunt truth is that they ran away as soon as they knew there was a problem, and by doing so, they invited a lot of what happened in 1992.

'To nail their lie in 1993, what about the balls sent to them from the Northamptonshire v Surrey game on 22, 23, 24 and 26 July 1993, and the one from Derbyshire v Lancashire a month earlier, which led to all the aggravation between the same two sides in the Benson & Hedges Cup final at Lord's a fortnight later?

'The ball from the Derbyshire match was photographed, and it is in about the same condition as the ball I photographed in the Headingley Test in 1992 between England and Pakistan. Those two matches were the subject of reports in 1993, and I made a verbal report of another match involving Surrey which I was loath to make official because of a plea from their acting captain Monte Lynch.'

The umpires in the Derbyshire v Lancashire match did not make a report, but the Derbyshire club did. The Northamptonshire umpires were Chris Balderstone and Ray Julian. Not only did they file reports about ball tampering, they also sent the balls concerned to Lord's but were bitterly disappointed when, yet again, no action was taken.

In the Surrey v Leicestershire match at the Oval on the 14–16 August 1992, the umpires were John Holder and Barry Dudleston. Holder was now off the Test panel, with his last Test at the Oval the previous year between England and the West Indies. He and Mervyn Kitchen had warned the England captain, Graham Gooch, about the condition of the ball on the third morning, Saturday. Both umpires expected a statement to be made about the incident, but it was not, and the Board still deny that any such incident happened.

Why? And why did they deny that any reports of ball tampering were made in 1993? The Derbyshire game against Lancashire had such a dramatic finale that it provoked an after-the-match reaction from the home players and club officers, that spilled into the Benson & Hedges final 12 days later. Needing 379 to win, Derbyshire were 243 for two with John Morris having hit a brilliant 151, but Wasim Akram then took six for 11 in 49 deliveries, and Lancashire won easily by 111 runs.

So incensed were the home players that, when their number 11, Ole Mortensen, was bowled by Wasim, he chased down towards the boundary to retrieve the ball and handed it to his colleagues. Umpires Vanburn Holder and George Sharp had inspected the ball regularly, but found nothing amiss. Nor did the TCCB when the Derbyshire club forwarded the ball to Lord's, and there the matter rested.

Then captain Kim Barnett says: 'We were cruising to victory, then suddenly we lost easily. All in an hour, when the ball swung huge amounts. It can happen, and Wasim is a world-class bowler, but the sudden change from nothing to everything was startling. Wasim was unplayable and I know our players were bothered about our collapse.'

Alan Hill was then acting secretary of Derbyshire, and he it was who sent four balls to the TCCB – two used by Lancashire and, for purposes of comparison, two used by Derbyshire. 'I cannot remember such a transformation in a match. Not just because of the collapse, but because the ball had hardly swung up until then, and suddenly it went miles. I know the umpires did not report any misuse, which is why I suppose the Board found it difficult to take any action.'

The only action which followed was the unfortunate incident in the morning session of the B & H Cup final between the same teams 12 days later. Understandably, the Lancashire side were incensed by the accusations and the action of Mortensen in grabbing the ball at the end of the match. Chris Adams had also queried the reason for the ball suddenly swinging. He asked Wasim to let him have a look at it, and was told that the damage was because Morris had smashed it so often into the concrete surrounds. What a coincidence that all the damage sustained was on one side of the ball only.

Derbyshire batted first at Lord's, with *Wisden* setting this scene. 'Much of the pre-match publicity surrounded events on the last afternoon of a Championship match between the two counties less than a fortnight before the final. Derbyshire had sent a ball used with startling effect by Wasim Akram during their second innings destruction to the TCCB for examination. Inevitable rumours of malpractice were quickly knocked down by the Board, but the mysterious saga and the ill-feeling it generated spilled into the final.'

As Adams quickly discovered when he walked in to bat with the score 32 for two. In steamed Wasim from the Nursery End, and let go a high full toss which Adams took on the left shoulder blade as he vainly tried to take evasive action. Umpire Barry Meyer had to decide if it was intentional or not and had some strong words to say to the bowler. Whether intentional or not, an apology takes some of the steam out of things, but what incensed the Derbyshire players most of all, and led to an altercation between batsman and bowler in the players' dining room at lunchtime, was that Wasim made no attempt to talk to Adams.

Adams says, 'I remember Mike Watkinson coming to ask me if I was all right but, having completely lost the ball from Wasim's hand and turned and ducked instinctively, I did not have a clue about what he did. As Wasim walked back to his mark, he half-raised an arm, but the Derbyshire boys reckon that was to tell the umpire it was an accident.'

Adams was out before lunch, and saw the incident replayed several times before he went to eat. As ill luck had it, the Lancashire players were seated when he went to the dining room and they were at the table immediately on the right as Adams went through the door. Also, Wasim was seated at the end of the table and so was the first person to appear in Adam's sights.

Human nature being just that, there are times when the other cheek is turned, and times when it is not – or, in this case, the other shoulder blade. Wasim was told by Adams what would happen if he did it again and that, accompanied by a bit of chest-prodding, was that.

The Derbyshire Chairman at the time, Chris Middleton, remembers the shock-waves that disturbed the normally ripple-proof waters at Lord's to such an extent that a peace-making meeting was arranged a few days after the final between representatives of the two clubs, the Cricketers' Association and the TCCB.

'The Board was worried that there might be bad blood between Derbyshire and Lancashire, and arranged a meeting at Edgbaston. In attendance were Kim Barnett and myself for Derbyshire, Tim Curtis as Chairman of the Cricketers' Association, David Hughes, Neil Fairbrother, Geoff Ogden and John Bower from Lancasire and Peter Bromage, Alan Wheelhouse and Tony Brown from the TCCB.

'I could have told them that there was no problem between the clubs. In fact, I went out to dinner on the eve of the final with some of the Lancashire committee. Also Neil Fairbrother was best man for John Morris, but the only problem was that beamer from Wasim. Peter Bromage started things off with a video of the incident, and then he and the other Board representatives saw the rest of us separately. Not individually, but each club in turn.

'The meeting finished, but after the Lancashire people had left, I showed the balls from the championship game, which I had collected from Lord's a few days earlier. The more you looked at the one, compared with the other three, the more obvious it was that something had happened to it. It looked as though a rotweiller had chewed it, and I remember Tim Curtis looking at it and saying that he found it difficult to believe that it had got into that state naturally at Derby, where we have a lush outfield and advertising boards as the boundary fence, with little or no concrete.

'He was right, but even if the damage had been caused by John Morris's onslaught, why was every scratch, cut and scuff on one side of the ball only? I can partly understand the difficulty the Board found itself in because of no mention about the ball in the reports from Vanburn Holder and George Sharp. But they should have looked at the ball and at what happened in the game, and taken action on what was overwhelming evidence.

'Kim Barnett said at the Edgbaston meeting that, prior to that game, Wasim had never swung the ball much at him over the years. When Kim went out to bat at number five, he shouldered arms to one which started at least two feet outside off stump and swung back so sharply that he was plumb lbw offering no stroke. Remember that John Morris had just smashed 151 with no trouble at all before Wasim came back and boomeranged the ball all over the place for his six for 11 in 49 balls.'

Strange things happen in cricket, but rarely does a match pattern, established over three and a half days, alter so dramatically. *Wisden* made these points: 'No Derbyshire match has ever produced so many runs, the aggregate 1497 passing the 1391 between Derbyshire and Essex at Chesterfield in 1904, but the conclusion was startling. Wasim Akram took six for 11 in 49 deliveries. Although the umpires inspected the ball regularly, Derbyshire were sufficiently concerned about its condition to send it to the TCCB.'

Wasim's six wickets included three lbws, one clean bowled and two catches to wicketkeeper Warren Hegg. Chris Adams recalls watching five wickets fall in no time. 'I saw John get one which swung away and across him. Kim then got the banana the other way, Matthew Vandrau was lbw, and Dominic Cork bowled, both with huge inswingers, and Mike Watkinson got Frank Griffith before I was lbw to Wasim.'

Has any game in history ended with a number 11 racing the fielders to the boundary in order to grab the ball and take it to his team-mates? And has a county club ever before sent a suspect ball to Lord's for inspection, knowing that the umpires had not reported it? Both actions suggest that, as far as Derbyshire players and officials were concerned, the ball that Wasim used in such devastating fashion after 48 overs of usage, had been illegally tampered with.

The statistical evidence is as overwhelming as that of the ball claimed by Middleton. Prior to the extraordinary climax to the match, 1483 runs were scored from 388 overs (3.82 runs per over) for the loss of 30 wickets. *The other eight fell in 15 overs at a cost of 15 runs.*

Fair of foul? Legitimate say Lancashire, the umpires and the TCCB. Derbyshire will never agree, as Middleton's remarks about the Edgbaston meeting make clear.

The charges and denials between both sides were many between 28 June and 10 July – all stemming from an alleged ball tampering-provoked beamer. Let Adams have the final word. 'I know I got wound up and I regret it now. But, although Wasim said nothing to me out in the middle, he did say it was an accident after the match when we were on the balcony for the presentations. I said, "Fair enough, that's the end of it".'

As it was regarding Derbyshire against Lancashire, but not Surrey six weeks later.

Surrey played Derbyshire at Ilkeston in a Championship match on the 19 to 21 August 1993, with two facts of particular significance. A year had now elapsed since Surrey were given a suspended sentence of £1000 in respect of a reported case of ball tampering in the match against Leicestershire at the Oval in August 1992. Remember, this suspended sentence was a follow-up of the letter dated 23 August 1991, warning the club of punitive action if there was a repetition of two reported cases of 'deliberate tampering with the ball' in 1991.

The second factor was the position of the Surrey captain if any further transgressions occurred. According to *Wisden*, referring to the 1992 season, 'The Surrey Chairman, Derek Newton, said the captain would be held responsible for any contravention by his players.' With England playing Australia at the Oval in the sixth Test, Monte Lynch was captain at Ilkeston. Waqar's 1993 season – his first since his extraordinary performances of 1991 – was good, but not outstanding. In 13 matches – the match against Derbyshire was his 10th – he took 62 wickets in 449.4 overs at an average of 22.69 apiece, and his personal strike rate was a wicket every 44 balls, compared with one every 26 balls in 1991, and one every 43 balls in his first season in 1990.

To develop the comparison between 1991 and 1993, Waqar took 69 more wickets in 1991 in 120 more overs. Statistics can prove or disprove many theories, but it is difficult to present a satisfactory explanation for his season of apotheosis, other than that of ball tampering, even if malpractice could only prove so damaging if allied to wonderful skill.

A final statistical point is that 1990 and 1993 produced for Waqar 129 wickets from 871 overs, compared with 131 from 570 in 1991.

At Ilkeston, Waqar bowled with a marked lack of success, except for a brief flurry of three wickets with the second new ball in a spell of five overs. Oslear chronicles the events thus, of a match about which, uniquely, he did not file an official report concerning what he saw as a clear breaking of Law 42.5.

'Late on the evening of 20 August, following the second day of Derbyshire v Surrey game, I started a report to the TCCB with *"It is my misfortune, but also my duty, to inform you of a further case of ball tampering involving Surrey CCC."* It was a report I never finished or submitted to the authorities, and people who know me and my determination to stamp out cheating of this nature might find my change of mind difficult to understand.

'I do not believe in turning a blind eye to actions of the sort carried out by Waqar on that day, or perhaps I should say, to two of the overs he bowled. Surrey were bowled out on the first day for 205, and Derbyshire got off to a great start with an opening partnership between Peter Bowler and John Morris, with their first wicket not falling until well into the second day.

'My colleague was Ray Julian, and we both inspected the ball frequently on the second day, and agreed that the Surrey bowlers were keeping it in good condition, and legally. At 101.3 overs, Monte Lynch called for a second new ball when the score was nearly 400. Joey Benjamin completed the over from my end, with Waqar then bowling the next seven overs from the opposite end.

'Nothing happened in his first three overs, except he bowled very fast. He had an exchange of words with Dominic Cork which was the usual stuff – full of comments about each other's batting and bowling, none of which was complimentary. Waqar had the last word, sending the off-stump back about 10 yards, and it was then that I knew that damage was being inflicted upon the ball once again.

'As I re-set the stumps, I picked up the ball and noticed some marks and a hairline cut, or perhaps I should say a nailine cut. Remember, we are talking about a second new ball, only six overs old, yet I recognised the marks as of 1992 vintage. As for the cut, that was how the damage was first initiated on the ball which I gave to Alan Smith on the afternoon of 23 August 1992, the day of the Lord's Texaco game. I asked fellow umpire Ray Julian to inspect the ball while the next batsman came in. He did so, but passed the ball back to Waqar without comment. Waqar got two more wickets in the 111th and 113th overs, both lbw, and when I had another look at the ball after the second lbw, there was the first sign that the quarter-seam had been raised. I again showed it to Ray, and he said "It didn't look like that when I inspected it."

'We both then realised that, to use a trade term, the ball was being "gobbed" at the end of an over with sweat and saliva, before the regular inspection took place. The seam is replaced and then dust is rubbed over it to make that side as smooth as possible. We made as big a show of the inspection as possible, making sure it was seen by the Surrey players, especially the captain.

'It worked, because Monte promptly took Waqar off despite just having taken three for 6 in the last four overs he had bowled. The score was 399 for six, and Surrey were chasing the other two bowling bonus points, yet off went Waqar and on came Tony Murphy. What surprised Ray and myself so much was that the tampering had taken place with a new ball, whereas most of my previous experiences, particularly with Surrey, did not happen until the ball had been used for between 40 and 50 overs at least...sometimes more.

'Yet the first ball had not been tampered with in 101 overs, but the second one was interfered with within seven overs. I was determined to report the matter, and after the close of play I photographed the ball which had then been used for 22 overs and three balls, only seven of which were bowled by Waqar. When he was taken off, I am sure efforts were made to obliterate the damage he had caused.

'I thought about it overnight and on the Saturday morning spoke at some length with Ray, because I did not want to put anything in my report which he could not substantiate. Ray made the point that Waqar's three wickets had nothing to do with any illegal tampering, and a world-class bowler had produced a world-class spell of fast bowling. Ray also made the point that only a month previously, he and Chris Balderstone had forwarded balls to Lord's from the Northamptonshire v Surrey game, and nothing had happened.

'I told him I knew how he felt, because I had already made four such reports involving Surrey, and this would be the fifth in two years. I felt that he was not keen to report, so I told him that it might be better if we waited before I wrote my report, and I would not send it unless we were both a hundred per jcent happy.

'We had chatted for half an hour in the middle, and as we walked off to prepare for the start of play, I noticed Monte Lynch exercising on his own and sat down with him to tell him of our thoughts. I told him we knew what had happened, and he said that he had taken

Waqar off as soon as he saw us looking at the ball. I accepted that, because I have always respected Monte as a true professional in every sense, and I was sure he would not have been party to that sort of cheating, even though Surrey were on the wrong end of a match they finally lost easily by six wickets.

'Monte then admitted that he was scared stiff of what action we might take, and said something to me which I immediately knew would make it impossible for me to file a report. "Don, if you send in a report about ball tampering, I will get the sack."

'He clearly meant it, and I was sorry to see such a likeable person, and someone who I regarded as a cricketing friend, so upset. I knew I could not cause him that sort of trouble, even though it went against all my beliefs to let an act of cheating by one of his bowlers go unreported.

'As far as I am aware, I have never been supported by the TCCB concerning any of my reports. I don't count that wet letter to Surrey, two years earlier, but it was that, plus the suspended fine in 1992, which finally stirred the Surrey club into a statement which meant something. Namely, that the captain would be held responsible.'

Perhaps Oslear would have acted differently if he was convinced his report would not have been acted upon. If that had happened, Surrey would not have been aware that the Derbyshire match would have been the second involving their team, which was the subject of a report following the Northamptonshire match the previous month. The captain at Northampton was also Lynch, so he had already used up one of his lives. Conversely, Oslear might not have filed a report if he knew in advance that it would go the way of all others.

He had committed a great deal to paper over the years. 'I had sent them six reports on ball tampering and at least five more for misconduct by players and, not only did I receive no support, in most cases I did not even receive an acknowledgement. That is why I had become so angry a month earlier when, together with all my colleagues, I had received that letter from Alan Smith reminding us of the need to maintain standards, and that we must not shirk our duty, even if we thought we might be marked down by captains. Talk about double standards! The only qualification about that phrase is that I am not sure that the Board officials I dealt with had any standards at all – except the one of avoiding trouble.'

Bitter words, but easy to understand.

'I told Monte to come and see Ray and myself at the close of play, and when I told Ray about Monte's fears, he agreed with me that we would not make a report. Derbyshire won just after 6.30 pm having scored 100 in 22 overs, and Monte had half an hour with us. I was still a bit uneasy at doing something I never thought I would, but we read him the riot act and told him the matter was closed.

'Before the Sunday league match, I spoke at some length to the Derbyshire Chairman, Chris Middleton, and we had a fascinating conversation about ball tampering. Like me, he had some photographs of balls that had been tampered with, and we compared them. Mine were of the balls used the previous year in the Headingley Test between England and Pakistan, and his were of those used two months earlier in the game between Derbyshire and Lancashire – the common denominator being the two Pakistan bowlers concerned.

'The photographs showed identical abuse, and Ray's reaction was significant. He said that the balls he and Chris Balderstone had sent to Lord's in July were in a worse state. If we had shopped Surrey again, it would have been two reports in five matches and four weeks.

'While we were talking to Chris Middleton, Monte came to us and repeated his fear of the sack, despite our assurances the evening before that Surrey would not be reported. He then asked us if we would talk to his coach, Geoff Arnold, otherwise it might be felt that he was siding with us against his player. We told him that we would have nothing to do with that, because the widening of the circle of people who knew about the matter was not desirable. He left and Mr Middleton said that the Surrey captain's fear of the consequences would stay with him a long time.'

Chris Middleton has one thing to add: 'I had seen the third day when we won in the closing overs, and I reckon I saw something else, involving Waqar and Monte. Waqar had had little success in his first couple of overs and I think it possible that, in a desperate effort to save, or even win the match, he started to work on the ball. All I know is that after his seventh over there was a long conversation with his captain, after which Waqar left the pitch holding his back. There had been no previous indication of a problem, and he turned out next day in the Sunday League. Also, remember that those games were of 50 overs in 1993, and he bowled his full ration of 10 overs with no problem at all. They were chasing prize money, and that win helped them towards their final finishing position of third.'

That is conjecture, but the following conversation between Oslear and Waqar is not. It took place in the umpires' room at the end of the

Sunday match, and after Ray Julian had departed for home. There were two others present at the meeting: Brian Holling of the Derbyshire committee and Brian Fitzgerald, a Lancashire member.

Oslear says that Waqar came to thank him for not taking any action. 'We sat and talked for about fifteen minutes, and I told Waqar that he was always under scrutiny, and that there were several umpires brave enough to report him if he continued with the sort of ball tampering I told him was illegal and, as far as I was concerned, constituted outright cheating. I also told him that he was considered to be one of the best three fast bowlers in the world, but people were already starting to question if it was his tremendous ability, or illegal interfering with the ball that brought him so many wickets.

'Waqar told me: "Apart from my action two days earlier, I have not tampered with a ball *for some time*." I would like to think he was telling the truth, but wondered if some of my colleagues would think differently.'

Oslear told Waqar that no report would go to the Board although 'I did not tell him of the reason. So ended my last contact with Surrey, the club who caused me most trouble in nineteen years on the list. I suppose it was typical of the game of cricket, that I should have finished my dealings with their players in a dilemma, the likes of which I had never known before. Duty is duty, yet I had dodged mine, even though it was for the most human of reasons.'

In the end, Oslear compromised. He kept his promise to Monte Lynch and made no reference to the ball tampering incident in his official report, but he did speak to Tony Brown about it at Lord's on 14 September. 'What prompted me to make a verbal report was because of the Board's false claim that they had not received any reports of ball tampering in 1993.' He reminded Brown that balls had been sent by the umpires of the Northamptonshire v Surrey game, and by the Derbyshire club following their game against Lancashire. 'The Ilkeston game was therefore the third game of the 1993 season in which either umpires or a county club believed that a ball or balls had been tampered with.'

Seldom, if ever, has an umpire finished a long career at such odds with the authorities. The final decision not to offer him a contract for 1994 was still to be made, but Oslear's 1993 season, together with the pending High Court case, made that decision a formality.

CHAPTER 8

Season of shame

Seldom has a Test series in England produced two more acrimonious matches than in 1992 at Old Trafford and Headingley between England and Pakistan.

The series got off to a soggy start at Edgbaston, but smouldered into life in the second Test at Lord's which Pakistan won by two wickets. Wasim and Waqar took 13 of the 20 England wickets, with the England batsmen suspicious of two collapses which cost them eight wickets in each innings for 83 and 67 respectively. This meant that England aggregated 280 for the loss of four wickets – the first two in each innings – but the other 16 wickets fell for the addition of 150 runs. Neither Wasim nor Waqar struck with the new ball, but nine of their 13 wickets with an older ball were bowled or lbw.

They produced high quality fast bowling which, coupled with deadly late swing, was too much for batsmen who were mown down despite being prepared for the ambush. As Ian Botham put it after he was clean bowled by an inswinging yorker from Waqar: 'I knew it was coming but still couldn't do a thing about it.'

Usually, it is a touring side which develops a siege mentality, but 1992 was to bring such an attitude from both sides – England, because of their growing suspicions about the methods used to prime the ball for unplayable spells of fast, swing bowling, and Pakistan, because they resented such charges and were convinced that they suffered from what they claimed was home bias by the umpires.

Pakistan have been consistent in recent years about their belief that 'neutral or independent' umpires would remove such a possibility from the minds of players. They had objected to various English umpires on past tours, with David Constant and Ken Palmer causing them most problems. Also, they were dismayed that John Holder was not on the TCCB's eight-man Test panel. The Pakistanis trusted and respected Holder, because he stood, together with John Hampshire, in the series between India and Pakistan in Pakistan in 1989/90. Another reason for their displeasure at his omission from the panel was because he had spoken to Graham Gooch during the Oval Test against West Indies the previous August about ball tampering and the matter had been hushed up.

That Pakistan view deserves sympathy and understanding, because no good reason has ever been given by the TCCB for failing to make public that some England players broke Law 42.5 on Saturday 10 August 1991 when the West Indies were batting. It happened in the morning session and within the first seventy-five minutes of play. My knowledge of the timing comes from a video recording of the BBC television transmission in the period when Raymond Illingworth and I shared the commentary duties. We spoke about the umpires, John Holder and Mervyn Kitchen having a conversation with Gooch, clearly about the state of the ball, and we then discussed the wording of Law 42.5.

Not often do I have the sort of proof as Oslear has of the Board's reticence about matters of controversy, but that is one instance which is on film. Holder's disappearance from the Test panel is claimed to be coincidental, and the Board will justify that, presumably, with markings and captains' reports, but the Pakistanis understandably find it difficult to believe that, in the opinion of the TCCB, there were eight better umpires for the 1992 series.

Meanwhile Ken Palmer's brother, Roy, was at the centre of one of the biggest on-field rows ever seen in a Test match, at Old Trafford in the third Test match of the England v Pakistan series, with the filial connection mentioned in dispatches by Pakistan.

The flashpoint incident began with a misunderstanding of a Palmer ruling on Aqib Javed's bowling to Devon Malcolm, and escalated into an unseemly harassment of the umpire by most of the Pakistan team, led by captain Javed Miandad. The handling of the incident, seen by millions on television, by match referee Conrad Hunte was widely criticised, particularly by the England captain and his players. Hunte felt it necessary to include both teams in a reminder of their behavioural responsibilities, and that incensed Graham Gooch, whose players did not offend in the match.

The Board also became edgy following a well-sourced article I wrote for the *Birmingham Post* on Monday 13 July. In it I mentioned the strength of feeling among the umpires that Roy Palmer had not been seen to receive backing from his Board, and quoted an unnamed senior umpire with Test experience. 'The Old Trafford affair was a disgrace, and so was the match referee's statement, but it's only the tip of the iceberg. Every time one of us stands up to them, we do so knowing we are not going to get backed.'

I also wrote about the ICC statement 'which takes no account of the repetition of criticism of the umpires by Intikhab Alam last Tuesday. The team manager is in no danger of being forced to make the sort of apology dragged from Mike Gatting in 1987 in Faisalabad by the TCCB.'

By an astonishing coincidence, Alan Smith wrote this letter to Roy Palmer, dated 14 July, the day after the *Birmingham Post* article so displeased the Board.

'Members of the Executive Committee were very keen that I should write to the three of you who were on duty at Old Trafford at the time to echo what referee Conrad Hunte has already said, namely, that the conduct of the umpires was impeccable throughout. We would not of course expect anything different and would like you to know that we unanimously believe these difficult incidents were very well handled. We should like to re-state our total confidence in yourselves, the other Test match umpires and, indeed, all the others who make up our first-class list.'

Exactly the sort of confidence-boosting letter Palmer might well have welcomed any time in the previous eight days since the fracas. Oslear had also drafted a letter to all umpires, following a story that they would refuse to stand in matches involving Pakistan unless an apology was given to Palmer. Oslear correctly pointed out 'that the matter is entirely in the hands of the Chairman of the ICC and their officers, and we are in no position to demand an apology. I also feel that if anyone refuses to stand, he would be in severe breach of contract.'

The letter was never sent following discussions with Tony Brown, and the tour rumbled on. Sir Colin Cowdrey travelled to talk to the Pakistan players and management at their next game against Durham at Chester-le-Street.

Hunte deputised for Clyde Walcott who was attending the ICC Annual Meeting at Lord's, but the former West Indies batsman, who was to succeed Sir Colin Cowdrey and become the first non-British

Chairman of the ICC on 1 October 1993, was back on duty for the Headingley Test. Walcott had a most difficult job to try to restore peace between the two sides, but he tried his hardest, as evidenced by the account of Oslear of that fateful game, preceded by the usual pre-match talk by the referee to both captains, managers and the three umpires, who were Mervyn Kitchen, Ken Palmer and Oslear, with the latter doing duty as third umpire for the first time that summer.

Oslear: 'I was still Chairman of the Umpires Association, and knew the strength of feeling among the umpires about what had happened to Roy Palmer at Old Trafford. It was no great surprise to me, because I believe the Pakistan players had been waiting for him and David Shepherd since their game against Somerset at Taunton on 13, 14 and 15 May. The ball was constantly inspected and I know the Pakistanis resented it.

'Both umpires were upset about the match referee's statement, and also about the fact that the Pakistan coach, Intikhab Alam, had escaped punishment despite twice criticising the umpires in direct contravention of the ICC Code of Conduct. He originally received a severe reprimand from the match referee for accusing Roy of "rude and insulting behaviour", and then repeated the remarks after the end of the Test.'

The ICC statement, issued the following Sunday 12 July, referred to a discussion between Intikhab, Sir Colin Cowdrey and Conrad Hunte concerning 'an alleged second breach of the ICC Code of Conduct'. The statement said: 'Intikhab Alam fully accepts the principles of the ICC Code of Conduct and has given an assurance that his captain and players are equally committed to support them. The Pakistan tour manager, Khalid Mahmoud, has also reinforced his cricket manager's words: "Our team is not looking to create trouble, but to play in the best spirit of the game."

'Sir Colin Cowdrey responded: "The matter is now closed. I shall be at Headingley for the fourth Cornhill Test match and be alongside the match referee, Clyde Walcott, when he has his customary talk before the match with the captains, the managers and the umpires."'

If Cowdrey believed that his interim visit to Durham had solved anything, he was soon proved mistaken. Oslear kept three sets of notes dealing with the preliminary talk, the Test match and the post-match disciplinary hearing.

'There were 11 of us present: Sir Colin, Clyde Walcott, Intikhab Alam, Khalid Mahmoud, Micky Stewart, Javed Miandad, Graham

Gooch, Ken Lawrence, Ken Palmer, Mervyn Kitchen and myself. Mr Walcott opened the meeting by saying that he was not prepared to accept dissent of any nature towards the umpires. Should any arise, he would deal with it in very strong fashion.

'The England captain then made it clear how upset he and his players were by the comments of Conrad Hunte at Old Trafford, because the match referee's statement included both teams in his warning about their responsibilities. He produced a letter he had sent in response. He then commented very strongly about the action of Aqib Javed when he ran through the crease when bowling to Devon Malcolm.'

This was the incident that upset the England dressing room more than any other. When play re-started after Palmer was surrounded by a Javed-led protest, a furious Aqib did one of two things which first-class cricketers deem as unacceptable, no matter the level of provocation. The first one is to bowl a beamer – a high full toss which a batsman can, at best, sight late, because he is automatically looking down towards the pitch as the ball is released, and sometimes, as happened with Derbyshire's Chris Adams in the following year's Benson & Hedges Cup final, does not pick it up at all.

The second utterly reckless ploy is the one used by Aqib – that of going through the crease. This is the deliberate acceptance of a call of no-ball by a bowler who wants to increase his chance of hitting a batsman by not releasing the ball until the back foot is close to the front crease. The current no-ball Law calls for *part of the front foot to be behind that line*, and the advantage gained by a pace bowler who thus releases the ball nearly four feet nearer the batsman than is legal, is considerable. Against a batsman of limited ability such as Malcolm, it is dangerous, which is why Gooch made such strong representations at the meeting.

The modern cricketer is not so fussy about bouncers at tail-enders, but beamers and through-the-crease deliveries are considered to be both cowardly and beyond the pale.

Having listened to the opening shots of the meeting, Oslear knew that the fourth Test was a ticking time-bomb. 'There was also a discussion about Law 42.8 dealing with short-pitched bowling, because it was when Roy Palmer warned Aqib at Old Trafford, that the bowler thought he was being done for too many deliveries above shoulder height, whereas Roy was warning him about intimidatory bowling to Malcolm. I found out that Khalid Mahmoud is a solicitor, but also found out he did not fully understand the Law.

'The England team manager, Micky Stewart, then raised the question of illegal ball tampering by the Pakistan bowlers and said that certain England players were in danger of no longer having the right attitude towards playing against Pakistan. The meeting was getting livelier all the time, and it was Javed's turn next. He claimed that the umpires were being too harsh in calling no-balls for the bowler's leading foot being an inch or so over the front line, and he also argued with Mr Walcott when he defended Roy Palmer for his decisions on Aqib's bowling.

'Sir Colin ended the meeting with a plea to both captains to try to ensure that things were made as easy as possible for the umpires, but the three of us could see that it was going to be a tough match. When the captains and managers left the room, I stayed on to tell Sir Colin that I was dismayed at what I had heard and that the tone of the meeting left a lot to be desired. I told him that a great deal of animosity existed between the two sides, and one incident could have dire consequences for the good name of cricket.'

Not exactly an under-statement from a man who is rarely in danger of being misunderstood, but perhaps even he was not prepared for the number of times an always bubbling match boiled over. The pre-match meeting had discussed dissent, ball tampering and the hope that umpires would not be constantly under challenge.

The other Palmer must have wondered what was in store for him.

The problems during the fourth Test at Headingley started towards lunch on the third day, when England were 270 for one, with Gooch then 135. Oslear writes: 'A second new ball was available after eleven overs on the Saturday morning, and the match situation cried out for it to be taken with England having started the day 19 ahead with nine wickets in hand.'

The man out was Michael Atherton who, in answering press questions about his 76 in a first-wicket partnership of 168 with Gooch, made the following naive sounding observation.

'It's nice to get in when the ball's new and not moving around a lot.' Naive? Perhaps not.

England continued to profit against the old ball, but only until lunch-time. Oslear says: 'During the interval, my two colleagues asked me to take the ball to the match referee, Clyde Walcott, because of its scarred condition. He inspected it but decided to take no action, even when it was in a worse state at the end of the innings.'

That innings closure was the most spectacular imaginable. England lost their last eight wickets for 28. Their last six batsmen scored two runs between them. A bemused David Gower was left stranded with 18 not out as Waqar turned figures of none for 97 into five for 117, with the wickets coming in 38 balls at a cost of 13 runs.

Oslear kept possession of the ball and says: 'It had then been in use for 113.5 overs. I compared it with the one used by England – only for 79.3 overs – but there was no comparison in wear or damage. The following morning, Ken Palmer brought Richard Hutton into our room and showed him the ball, with all the damage on one side. He asked if he could take it and photograph it, presumably for *The Cricketer* magazine of which he is Editor, but I refused.

'I put both the England and Pakistan balls back into my boot bag, and did not see them again until two days later when I emptied the bag as I changed for my game at Markse-on-Sea. I realised then that I should photograph them. I did, in black and white, but later had them done in colour which revealed the damage much more clearly.'

The first flare-up in the match came in the fifth over of England's second innings, when Ken Palmer gave Graham Gooch not out in a run-out incident which television proved to be a wrong decision. Slow motion replays showed that Gooch was a couple of feet short of the crease, but the umpire did not think it was close. It seems that, only when he returned home at night and saw the incident again, did he realise he had made a mistake. (The use of television technology to assist the third umpire to decide line decisions was to be unveiled in South Africa four months later, and the experiment was so successful that it was adopted world-wide within three years.) It proved that a close decision in a fast finish is virtually impossible for the human eye to get right – it has to compute the bat, ball, a crease and the stumps, four feet apart, and any extraneous activity from the wicket-keeper or fielder which might negate the appeal, if he has broken the stumps before he has gathered the ball. When close finishes are replayed in slow motion and then normal speed, the viewer is able to see the impossibility of consistently making the right decision. A few years ago, Devon Malcolm was given 'in' at Lord's during a one-day international, only for a slow motion replay to show he was well out. The incident was then replayed at normal speed, and he looked to be safe behind the back line, never mind the front one.

Palmer got it wrong, but understandably so. Equally understandably, the Pakistan players felt they had been wronged –

and by a man to whom they had objected on a previous tour. The game was on a knife edge, with England needing 99, and the tourists were never in danger of missing a wicket because of a lack of appeal. Waqar and Mushtaq Ahmed took two wickets each and, at 65 for four with Mark Ramprakash on a pair, the atmosphere was electric.

Only one man seemed unruffled, David Gower, whose calming presence in the middle of what was now a white-hot kitchen, was a source of comfort, both to Ramprakash and, as he freely admitted after the match, the England captain. It was the supreme irony. The man whom Gooch had kept out of the England side was now to nail down a win that could so easily have been blown away by a Pakistan side whose volatility is particularly difficult to combat.

The tourists had three substitutes on the field and, if it is not a record for one of them to be fined for dissent, it should be. Gower, when on 7, was given not out to a caught-behind appeal from Mushtaq. Rashid Lateef, not playing in the game, compounded wicket-keeper Moin Khan's dismayed reaction of charging down the pitch towards umpire Kitchen, by hurling his cap to the ground and then kicking it away.

England finally won, with Gower 31 not out and Ramprakash unbeaten with 12, but what an aftermath to the game. Broadsides were fired from opposite press camps, with a *Sunday Telegraph* article – not penned by the cricket correspondent, incidentally – using the word 'cheats' about Pakistan cricketers, and that country's senior cricket writer using the same words about umpires Palmer and Kitchen, who somehow managed to keep a vestige of control over the noisy contest.

The words came and went, but those of match referee Clyde Walcott went on record as he implemented his pre-match warning that 'I will not tolerate dissent in any form'.

Oslear records that the disciplinary meeting began at 6.20 pm. 'Present were Clyde Walcott, Khalid Mahmoud and Intikhab Alam, Rashid Lateef, Moin Khan and their captain, Javed Miandad, and the two umpires, Mervyn Kitchen and Ken Palmer, the Yorkshire Secretary Chris Hassell and myself. Mr Walcott said that the two Pakistan players were there to answer the charge that they had brought the game into disrepute by excessive appealing and showing dissent to the umpires.

'Moin Khan was told that he had appealed excessively and also ran down the pitch towards the umpire. He was told that no action would be taken on this occasion, but that he should go away and think about how best to conduct himself in the future. Moin said that he did not believe he had misbehaved and his captain said that it was only over-excitement that prompted the behaviour.'

Javed believed he had made a valid point, and it is worth considering. Pakistan cricketers are volatile by nature and, usually, technique. Those twin characteristics are both a charm and a curse, with little attempt ever to row in mid-stream. Small things inspire them, and incidents which are considered minor to other sides cause the lid to be blown off the behavioural pressure-cooker. They are a fiercely proud nation and, sometimes, see trouble where there is none. Slights, imaginary and real, are seldom separated, and they live and play by different standards. They are often truly puzzled by the reaction of others to what they see as normal and acceptable behaviour. Different nation, different culture, different standards. Not better or worse, just different. Critics will argue that, among the majority of the other major cricket-playing countries, it is always Pakistan who are 'different', and it is difficult to refute the charge that most of the serious incidents in Test cricket are in matches in which they are involved.

On this occasion, Javed was commended by the match referee for the way he tried to calm his players down – singular praise coming, as it did, in the match following Javed's own questionable performance at Old Trafford.

Oslear picks up the story. 'Moin Khan left the meeting at 6.45 pm to leave Rashid Lateef to face the more serious charge. He was defended by his manager, Mr Mahmoud, who said that his act of throwing down and kicking his cap was an isolated expression of disappointment.'

It might have been but again, as with Javed's defence of over-excitement for Moin, the act of the substitute fielder is worth analysis. He had neither batted nor bowled in the match. He was not querying a decision against himself, but so immersed was he in the Pakistan cause that he found it impossible to contain his feelings at a crucial stage of the day's play. It took the meaning of the word 'commitment' to beyond its ultimate and, as far as Walcott was concerned, to an unacceptable limit.

Oslear again: 'Mr Walcott told him that his first thought was to suspend him, but he had decided against it and his decision was that he would be severely reprimanded and fined 40 per cent of the

Pakistan match fee. Mr Walcott added that the player was escaping lightly, but Javed started laughing at this point. He said he thought it was a joke that anyone could be fined an amount of money they had never received, because the player had still to make his Test debut.'

Javed missed a big point. Touring sides do not have a match fee, rather a fee for the tour. ICC fines are therefore based upon that country's most recent home match fee, which is lodged before the start of a series. Therefore, Lateef's fine – about £115 – would be paid out of his touring fee, and based upon the fees paid for Pakistan's last home series.

Oslear says: 'Mr Mahmoud argued strongly that it was punishment enough for the player to appear at the hearing, and I thought Mr Walcott would rescind his decision. But he stood firm, despite Mr Mahmoud saying that the punishment would be 100 per cent worse when the English press got hold of the story. He said there was bound to be adverse publicity. The meeting closed and everyone left the room, only for the Pakistan captain and managers to return.

'They complained to Mr Walcott about the performances of the umpires throughout the match, which I thought was unfair, as the umpires were not there. If they felt that strongly about it, why not say so at the proper time when they were there? There are times when cricket officials – and cricketers – do not deserve respect, and this was one of them.'

It did not seem possible for relations between the two sides to worsen further after the Tests at Old Trafford and Headingley, but cricket and the impossible often meet head-on – as happened on 23 August at Lord's. History of the wrong sort was created, with the resultant mutual acrimony between administrators and players, arguably, worse than any between two countries since the Bodyline series in 1932/33.

At that time, England have no plans to tour Pakistan during the remainder of the decade, although the 'A' side went on a bridge-building tour in October 1995. Pakistan's invitation to tour England in 1996 was issued and accepted much later than is the norm, and the sixteenth series between the countries was the twelfth of three matches. England had lost the last four, with the previous victory back in 1982, when Bob Willis led his side to a 2–1 win.

Accusations of ball tampering are at the heart of most of the bad feelings, certainly as far as the England players are concerned, but it is worth summarising the views of other countries before condemning or excusing.

Oslear, because of his carefully maintained records, has detailed several cases of alleged ball tampering involving Pakistan bowlers, either individually or, as happened in the 1992 tour of England, the team. He itemises complaints at Old Trafford and Headingley which were not acted upon, and those which were, at Lord's in the Texaco match. What about other countries?

The two most vehement charges came from New Zealand and West Indies in their successive tours of Pakistan between October and December 1990. The New Zealand series got off to a far from cordial start with Imran deciding not to play, because 'rather than sending a second-string team to Pakistan, the New Zealand Board would have been better off postponing the series. By not doing so, Test cricket is going to be discredited in what is likely to be a mis-match. For me there is no motivation in playing against a New Zealand team minus their six top players.' (John Wright, Jeff Crowe, Andrew Jones and John Bracewell were among those unavailable for selection.)

New captain Martin Crowe soon stirred things up with this comment on the Pakistan Board's plan to appoint neutral umpires. 'We don't know anything about the two guys appointed, but we believe they will be better than having two Pakistani umpires.' The home Board understandably objected to those comments and decided to appoint local umpires after all.

Wasim and Waqar took 15 wickets in the first Test, won by Pakistan by an innings and 43 runs. The home side won the second Test by nine wickets, and left Imran with no need to apologise by losing the third Test by 65 runs. New Zealand manager Ian Taylor admitted that his team deliberately damaged the ball in the final game in which Chris Pringle took 11 for 152 after taking two for 190 in the first two Tests.

Taylor said that his players reacted to what they felt was similar ball tampering by the Pakistanis. 'I am not sure how they did it – whether they used fingernails or sandpaper. *I would not have been surprised if they used knives.*' He said that he had spoken to the umpires about the practice, but they had taken no action.

It was Waqar's third series and he took 29 wickets at an average of 10.86 with a wicket coming every 30 deliveries. West Indies were next on the menu, captained by Desmond Haynes and managed by Lance Gibbs. The latter confirmed that, when his party arrived a week after New Zealand had departed, a message was waiting for him from Ian Taylor warning him to guard against ball tampering.

Imran returned against opposition more of his mettle, with Javed standing down 'voluntarily and willingly in the greater interest of the game and the country'. The first Test went to Pakistan by eight wickets with Waqar and Wasim, just as they did to start the series against New Zealand, taking 15 wickets. West Indies won the second Test by seven wickets and the third was drawn.

The admirable aim of Haynes to say nothing about anything controversial did not last long. Asked about the wisdom of playing the first one-day international the day after arriving in Pakistan, he said, 'I'm not here to complain about anything.'

On the second morning of the second Test in Faisalabad, 25 days later, the West Indies captain publicly drew the attention of the umpires to the alleged intentional attempt of the bowlers to damage the ball. The innings was only 11 overs old when Haynes played a defensive stroke to one from Wasim, whereupon he immediately picked up the ball and asked umpire Khizar Hayat to scrutinise it. Pakistan Board officials later denied any improper action and countered by asking the West Indies tour management to compare the ball Haynes had complained about with one the tourists had used. They claimed the West Indies' ball looked even more damaged. (It was, however, 54 overs old, which surely made comparisons difficult.)

Haynes said that he thought the Pakistanis were scratching the ball with their fingernails to roughen the surface, with his comments endorsed by the New Zealand coach, Warren Lees, now safely back home. According to Lees: 'They [the Pakistan bowlers] scored one side of the ball so that became furrowed and eventually took on the texture of suede, while the other side was kept shiny. We made an official complaint to Mustapha Khan, the assistant secretary of the Pakistan Board, but there was no action from him or the umpires.'

Lees confirmed that, following experiments in the nets before the third Test, New Zealand bowler Chris Pringle doctored the ball with remarkable results. Meanwhile Haynes pursued his complaint in his official tour report with Imran, not for the first time, vehemently denying claims he was later to admit had some substance. 'Haynes should ask his pace bowlers if they have ever lifted the seam,' said Imran.

Ted Dexter, England's then Chairman of Selectors, widened the debate thus. 'In some ways, I don't object to people damaging the ball because, by and large, a damaged ball has always been to the detriment of the fielding side. For the first time it seems that somebody had found that, by damaging it, they can make it swing. That could be a good thing because it makes the bowlers pitch the ball up and, if the ball swings more, maybe not so many bouncers will be bowled.

'But at the same time, something like that could damage the balance of the game. If the ball swings so much that there is no point in ever spinning it again, then the balance has gone the wrong way.'

Sir Richard Hadlee has gone on record as wanting to amend Law 42.5 to allow some sort of roughening, because of the high degree of skill needed to maximise any assistance obtained. He has a point, proven by the comparative records of Waqar and Aqib. The latter, a good but not outstanding bowler, has played in around half the number of Tests of Waqar, but only has a quarter of his wickets and at twice the cost, despite using the same ball.

The same sort of pattern is shown when comparing their respective seasons for Surrey and Hampshire in 1991. They both played in 17 games, but Waqar took 113 wickets from 570.1 overs, and Aqib 53 from 485.1. For someone like Waqar the pitch is irrelevant, which is why the fact that he bowled half his overs on the best batting pitch in the country, the Oval, proved little restriction.

What the authorities must address is the need to strike and maintain the balance referred to by Dexter. They need to loosen the Law, and thus recognise that, in the minds of bowlers from the sub-continent, there is little, if any, difference in doctoring the surface of one side of the ball by roughening it, and the other by producing a high polish as has happened in English cricket for years, with illegal substances.

The skill element cannot be over-emphasised, which goes some way towards justifying the resentment of the Pakistanis when they are accused of being cheats. Some way, but not all. The fact is that, whether Sarfraz Nawaz was or was not the discoverer of the principle of reverse swing, it has had a bigger effect upon cricket than any other bowling tactic of modern times.

What Waqar and Wasim have achieved is a magnificent amalgam of pace and swing. They bowl at no less speed than the West Indies fast bowlers, yet can still swing the ball more than genuine medium pace swing bowlers. As a result, they have become the deadliest old-ball bowlers in the history of cricket, and it is not all down to illegal tampering. A sensible change of Law 42.5 would preclude the sort of allegations made against them in the past having any relevance in the future.

At times, more sinned against than sinning, the Pakistan players seem to invite trouble by actions other than tampering with the ball. There is a view that they are like a naughty child. Give him a couple of centimetres and he will take the a lot more. Put another way, if the ICC and TCCB authorities had stood their ground, it would have been better for all concerned. As it is, notwithstanding the expressions of goodwill which preceded the resumption of cricket between England and Pakistan for the tour of England in 1996, the first controversial incident was still likely to refuel embers which are always smouldering.

Few cricketers are helped by the press they receive. Consider these words written by Pakistan journalist Qamar Ahmed in support of his country's cricketers in 1992. 'Sadly, the tour ended in acrimony, amid allegations and accusations of ball tampering. The accused, the pace trio of Wasim Akram, Waqar Younis and Aqib Javed, have all played county cricket and come through the hawk-eyed scrutiny of English professional umpires with reputations untarnished…but now they were playing for Pakistan.

'Even before the team arrived, the hate campaign had begun in the pages of the British gutter tabloids, and through the blinkered views of some of the so-called cricket correspondents, one of whom even went on to write that the ball was being tampered with by Pakistan in the World Cup final – in which two balls were used, one of which was handed to the umpire after each over.'

Fair point, unlike this comment, clearly written from the heart.

'Therefore the Pakistan team was not surprised at the allegations; they had arrived on tour anticipating the allegations, a hostile and ignorant rag press, and inconsistent umpiring, the worst fear of any touring team. *In the end their fears were justified.*'

The coverage of the Lord's Texaco match by Qamar Ahmed is wild and inaccurate. 'Pakistan, keen to have their name cleared of the suspicion and allegations made, asked the ICC to publish the umpires' verdict and referee's report as to why the ball was changed, but the ICC, instead of coming up with an answer, hushed up the controversy, apparently for legal reasons. It is a verdict which speaks a lot for the workings of the ICC and the role of its referees, whose job mainly is to impose fines for slow over rates and undisciplined acts by players or officials. The referee is completely powerless to challenge any umpire's decision, the inconsistency of some of the umpires, *or the home bias that unquestionably exists in every country.*'

If the writer believes that phrase, he is, presumably, echoing the thoughts of the Pakistan players, and that provides a ready explanation for attitudes and actions which appear to be confrontational. Perhaps he should listen to John Stephenson, then Secretary of ICC, who was improperly pressurised after the match by a senior Pakistan Board official. Manager Khalid Mahmoud later apologised for the approach which was aimed at any statement containing the lie that the ball was changed because it had gone out of shape.

There is more from Qamar Ahmed. 'The myth that the English umpires are the best has now been shattered, at least in the eyes of many Pakistanis and many millions who were able to watch their performance by satellite. No wonder then that the Gooch run-out decision was blown up into huge posters and stuck on the back of buses and street walls all over Pakistan with "Shame of a professional umpire" written all over it.'

To be fair, the British press is not snow white, as they showed in some near-hysterical coverage of the change-of-ball incident at Lord's. Given a kick-start by the unofficial briefing by Press Officer, Ken Lawrence, they ploughed in with word-processors on fire. 'Cowards' (the authorities) and 'Cheats' (the Pakistanis) were just two of many similar headlines.

Tony Lewis used different words, but the meaning was just as clear. 'Seeing sportsmanship throttled is a demoralising experience. Cricket without it is no more than a war game loaded with lies, propaganda and now legal writs.' That was in the *Sunday Telegraph*, but another broadsheet pundit marched to a different drum. Simon Barnes of *The Times* wrote, 'If at first you don't succeed, whinge. Everyone knows that ball doctoring is as much a part of English cricket as the tea interval.'

The 1992 Pakistan tour of England was not an isolated example of a series of events which reflected little credit on anyone. The next few years would witness a plethora of charges concerning alleged tampering with a cricket ball...most notably, an incident concerning none other than the captain of England.

CHAPTER 9

A pocketful of trouble

Saturday 23 July 1994 produced the biggest captaincy storm of any Lord's Test, with England's Michael Atherton the victim of television's all-seeing eye and accused of ball tampering.

The third day of the historic Test against South Africa was one of the hottest and most humid of the summer, and England were on the rack. They had been bowled out for 180 in their first innings, some 177 runs adrift of South Africa's first innings total, and their opponents were closing the coffin lid with a string of consistent partnerships as England struggled in the field.

At 2.50 pm, the England captain brought back Darren Gough, and was seen to walk towards him to discuss field placings. He had the ball in his left hand, and was seen, on camera, to bring his right hand out of his trouser pocket and transfer something to the ball. The substance was rubbed on and around the seam while he was talking to the bowler, with the BBC commentator Tony Lewis contenting himself with an observation about 'Aladdin's lamp'.

Bearing in mind the legally delicate climate about allegations of ball tampering, the restraint of Lewis was well advised, but the reaction to the live television pictures beamed to South Africa was predictably excitable.

The incident was replayed several times, and it was difficult to refute the damaging nature of the pictures. Clearly, Atherton was doing something, but what exactly? The South African team coach, Mike Procter, was shown the footage and immediately told his players. They were privately annoyed, but publicly said not a word, rightly leaving the authorities to resolve the bizarre looking incident.

Match referee Peter Burge had no alternative other than to ask Atherton for an explanation, and this he did at a hearing convened shortly after close of play. The England captain took his cricket trousers to the hearing, and when asked by Burge if he had anything in the pockets, said 'no'. Subsequently, however, he was to say that he thought the question referred to artificial substances, such as abrasive filings or any aid to scuffing the surface of the ball.

Burge issued a statement which was curiously worded in that he said he had an explanation from Atherton which he accepted, although Burge did not offer what that explanation was. He referred to what he saw as Atherton's 'unfamiliar action' and to whether it contravened Law 42.5 and its reference to 'artificial substances to alter the condition of the ball'. Having accepted the player's word that the trouser pockets on offer at the hearing contained nothing, Burge declared the matter closed.

Not as far as the media were concerned. The story made the Sunday morning national newspapers, and further even more damaging television pictures meant that the country's national daily correspondents were queuing for the follow-up. Chairman of Selectors Raymond Illingworth recognised the danger of saying nothing further, especially when Atherton admitted to him that he had dust and dirt in his pocket and had therefore lied to the referee.

Illingworth also accepted the captain's avowal that he was not trying to tamper with the ball, but simply trying to keep it dry and free from sweat in order to help the ball to reverse swing.

Desperately short of time in a day in which England were to be bowled out for 99, the Chairman of Selectors proceded to construct an exercise of attempted damage limitation. He had to pre-empt Burge taking secondary action which could extend to suspension and, therefore, the possible removal of Atherton's captaincy by the Test & County Cricket Board.

Before a press conference, hastily convened at the premature end of the match, Illingworth went to Burge and said that he had decided to fine Atherton two amounts of £1000, one for lying and one for using the dirt – although that in itself was not an offence as it was not considered to be an artificial substance. (The amount of £1000 was the maximum allowed under the terms of Illingworth's contract.)

Illingworth gambled that Burge would not take any further action, and so England would keep their captain. Quite a strategy, considering that the tabloid press were convinced that the bad blood between manager and captain was such that Illingworth was looking for the first excuse to force Atherton out of the job.

The press conference was messy, with Atherton unaware that live television cameras would be there, and it solved little. As the editor of *Wisden*, Matthew Engel, wrote: 'Over the next 48 hours, there was a tidal wave of public emotion in which almost everyone from the cricket correspondent of the BBC to people who had never seen a match in their lives demanded Atherton's resignation.'

Illingworth and the TCCB publicly registered their support of the England captain, and the umpires revealed that the condition of the ball had not been altered. Atherton himself was hounded for four days while trying to take a break in the Lake District, and finally called another press conference the following Friday 29 July at Old Trafford at which Engel wrote: 'He did not entirely explain away the pictures, but stressed repeatedly that he had never cheated at cricket.'

Although the television cameras showed particles of dust adhering to the seam and therefore could, conceivably, alter the turbulence factor so crucial in swing and reverse swing bowling, the general verdict was that Atherton's actions were silly, rather than legally culpable under Law 42.5.

Overseas reaction was more sceptical. The chief complaint of the South Africans was that the incident deflected much of the credit they deserved for winning the Test by 356 runs. A couple of former Test captains, including Sir Gary Sobers, asked why, if Atherton wanted to keep his hands dry, did he not have a small towel in the pocket?

Not guilty or not proved? Mike Atherton would be the one to answer that question. Don Oslear, though, has his own opinion.

'To my mind it was ridiculous for Mike Atherton to have done something which he admitted was an abuse of the Law, particularly as less than two years earlier on the same ground, an even bigger row followed another alleged case of ball tampering. Mike is an intelligent individual, and someone I considered throughout my career to be a sportsman and a gentleman. In my opinion, he abused the second sentence of Law 42.5 which states that 'No one shall rub the ball on the ground or use any artificial substance or take any other action to alter the condition of the ball.' He did not rub the ball on the ground, but it is just as wrong to rub the ground on the ball – earth to pocket, fingers to earth, fingers to ball, earth to ball. Earth is an artificial substance, in my opinion. He therefore certainly did take action to alter the condition of the ball.'

But not according to the two umpires, Dickie Bird and Steve Randall, both of whom told the match referee that the condition of the ball had *not* been changed.

Oslear continues: 'As Mike has stated, he will have to live with suspicion for the rest of his career. Others have pointed out that had he been playing for Pakistan, there would have been a hue and cry for his hide.

'To my mind, only two people come out of the sad affair with any credit. Ray Illingworth came down as hard and as quickly as possible upon the England captain, punishing him with the maximum allowable fine. Surprisingly, Mike Atherton also emerges from the affair with some small credit. At no time did he try to bluster excuses. He took the punishment and the criticism, and has surely come out a wiser man.'

Interestingly, on England's 14-week tour of South Africa in 1995/96, Atherton was not once reminded of the incident – not by the home press nor their crowds, all of whom were generous and extravagant in praise of his batting, especially in the Johannesburg Test. Even towards the end of the tour, when he appeared to be uncooperative with the media to the point of sullenness, the Lord's incident was never mentioned.

The final month of 1995 produced two further allegations of ball tampering. At Perth, in a Test which started on 8 December between Australia and Sri Lanka, the tourists were officially called for ball tampering by match referee Graham Dowling from New Zealand.

As Australia scored 617 for five, it seemed an odd accusation from Dowling that the Sri Lankans had 'clearly tampered with the ball in the 17th over the innings.'

There were two other curious factors. Firstly, if the evidence was so clear, why did Dowling choose to take no action other than a public warning? Secondly, why did Sri Lanka subsequently challenge the referee's statement and threaten legal action? It seems that, because the umpires did not change the ball, the alleged evidence was no longer available.

The second instance involving alleged interference with the ball occurred a week later on 15 December at Kingsmead in the third Test between South Africa and England. Sky Television pictures showed South Africans Craig Matthews and Shaun Pollock apparently tampering with the ball, although match referee Clive Lloyd decided to take no action after talking to both bowlers.

Matthews was brought on for his first bowl of the England innings with the score 34 for two. As his captain, Hansie Cronje, spoke to him about field placings, the bowler was seen to be running thumb and finger around the outer part of the seam, apparently lifting it in order to get extra purchase when the ball landed on it.

Matthews defended himself by saying that he was removing debris from the outer seam, and was also trying to remove some scuff marks from the shiny side of the ball adjoining the seam by wetting thumb and finger and running it around and alongside the seam.

Match referee Clive Lloyd accepted the explanation, as he did about far more damaging footage showing Shaun Pollock gripping the ball with a two-handed, clench-fingered hold around the centre seam which he appeared to be pulling apart.

The bowler was first reported as saying that he could not remember the incident, but the eventual party line was that he was trying to push the seam together, not pull it apart. That version was greeted scornfully by the England party, who pointed out that a more viable explanation was that the two-handed grip might have been trying to probe the join between the main seam and the quarter-seam. In the end, Lloyd warned both players to be more careful about whatever they did with the ball, because of the probing nature of modern television coverage.

Imran Khan believes that a relaxation of the present Law would prevent a repetition of the many acrimonious accusations about ball tampering. In an article for the *Daily Telegraph* he says: 'It is because the laws are impossible to implement, as well as being highly impractical, that ball tampering has become an acceptable part of the game among the players. If I was on the Pakistan Cricket Board, I would insist that the ICC clarify the relevant Laws so that Pakistan fast bowlers do not have to spend their time justifying their ability to swing the old ball, and proving it to be within the Laws of the game.

'I propose that bowlers should be allowed to lift the seam or scratch the ball, as long as they do not clearly alter its condition according to the standards set by the ICC.'

One would have to say that, surely, this is such a contradiction of terms as to be impossible to do.

Imran continues: 'The umpires should change the ball if they feel either it has been altered either by the bowlers or, as the Sri Lankans claimed, by hitting the concrete outside the boundary fence.'

This is the oldest defence of all – yet why does the boundary concrete only ever roughen one side of the ball?

And about changing the ball because of unfair play, Imran has this to say: 'It [the ball] should not be changed due to unfair play so that a player or team are not, by mistake, accused of cheating. Unfair play should only apply if an outside substance is used, such as a bottle top.

'Thus court cases can be avoided where players feel slandered. Newspapers will not be printing sensational headlines calling bowlers cheats, just because they get a photograph with a player's fingernails on the ball surface. Neither will teams try to cover up their own failures by accusing the opposition of ball tampering. Above all, the game of cricket will not have to suffer from a damaging controversy which has the potential to destroy cricketing relations between countries.'

More a case of wishful thinking, perhaps?

Betting and Bribery

CHAPTER 10

Malik in stormy waters

The betting world is full of shadows and whispers. It is a world split into two, with one section dominated by legal bookmakers, and the other by an illegal fraternity which, predictably, is the one which bedevils sport. Cricket has been a gambling medium for over 200 years, but no bigger shock wave has rocked the sport than the one which swept Salim Malik out of international cricket between 15 February and 21 October 1995.

The former Pakistan captain was charged with offering a bribe to two Australian cricketers, Shane Warne and Tim May, before the start of the first Test between Pakistan and Australia, which started at Karachi on 28 September 1994. Over two centuries earlier the MCC had made provision in their regulations to try to control the striking of bets in challenge matches. Bookmakers would stand around the Lord's pavilion and players were constantly approached in efforts to influence the result of a game. William Lambert, the leading all-rounder of his time, was banned from Lord's in 1817 because the MCC said he had thrown a match, and towards the end of the 19th century, the volume of open betting was minimal, although prior to 1884, four of the Laws of Cricket were to do with betting.

The only modern instance of a cricketer being involved in betting against his own side concerned the former Pakistan Test batsman, Younis Ahmed, who was sacked by Worcestershire for backing Leicestershire to beat his team in a Sunday match in 1983. The player's defence was that he had placed the bet at generous odds as a way of covering his win bonus if Worcestershire lost. The club took the view that his bet would have been made public, if not at the time then later, and the player would be in an untenable position had he dropped a vital catch or got out at an important stage of the match.

There is little doubt that Younis was guilty of nothing more than naivety. He talked freely in the dressing room of the quoted odds for the Sunday fixture against Leicestershire, before the start of the Saturday match against the same side in a Benson & Hedges Cup qualifying match. He did not place a bet then, nor before he went out to bat late in the afternoon. Moreover, he could have played a long innings and therefore been unable to place the bet when he came off because the bookmaker's office would be closed.

However, he got out cheaply and, sitting in the dressing room, heard his colleague Paul Pridgeon say that he was going to check on some results, and did he, Younis, want that bet on Leicestershire? He said he did and it was placed, only for Pridgeon to realise within minutes how dangerous a situation could develop. He informed the club and Younis was sacked. (This was despite claiming that his bet was no different from the famous one placed by Rodney Marsh and Dennis Lillee at Headingley in 1981, when the two Australians placed £20 between them at 500-1 against an England win, in the belief that if a cricketing miracle happened, they would be compensated by £10,000. Thanks to Ian Botham, their bet is now part of cricketing folklore, and Ladbroke's have never offered such long odds again, no matter how impossible it looks for one side to win.)

The Malik story was brought to light in Sydney by Phil Wilkins, who won an award in September 1995 for his journalistic scoop. The facts were startling. Sworn affidavits by two Australian players, Shane Warne and Tim May, alleged that Malik offered them £35,000 to throw the first and third Tests, in Karachi and Lahore, of the 1994 Australian tour to Pakistan. Another player, Mark Waugh, also claimed he was approached with an offer of over £60,000 if he performed badly.

The Australian manager in Pakistan was Colin Egar, and he did not learn about the alleged approaches until the third Test, just before the end of the tour. According to Wilkins: 'Intimidation and an underlying fear of retaliation from Indian based bookmakers, who have infiltrated deep into cricket circles internationally, were at the root of the players' reluctance to inform their team management of the offered bribes.'

As money from gamblers in Dubai which is linked with hashish, heroin and arms dealings is relayed to Bombay, the Australian players were right to feel intimidated, and also right to refuse to return to Pakistan to testify at a later date, as they were requested.

The story asked many questions, most of which have still to be answered. Wilkins explained why it took four months for the alleged bribe story to surface, but then tackled the Australian Board to ask what action they had taken since Egar had relayed the facts to them. The Australian Cricket Board revealed that it had asked the International Cricket Council to consider allegations of bribery in cricket on the sub-continent in September 1994, prior to the tour.

Moreover, when they heard about the approaches to their three players, the ACB asked the match referee, New Zealand's John Reid, to investigate for them. He said, 'I was asked to look into betting, but personally did not hear about any offer to the Australians. Nobody approached me on or off the field about bribery.'

Of course they didn't, some would say. Not in the middle of the final match of the tour. The bird had already flown.

It is worth establishing the volume of betting on cricket in England. There, the Test & County Cricket Board sanctioned Ladbrokes' request to instal betting shops on county ground headquarters around the country twenty years ago. Not all of the eighteen clubs offer the service, but the six Test match grounds do. Betting is usually on the result of the match, or on a sessional basis in which punters are asked to forecast the number of runs scored and wickets taken. Odds are laid against which batsman will score most runs and which bowler will take most wickets, and there is no ban on cricketers in the match placing a bet. The Board have carefully monitored the situation but, so far, have not found it necessary to legislate against a cricketer placing a bet.

Another strong market comprises odds against each club winning one or more of the four English domestic competitions, and teams and their committees will often have a flutter. The most spectacular coup was landed by the Warwickshire committee in 1994, when the side won three competitions and the gross winning returns were over £200,000 – only for the small print to be invoked after a dispute which went to the *Sporting Life* arbitration service, who ruled that they would receive a limit of £100,000 for their original stake of £82.50.

This type of betting is legal, and therefore easier to control than the illegal sort, which flourishes in Pakistan and India. The bookmakers are based in the stock exchanges of Karachi and Bombay, with the latter city providing by far the bigger operation. Pakistan journalist Qamar Ahmed says: 'Bets can be placed in Bombay on Test matches anywhere in the world. We are talking about millions of dollars riding on a single match.'

There are around 20 big bookmakers in Bombay and 200 smaller ones, and virtually every one is illegal which means that they deal in 'black money' – the sort which is undeclared for tax purposes. Betting on horse racing is legal, but the amount wagered is said to be only about 5 per cent of that bet on cricket. The international one-day tournaments in Sharjah quickly became targets for the betting ring, and there are many stories about matches allegedly fixed between the participating sides, which usually include India and Pakistan. The televising of one-day cricket produced a betting explosion, and Tony Lewis, who commentated on several Sharjah tournaments, has this to say about the final of the Australia-Asia Cup between Pakistan and India on 18 April 1986.

'I was commentating on the closing overs of a tight match, and the crowd atmosphere was electric. The loyalties of an all-ticket crowd of 15,000 were evenly divided and mostly made up from the large number of Asian expatriates working in Sharjah. There had been a roaring black-market trade for what was a dream final, and the noise was more like that of a football match than a game of cricket.

'The ground is about four miles out of Sharjah, and the only buildings nearby are blocks of flats and often you can only see the city through a haze of grey sand. What adds to the atmosphere is the fact that more betting takes place on the Sharjah ground than anywhere else I have seen. More people than not have mobile telephones which they use to contact the Bombay bookmakers sometimes two or three times an over.'

The telephone link from the Bombay bookmakers to the ground in question is crucial. I have been in press boxes in England, India, Pakistan and South Africa where the equivalent of the White House 'red telephone' has been quickly established, with the hot line kept open to keep the bookmakers ahead of the game as far as toss, weather and the minute-by-minute state of the game is concerned. In fact, the intelligence system sometimes deals in seconds – I heard an Asian journalist actually get a bet on while the ball was in the air and the fielder was circling underneath. A gabbled bet down the telephone was accepted at better odds than was the case three seconds later when the catch was taken. It could have been dropped of course, in which case the bet would have been immediately devalued, but that is one of the charms about betting.

I also saw at first hand in January 1995 in Johannesburg, the attempts made by Asian bookmakers to infiltrate the press box for the inaugural Test match between South Africa and Pakistan at the New Wanderers ground, so that they could prime their Bombay base camp with information. Dr Ali Bacher, Chief Executive of the United Cricket Board of South Africa had a long list of applications from Pakistan and India for press accreditation. He had not heard of many of either the applying journalists or the newspapers for which they were supposed to work.

I suggested that he consult Qamar Ahmed who was in the country to watch his 200th Test match. He nearly wore out his blue pencil in drawing lines through most of the applications which, he said, came from bookmaking circles.

In itself, betting on a large scale on events involving human beings is not harmful, but the temptation factor of trying to dispense with the chance factor is considerable.

The biggest post-war British bookmaker was William Hill, whose golden rule in betting for years was 'never bet on anything that can talk'. He soon changed his mind, however, and pioneered the first fixed-odds football coupons over fifty years ago, but the maxim is still a sound one. Sport in general and cricket in particular is all about errors. Who makes the least usually wins, particularly of the unforced sort. Pressurised errors are more forgivable, but not to the man who has thousands of pounds riding on the ability of a batsman or bowler to hold his nerve when the battle is at its fiercest.

That Australia-Asia Cup final described by Tony Lewis was won by a last-ball six by Javed Miandad which did several things. It won a game Pakistan seemed to have lost to India. It won Javed a Mercedes car and a jewel-encrusted watch worth a small fortune. And it settled bets worth millions of rupees back in Bombay, with half of the mobile telephones in the crowd having been successfully used with the speed of a world class touch-typist, and the other half suddenly still and quiet.

It was on the same ground against the same opposition in 1991, that Imran Khan caught wind of the intentions of four of his team to bet on India. He promptly called his players together and told them that their earnings of $20,000 would be bet on themselves. Pakistan won the game easily by 72 runs, but not without controversy as India claimed that three crucial lbws given by the umpire – Ravi Shastri for 15 and Mohammad Azharuddin and Sachin Tendulkar for ducks, all to Aqib Javed – were the result of bias against them by Moslem organisers.

Pakistan have figured prominently in accusations of fixed matches, mainly because gambling interests have infiltrated the country's cricket, and the instability of the game's administration means an absence of control. In the period between September 1994 and February 1995, allegations were made of one-day matches against Sri Lanka in that country and in Australia, as well as two five-day Tests against South Africa and Zimbabwe – whose first-ever victory in a five-day Test was achieved by an innings with two days to spare.

No fire, but sufficient smoke for the Australian Cricket Board to ask their Pakistan counterparts to hold an inquiry. This took place soon after Australia's arrival in Pakistan in October 1994, but the investigation, predictably, proved inconclusive. Hard evidence could only come from the bookmakers, and as all betting is against Islamic law, the silence was deafening. Enter Sarfraz Nawaz – never far from controversy and then a special adviser to Prime Minister Benazir Bhutto – who let fly with a series of accusations, claiming that:

1. Pakistan cricket was corrupt.
2. Betting runs into millions of rupees.
3. The Texaco match at Trent Bridge in 1992 between England and Pakistan was fixed.
4. Secret-service agents have tapped telephones and examined bank accounts of several Pakistan Test cricketers and their relatives.
5. Pakistan were paid 30 million rupees to lose the 1987 World Cup semi-final against Australia in Lahore. The money was paid by, among others, Asif Iqbal, former captain and colleague of Sarfraz.
6. Imran Khan 'is a cheat and an adulterer and should be stoned to death'.

Not bad for starters, especially as, with the exception of Salim Malik, every such allegation of fixing matches that has been floated has quickly sunk into an ever muddied pool of innuendo. Only points 3, 4 and 5 are worth comment. I saw both matches he names. In the Texaco match, England won at Trent Bridge by 198 runs. Their 363 for seven was the highest ever scored in a one-day international (although the score came from 55 overs and the previous highest of 360, scored by West Indies against Sri Lanka in a World Cup match in 1987, was in a 50-overs match). When a side faces such a big total, they must attack from the first ball, with the consequent increased chance of a collapse.

As for the Lahore semi-final between Pakistan and Australia, that was a hard-fought contest in which Imran Khan stood his ground late in the match for a catch claimed by Greg Dyer, but was given out by Dickie Bird. The winning margin was 18 runs and Javed Miandad's 70 kept his side in the match. Pakistan manager Asif Iqbal asked for a Board investigation and said that he believes many rumours are started because Pakistan supporters cannot conceive of defeat by legitimate means.

Malik has another theory, based on opponents to his captaincy in Pakistan, that he acquired in controversial circumstances when Wasim Akram was forced out by player revolt. That so-called mutiny was reportedly led by Waqar Younis, since which time the two fast bowlers have seldom played in the same Test side. It was usually one or the other, but rarely both, until Wasim regained the captaincy against Australia in October 1995.

The claim of Sarfraz that bank accounts have been examined cannot be dismissed out of hand. Khalid Mahmoud was tour manager in England in 1992 and in South Africa and the West Indies in 1993. He says this: 'Quite a few players' living standards have improved so quickly that their involvement in gambling seems to be closer to fact. My comments are made in the context of betting allegations, not bribery. I have not spoken to anyone about the bribery thing. I am totally shocked to hear that, if it is true.'

Asif Iqbal is at the centre of another bribe story, this one concerning his last Test match for Pakistan against India in Calcutta, on 29 January 1980. India were captained for the first time by Viswanath, and the story is that large bets were placed on two things happening: that India would win the toss and that they would gain a first innings lead. Asif was alleged to have lost the toss under curious circumstances, and then declared his side's first innings close at 272 for four in reply to India's 331.

The losses of the Bombay bookmakers were so large that they cancelled all bets. Asif's answer to that charge is this: 'I didn't even know betting existed then. As for the people who made the allegations about the toss – were they there when the coin went up? As far as declaring is concerned, the players had a chat and we felt that losing a series 3–0 is little different from 2–0. Anyway, we dropped a couple of catches.'

A review of the administrative upheavals within Pakistan cricket will give a major clue as to why, on and off the field, it resembles a rumbling volcano that is never far from eruption. British critics of subcontinental cricket should realise the vivid contrast in styles of administration. There is no such thing as an Establishment. Continuity does not survive long in a hot-house of warring factions, many of which are politically based.

The wider stream of the country's political system has been eroded by many regional and religious disputes, and it is impossible for Pakistan cricket to avoid being affected by upheaval. The Pakistan Board has long been used as an instrument of patronage for the military, the government and commerce. For instance, in 1993, following a bitter row about the mishandling of television revenues, the State President, Farooq Ahmed Khan Legari, sacked the old Board of Control and appointed an ad hoc committee in its place.

Javed Burki became the chairman, and what a bag of trouble he inherited from the team's tour of southern Africa. Dressing room arguments about the division of betting winnings, and the usual players' perks, soon festered into the public domain. Rashid Lateef complained he was being slighted by his captain, and was reprimanded by Burki, together with his team-mate and friend, Basit Ali. Much has been made of the retirement of the two, announced before the end of the third Test of the 1993 series in Harare, but it seems they jumped ship before they were pushed, having learned that they were about to be sent home.

Earlier, Waqar suddenly declared himself unfit for the final match of the tour of South Africa, the inaugural Test, after telling travelling journalists that he wanted to leave a tour which was on the point of falling apart. The undercurrents prompted this comment in a Lahore newspaper, penned by Kamila Hyat: 'The atmosphere of deceit and paranoia prevailing within Pakistan cricket has now reached a point where almost nothing is taken at face value.'

The touring party was now in total disarray having lost the best-of-three one-dayers to South Africa after straight defeats in Cape Town and Johannesburg, and then sank without trace in the inaugural Test. There followed the crushing defeat in the first Test against Zimbabwe in February, which was prefaced by a toss of the coin which ended in pure farce.

The coin used by home captain Andy Flower was one with a fish-eagle on one side, and building ruins on the other. Quite naturally, Malik called 'Bird' and was right, only for match referee Jackie Hendriks to disallow the call on the basis it must be either 'heads' or 'tails'. The second toss went to Flower, and so the course of the historic game was altered irrevocably.

Poetic justice in a way, because Malik was one of the captains involved in a toss which led to all tosses in international cricket now being supervised by the match referee. The match in question was the first Test between New Zealand and Pakistan, played in Auckland on 10, 11 and 12 February 1994.

Malik's call was an indistinct mumble, from which New Zealand captain Ken Rutherford understood nothing. The Pakistan captain bent down, looked at the coin and said, 'You bat, we'll field.' Wasim and Waqar took 15 wickets, passing 200 and 150 Test wickets respectively, and Pakistan won by five wickets in a match in which only 198 overs were bowled for the 35 wickets which fell.

Rutherford was unimpressed, but there were no communication problems in the next two Tests or the first four one-day internationals, and Malik called clearly and wrongly five times. The equaliser, if that was what it was, came in the final match of the tour, the one-day international in Christchurch on 16 March.

Rutherford spun, Malik's call was again a mumble which could have been anything, so the home captain settled things his way. He picked the coin up and said, 'We'll field, OK?' Salim nodded sheepishly and New Zealand won by seven wickets to register their only win of the tour against Pakistan.

The story of the two tosses prompted the ICC to instruct their match referees that, in future, all tosses would be supervised, and so another tradition of the game has disappeared. John Reid took his brief a step further in the 1995 series between England and the West Indies, and spun the coin, rather than allow Michael Atherton to do it.

There are many instances of confusion arising from the apparently simple matter of tossing a coin. Tony Lewis tells of a time when he captained Glamorgan at Taunton against Somerset, led by Roy Kerslake, another Cambridge Blue. Kerslake tossed, Lewis called wrongly, only for Kerslake 'to ask me what I wanted to do. I told the truth and said I would like to bat. We did and won the match, but curiosity made me ask Roy why he had asked me the question. He said, "Well, actually, you were on my slightly deaf side and I wasn't sure what you had called."'

On tour in Australia in 1962/63, England captain Ted Dexter lost the toss against Western Australia, whose captain, Barry Shepherd, invited him 'to take a blade'. The upshot was that both sides walked out to field together. Western Australia because their captain's instruction was a reference to the blade of the bat. Dexter, like Lewis and Kerslake, was a Cambridge Blue and, never having heard the phrase before, worked out that it referred to a blade of grass; ergo, England, or MCC as they still were in state games, were being told to field.

The third story of misunderstanding has no Cambridge connection – not unless Kepler Wessels or Mohammad Azharuddin studied under assumed names. The match was the first one-day international between South Africa and India in Cape Town on 7 December 1992.

The toss for the day-night game took place at 1.45pm and was done before the television cameras of the South African Broadcasting Corporation. Their chief commentator was Trevor Quirk, a former wicket-keeper for Northern Transvaal. He did not hear Wessels explain to Azharuddin the identification of the home captain's lucky coin, which had a different animal's head on each side.

Wessels told the Indian captain which head was 'heads' and which head was 'tails', so the ingredients for a mix-up were there. Azharuddin called 'heads' but, before Wessels could say what he wanted to do, as the 'tails' he had explained came up, Quirk, in all innocence, said to Azharuddin, 'Heads it is. What are you going to do?'

A now completely confused Indian, of whom there is no nicer or more honest international captain, said that India would bat. They did, with Wessels not referring to the Quirk-induced mix-up until after the match, when he told the broadcaster that he had got it wrong. South Africa won by six wickets with three balls to spare, with the second match, played two days later at Port Elizabeth, producing the infamous incident in which Kapil Dev ran out Peter Kirsten, as the former ran in to bowl and, without warning, held onto the ball, broke the stumps as the non-striker backed up too far.

News of the alleged approach by Malik to Warne and May in September 1994 was kept to members of the Australian party until the third Test of the tour of Pakistan, when manager Colin Egar was told. He informed his Board, and so the story edged nearer to the public domain. The award-winning journalist, Australian Phil Wilkins, picks up the story.

'It all blew up immediately after the Ashes series against England finished in Perth in early February 1995. I was desperately trying to tidy things up, because we were all off to New Zealand and then the West Indies to complete the longest and most crowded Australian season I have ever known. I got a telephone call from someone who told me that a big story was about to break. I thought he was referring to the fact that cable television was reported to be interested in doing another Kerry Packer and buying up players, as happened later in the year with rugby.

'"No, it's bigger than that," I was told. Then I was given the names of the players involved and informed that the Australian Board were putting everything they had got to the ICC, so I had to do something. I had spoken to Tim May and Colin Egar, but could not raise Shane Warne or his agent. I met my telephone caller, and was soon convinced I had to do the story. I knew that the [Australian] players in Pakistan were frightened what might happen if the story broke while they were out there, which is why they kept it under wraps until nearly the end of the tour.

'Tim did not want to be quoted because, in his own words, "It's too big". As it was. I tackled the Board and was told by chief executive Graham Halbish that it was true that the manager did not learn about the approaches to his players until the final Test. He said, "That is the truth, and the Board is completely satisfied with Colin Egar's conduct on the tour."

'I know that when our Board asked John Reid, the match referee, to investigate, he found a wall of silence, and that is because of the fears of the players about the possible consequences if they co-operated.'

Wilkins continues: 'What I thought was extraordinary was that, only after a five-Test Ashes series against England [some five months after the alleged incident] did our Board send information about the scandal to the ICC "on request". This information included statements from three players, Warne, May and Mark Waugh; and the entire Australian party in New Zealand to play in a quadrangular tournament was forbidden to make any comment.

'We went from there to the West Indies, and we were only a couple of weeks into that tour when we learned that the ICC had passed the papers to the new Pakistan Board for them to investigate. The old body was called the Board of Control for Cricket in Pakistan, but that name was now changed to the Pakistan Cricket Board.'

A cynic might read something significant into the removal of the word 'control' from the title but, undeniably, a more stable looking regime had been put in place.

Wilkins again: 'The first sign of penetrating the administrative logjam came when we heard that Malik had agreed to be investigated, but only providing that Warne and May would travel to Pakistan so that their evidence could be examined. Understandably, as far as I was concerned, they refused on the grounds that they did not think they could be guaranteed safe passage in and out of the country. Without trying to over-dramatise things, the Australian players were very fearful of the personal consequences if they travelled to Pakistan. As far as they were concerned, they had been approached by Malik, presumably acting on behalf of illegal bookmakers.

'They had turned him down flat, and had kept quiet mainly because they took his approach seriously and were not prepared to take the slightest risk about their safety. The Pakistan authorities made much of the fact that the alleged approach was not made public for nearly five months. Well, that is the reason.'

What cannot be over-emphasised is the dreadful consequences of any cricketer accepting a bribe, or placing a bet on the opposition. If Malik's alleged approach had been accepted, it must be assumed that fortunes, small and mostly large, would have been wagered on Australia losing the first Test.

They did just that, but under such dramatic circumstances that no investigation would have cleared them of duplicity. Pakistan won what was only the eighth Test victory by one wicket in the history of cricket. Not only that, Pakistan triumphed thanks to an unbroken tenth wicket partnership between Inzamam-ul-Haq and Mushtaq Ahmed of 57, the last four runs of which were four byes off a missed stumping conceded by wicket-keeper Ian Healy. Furthermore, the ball went through his legs, off the bowling of Warne – one of the two players approached.

The betting world being what it is – a market-place of rumour and counter-rumour – how long would it have taken to surface that Warne and May had agreed to Malik's proposal? The fact that they refused it, and the match ended as it did, is a supreme irony.

A goalkeeper's basic fumble. A missed putt of six inches, like the back-hander missed swipe by Hale Irwin which cost him at least a share of the Open Championship at Royal Birkdale. A missed conversion from in front of the posts, like the one Don Fox kicked wide for Wakefield against Leeds to lose the Rugby League Cup final they would otherwise have won at Wembley. Stephen Hendry missing a black off the spot. Devon Loch stumbling on the flat, a few yards short of the winning post of the Grand National with Dick Francis on board. All these are typical examples of things in sport which cannot happen – except they do. Human beings are exactly that – not mechanical, metronomic bodies who are incapable of an error.

Back to Karachi, where Pakistan had never lost a Test and were not to lose against Australia. The game was the first one Australia had played without Allan Border for 153 Tests, and the first one in which Malik captained his country at home. If Warne and May are to be believed, he was so keen to win the game that he was prepared to pay for a guaranteed result. His after-the-match quote, following the highest of the previous seven last wicket partnerships to win a Test, was: 'Until the last ball, we weren't expecting to win. We were praying in the dressing room and I still can't believe it.'

At the end of the fourth day, Pakistan were 155 for three, needing 314, with Malik out just before the close off a bouncer from Joe Angel. The delight of the Australians at the fall of the third wicket seemed excessive at the time but, perhaps, not so now. That removed one of the central figures of the bribery imbroglio. The other, Shane Warne, dominated the final day's play, taking four of the six wickets to fall. Imzamam was the batsman who gave him the charge and missed; Healy missed it too, although he claims that the ball flicked the batsman's pad on the way through.

Either way, Pakistan won a match fair and square which, so Warne and May allege, Malik tried to influence in a manner that was improper, and bordered on the legally criminal. Prison sentences have been served by proven cases of sportsmen accepting money to throw games – footballers Tony Kay and Peter Swan went to prison thirty years ago for just such an offence.

On 7 March 1995, Salim Malik and coach Intikhab Alam were suspended, with the former captain given seven days to reply to the charges. Nobody has ever suggested that Intikhab was involved, although he has paid the penalty for not knowing more about stories that, by now, were beginning to seem credible. In Zimbabwe in February 1995, the beleaguered Pakistan tourists now had another story to deny – that they had thrown one, if not both of their back-to-back Test defeats in Johannesburg and Harare within the space of fourteen days.

A defence that the story was untrue because the players were asked to *re-affirm* an anti-betting oath on the Koran only made things worse. Re-affirm? So when had the original oath been taken? Before the start of the tour of southern Africa was the answer. And what was the oath?

According to Intikhab, it was that the players would 'not take bribes to throw matches or perform poorly'. No mention of betting, and how can a player avoid, on occasions, 'performing poorly', no matter what oath he has taken? If an oath could solve that problem, there would never be another duck, or a wide, or a dropped catch.

The mysterious 're-affirmation' was confirmed by Intikhab in the middle of February 1995, but only with the greatest reluctance and four days after he denied to journalists that any such oath had ever been taken.

He explained: 'There were so many rumours prior to the tour and we didn't want any problems'. He then said that similar oaths on the Koran had been taken by Pakistan sides for many years. Javed Burki went on record as saying that 'I do not think it is possible to throw a Test match, but God forbid if we find the slightest hint of impropriety, we'll take immediate action'. He also said that stories about Pakistan throwing matches a few weeks earlier in South Africa had appeared in the Pakistan press. 'We asked for names, but none were forthcoming.'

In March, Malik was allowed to play in domestic cricket while investigations continued, with the captaincy now like a game of musical chairs. Moin Khan was appointed for the Asia Cup, but chicken-pox did for him and Saeed Anwar took over. That was the tournament in which Wasim joined his colleagues late after a dispute with his Board about whether his wife could stay with him in his hotel.

Pakistan surprisingly lost to Sri Lanka in the Asia Cup in Sharjah and, on their return home, Rashid Lateef – former vice-captain – and Basit Ali announced that they had decided to reverse their decision to retire. The reason? 'We are satisfied with the new Board's handling of bribery allegations and other issues.'

A contrasting view was given by Wasim Akram, whose 'derogatory remarks about the administration in an Indian magazine' meant he faced disciplinary action. Some things never change. On the managerial front, Khalid Ibadulla, a Warwickshire playing colleague of mine in the 1960s, came and went, to be followed by Mushtaq Mohammad.

The captaincy was next given to Rameez Raja for the disastrous home series against Sri Lanka. All sorts of history was made by Sri Lanka. By winning the series, they did something that neither England nor India have done in five tours of Pakistan; Australia have failed in four attempts, New Zealand three, the West Indies two and Zimbabwe once.

This was Sri Lanka's fourth tour, and they seized their chance, made available by the troubles, on and off the field, which had beset Pakistan cricket in the first nine months of 1995. It was the first home series Pakistan had lost for fourteen years, and they had not previously lost two consecutive home Tests since Richie Benaud's Australians won in 1959 at Dacca and Lahore to clinch a three-match series.

The Dacca match was played on matting, after heavy rain made it impossible to use the new grass pitch, and the unlikely bowling hero for Australia was not Alan Davidson, Ian Meckiff, Ray Lindwall or Benaud, but Ken Mackay whose second innings match-winning figures were 45–27–42–6. Batting conditions were clearly not the best, with match aggregate figures of 671 runs from 333.3 overs. The third Test in Karachi was drawn, with the second slowest ever day in Test cricket – Pakistan scored 104 for five – watched for the first time by the President of the United States, Dwight D Eisenhower.

An interesting link with that match and the 1995 troubles is provided by Intikhab Alam, who became the first Pakistan bowler, and only the tenth ever, to take a wicket with his first ball in Test cricket when he bowled Colin McDonald. Intikhab was then three weeks short of his 18th birthday.

Back to Salim Malik. He originally threatened to sue the Australian newspapers which broke the story, and then followed up with legal threats against his own board, but never implemented them before they cleared him in October.

A Calcutta sports editor, Ayaz Memon, is in no doubt that betting is now a huge operation on the subcontinent, and is uncontrollable by the authorities. 'Pakistan needed 180 to beat Australia in Sri Lanka last year and I had the equivalent of £500 on them. Even when they needed 60 to win with seven wickets in hand, the bookmakers offered me generous odds and I was sucked in. A bookmaker friend told me later that the match was fixed.'

Betting promotes many similar stories, with many of them spoken out of damaged pockets, but there can be little question that the Pakistan authorities have a problem. But how do they deal with it? Have they done a deal with Malik? In return for dropping threatened legal action against them, one theory suggests that the Board will not pursue their investigation.

Whether true or not, the idea underlines the near-impossibility of nailing down the truth. Why are most of the supposed betting stories to do with Pakistan? And why did Salim Malik become involved, if he did? An English Sunday broadsheet investigated and believed that the collapse of a bank, with which Malik was connected, left him with financial problems – not all of them his own.

It seems that, in recent years, Malik introduced prospective clients to the bank. The bank's investment record was variable and, so it is believed, many of their clients suffered losses for which Malik may well have felt ethically responsible. Whether true or not, the fact remains that while rumours have been flying around for some time about the involvement of Pakistan cricketers in betting, it was only during Malik's brief reign as captain that the first ever direct charges were made from people other than from the subcontinent.

Before the case is examined, for and against Malik, the events since early March 1995 are significant. The ad hoc committee suspended him from first-class cricket: 'Based upon the evidence available to it, the committee has asked Salim Malik to show cause why disciplinary action should not be taken against him'. It also ruled that Rashid Lateef and Basit Ali had committed 'a serious breach of contract by flying home before the end of the tour of Zimbabwe'.

Two weeks later, the committee withdrew Salim's suspension and formally asked the ICC to arrange for Warne and May to visit Pakistan and present their charges and undergo cross-examination. The committee declared that 'Salim must be considered innocent until proven guilty. He is free to play cricket during the inquiry.'

Fine words, but meaningless once the ad hoc committee was wound up and the new Pakistan Cricket Board was formed. The new structure was politically orchestrated in a way that cricket authorities in other countries would not tolerate. The fact that it did not cause a ripple in Pakistan cricket's sea of troubles says much about the country.

Chairman Syed Zulfiqar Ali Shah Bokhari had been appointed by President Leghari, an old school friend – both men went to Lahore's Aitchison College. Bokhari is a member of the Punjab feudal elite, a governor of the State Bank of Pakistan and a politician who has experience as the Prime Minister's ambassador to Spain.

Not that he had unlimited powers, because the new constitution gave more control to chief executive Arif Ali Khan Abbasi, who was a member of the former ad hoc committee. Treasurer was Salman Taseer, a prominent member of Bhutto's People's Party of Pakistan. That appointment may not be unconnected with the governmental wish to maintain control over Pakistan cricket in the run-up to the 1996 World Cup.

Waqar Younis giving due care and attention to the seam. Note that the Law allows him to clean the seam, but not to pick or lift it. The position of the right forefinger in relation to the angle of the seam appears to suggest that the contact point of finger and ball is away from the seam.

Above: The only postwar father and son combination to play for England and open the innings – Micky and Alec Stewart. The younger Stewart was to be involved in further ball tampering controversy in his position as captain of Surrey.

Right: Intikhab Alam, team manager of Pakistan during their troubled tours of England in 1992 and Southern Africa in 1994-95. He was sacked in March 1995 and reappointed for the tour of Australia later that year and the 1996 World Cup.

The second new ball used by Surrey in the first innings of their match against Derbyshire at Ilkeston, 1991. Waqar Younis was Surrey's main strike bowler that day, and while this photograph shows the ball after 22 overs, according to Don Oslear it was in a similar condition after just 8 overs. The cuts, or nail marks, can be seen on both left and right sides of the cross-seam. Its condition mirrors that of the ball which Oslear presented to A C Smith after the Lord's one-day international involving Pakistan in August 1992.

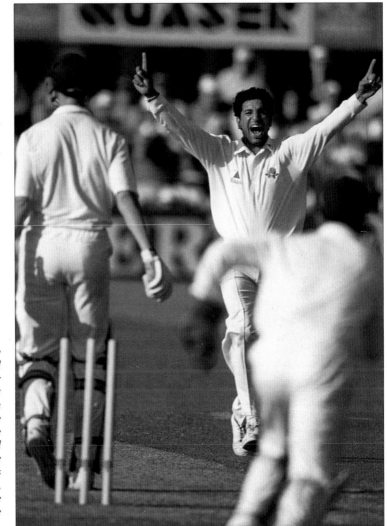

Right: Wasim Akram bowls Alan Mullaly in a Benson & Hedges semifinal at Leicester in 1993, in a devastating spell of swing bowling in which he took five for 2 in nine balls. The eventual final between Lancashire and Derbyshire was the scene of the beamer incident between Wasim and Chris Adams.

Below: The ball used by Lancashire in the second innings during their four-day game against Derbyshire at Derby in July 1993. Note the alarming difference between the treated and untreated sides. On the left, the gouging marks are all too plain to see, while the nail cuts on the right photograph are prominent in two places.

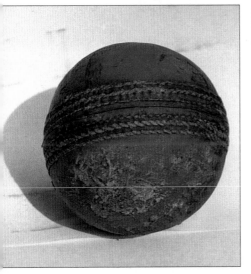

Left: Sir Colin Cowdrey, whose four-year reign as Chairman of the ICC included the return of South Africa to official Test cricket, and the introduction of the Code of Conduct, match referees and an international panel of umpires.

Below: Chris Lewis unceremoniously points Craig McDermott to the dressing room during the England v Australia Adelaide Test of 1995. Match referee John Reid fined Lewis and expressed his disappointment because he had specifically warned both captains about the ramifications of such actions.

Opposite page
Right: Jo Angel has a run-in with umpire Khizar Hayat in the first Test in the betting-bedevilled series between Pakistan and Australia in Karachi 1994. Angel was subsequently fined and severely reprimanded.

Below right: Alec Stewart acts as peacemaker between Phil Tufnell and the umpire at the MCG against Australia A in a Benson & Hedges World Series game in December 1994. Tufnell had tossed the ball away after an appeal for caught behind had been turned down – and was fined 30% of his match fee by referee John Reid.

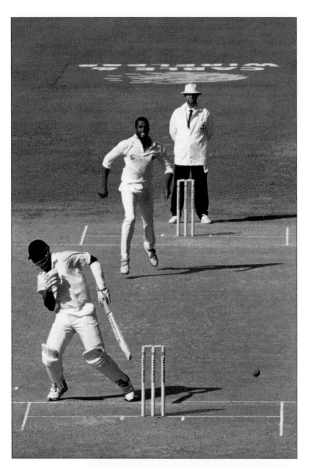

*West Indies v England, First Test,
Kingston, 1994. Tail-ender Devon
Malcolm is hit by a ball from Courtney
Walsh in a series of short-pitched
deliveries from around the wicket that
went unpunished by umpire
Ian Robinson.*

*Umpire Dickie Bird, who announced th[at]
he would retire from international crick[et]
during the 1996 summer Test series, giv[es]
Kenny Benjamin his views on intimidat[ion]
during the 1995 Headingley Test.*

Shane Warne bowls from around the wicket into the rough ... which was the sort of justice the Aussie spinner felt had been meted out after the ICC failed to follow up on alleged attempts at bribing players by Salim Malik.

In the First Test between South Africa and Australia at Johannesburg in March 1994, Warne bowled Andrew Hudson in his first over, the 44th of the innings, and unaccountably lost all self-control, despite Ian Healy's peace-keeping efforts. The bowler was fined 10% of his match fee and severely reprimanded.

Merv Hughes bends the ear of Graeme Hick in the Second Test between England and Australia at Lord's in 1993. The Australian got away with this one, but he was less fortunate in the following series against South Africa in 1994, when he was fined 10% of his match fee for verbally abusing the batsman during the First Test in Johannesburg. Then, within 48 hours, his own Board took away the other 90% of his match fee (as they did to Shane Warne), because of the perceived weak action of referee Donald Carr.

New Zealand bowler Chris Pringle, who is on record as admitting he tampered with the ball during the Third Test of the 1990-91 series against Pakistan in Faisalabad, where he took 11 wickets including a career best seven for 52. His previous two Tests had seen him take two for 180.

England v South Africa, Oval Test, August 1994. Mike Atherton indicates that he thought he had hit the ball from Fanie de Villiers from which he was given out lbw. Match referee Peter Burge decided that this action from the England captain crossed the line between disappointment and dissent.

Abbasi had fifteen years experience in cricket administration, which says much for his durability in a constantly changing scene. On behalf of the new board, he endorsed, publicly, Salim's right to a fair hearing. Privately, it seems his attitude was different, as he apparently said that the former captain's career was over. On 30 March, Khalid Ibadulla was announced as the new Pakistan cricket manager, succeeding Intikhab Alam, and there were sweeping changes in the squad announced for the Asia Cup in Sharjah. Out went Salim, his brother-in-law Ijaz Ahmed, Akram Raja and Kabir Khan. Waqar was still unavailable because of the injury which precipitated his departure, ten weeks earlier, from the tour of Southern Africa, an injury from which, vainly, he tried to convince Surrey a few weeks later, he had recovered. (Medical opinions were exchanged before Surrey decided to sign Australian Carl Rackemann for the 1995 season.) Also missing were the still 'retired' Rashid Lateef and Basit Ali.

The Pakistan Board announced that it had 'directed the selection committee to ensure that players who have consistently exhibited undesirable attitudes and behaviour are not considered for selection'. Pakistan's laws of libel are rather looser than those of the Western world, where such a statement would have been seized on by avid legal advisers for omitted players. For instance, in 1984, when Ian Botham returned from Pakistan and made his notorious 'mother-in-law' jokey reference to Pakistan, Sarfraz Nawaz was quoted in his national press as saying that the remarks 'were those of a dope-crazed fiend'.

It is only when the differences in culture and law are considered between Pakistan and, say, England and Australia, that critics of the militarily run country can begin to understand why some things are done as they are.

It is difficult for British people to understand laws allowing the tongues of liars to be cut out and the hands of thieves to be cut off, not to mention a scenario like the Prime Minister of the day dissolving the Test & County Cricket Board and appointing members of parliament to run cricket.

So, although Salim had been declared innocent until proven guilty, by omission from the party he had been found guilty of something. But what? Three reasons were given by different officials.

1. There was enough circumstantial evidence against him about betting.

2. He would have been booed by the Sharjah crowd and 'a national humiliation of Pakistan had to be avoided'.
3. He had been left out because of 'acts of indiscipline' committed under his captaincy in Zimbabwe.

The latter point was made by Abbasi, although there was no accompanying statement about which players had committed the acts, nor what punishment was meted out. The two players who broke their contracts, Rashid Lateef and Basit Ali, escaped punishment, which could explain why they were satisfied with the way the new Board had handled the betting and bribery allegations.

Both players said they had been 'under all sorts of pressure to change their minds' and two other factors entered the equation which was aimed at balancing the past, present and future with as little long-term damage as possible. As an exercise, it would be easier to square a circle, or refill an empty tube with toothpaste. Or convince Don Oslear that the Test & County Cricket Board were the best employers he had ever worked for.

The first factor was the regional one and one far from peculiar to Pakistan – take for instance North v South in English cricket, a five-pointed inter-island tug-of-war in the Caribbean, or New South Wales against the rest in Australia, and so on.

Rashid and Basit are from Karachi and Salim from Lahore, with regional favouritism advanced as the reason for their different treatment. The second factor was more sinister. It was alleged that Rashid had threatened to incriminate other players in the betting scandal if he was kept out of future teams.

What is clear is that the ICC would have been the best body to organise the inquiry, but it was deemed constitutionally correct to refer it to the Pakistan authorities. The problem facing everyone was how to snip through the bureaucratic labyrinth of interests, both vested and conflicting, in Pakistan. If a more democratically elected TCCB in England can still dodge nasty smells in their own game, how can an arbitrarily appointed authority such as the one in Pakistan be expected to set a disciplinary example to the rest of the cricket world?

As Lahore journalist Kamil Hyat exlains: 'Allegations of match-fixing have become a convenient tool in the hands of anyone who wants to malign particular individuals or the Pakistan team – for any number of reasons, linked with the power struggles which periodically shake cricket in Pakistan. Each time an individual or group wishes to drag someone down, it is all too easy to feed the press with these insinuations. Of course, this also means that a valid charge may be dismissed too summarily as yet another symptom of the same malaise.'

The Salim Malik affair achieved a rare thing. It tore asunder a Pakistan team which, mostly under the paternal influence of Imran Khan, had risen to the peak of world cricket. He and Clive Lloyd are the best examples of strong characters who were able to unify teams that, under lesser captains, were pulled apart by race or region. It helped that both men were great cricketers, but few other outstanding performers who have captained their country have commanded the same dressing room respect.

An examination of Pakistan's captains in the past fifteen years, prior to Salim taking over, reveals that only Zaheer Abbas interrupted a run between Imran and Javed Miandad who, between them, led Pakistan in twenty-five out of thirty-one series played against England, Australia, West Indies, New Zealand, India and Sri Lanka. The split is surprisingly even, with Imran leading in fourteen series and Javed eleven. Small wonder that, after fifteen years in which Pakistan were captained by two of their greatest ever cricketers, the next man in would have a difficult task. Especially as the accession to the throne came after a particularly bloody palace revolution which deposed Wasim Akram. That is the background to the biggest scandal in international cricket in living memory.

CHAPTER 11

Guilty or not guilty?

Salim Malik is the first cricketer to be put out of modern international cricket because of allegations about an involvement in betting and bribery. There is a distinction between the two words, but one that is all too easily blurred when rumours start about sides betting against themselves. That is not bribery in the strictest sense; the *Chambers 20th Century Dictionary* definition of a bribe is, 'Something offered to influence the judgement unduly or corrupt the conduct'. A bet is defined thus: 'Something staked to be lost or won on the result of a doubtful outcome'.

Therefore, by definition, cricketers betting on the opposition to win believe that they can remove the doubt about the outcome. The same object is at the centre of the allegations about Salim made by Warne and May. They claim that he wanted to pay them to perform badly in order to enhance his side's winning chances. That is bribery which, presumably, once given and accepted, would have been followed with large wagers on Pakistan to win the Test matches in question, and with them the series.

The irony is that Pakistan won the first Test and survived the wrong end of the other two, mainly due to superlative batting performances by Salim. His scores were 26 and 43 in the first Test in Karachi, 33 and a career best 237 in an improbable draw at Rawalpindi after the home side followed on, and 75 and 143 in another draw in Lahore. In this game, Pakistan were effectively 25 for five in their second innings with a day and a half left, so Salim's 143 sealed the series win the Australians insisted he tried to buy five weeks earlier.

The difference was that if there was no bribed guarantee, the big players concerned would not then risk their rupees. There is no safer bet than in a two-horse race, where inside knowledge suggests that one horse is guaranteed to under-perform.

Defenders of the five-day faith insist that it is impossible to fix a five-day Test, unless an entire side is bought up. Perhaps so, but a briber can achieve most of what he wants if he knows that two of the opposition's main bowlers, who will bowl half the overs in the series, will not perform to their potential. Anyone trying to fix a soccer match concentrates on buying the favours of defenders and not forwards – as in the proven cases of the Sheffield Wednesday pair of Tony Kay and Peter Swan, and in the case involving charges against goalkeeper Bruce Grobbelaar.

To develop the point, once the bribed bowlers prove expensive, the captain takes them off and has to rely upon support bowlers. Buy a couple of batsmen, and they might get the ducks that come to any Test batsman at any time – but that still leaves three or four batsmen capable of scoring a hundred. No, it is bowlers who have to be bought.

The case for the prosecution against Salim is purely circumstantial, except for the still unsupported charges laid by Warne and May. It is based upon interpretations put on his, and his team's performances in southern Africa, and is typical of accusations which are often made in sport to explain the inexplicable.

Consider these instances in Cape Town and Johannesburg in January 1995, followed by the Harare Test against Zimbabwe two weeks later. Pakistan had dominated the qualifying stages of South Africa's quadrangular tournament – the two sides knocked out after each team played six matches were New Zealand and Sri Lanka. The latter team was eventually 'rained' out of the tournament in their final game against South Africa, having beaten the host country in their first game at Bloemfontein.

That match provided the biggest upset of the tournament, with South Africa quoted at odds of 1–3 only to collapse against spin and lose easily. I saw the match and was told of regular telephone calls to the Orange Free State office from an increasingly dismayed caller from Dubai, who was checking on the progress of his 'certainty' bet of US$1 million on South Africa. His winnings would have been a tax-free US$333,000. Nobody suggested that Hansie Cronje and his players had 'taken a dive', because had South Africa not reached the finals, it would have been a marketing disaster which would have hit home coffers and the pockets of the players alike.

Dr Ali Bacher, Chief Executive of the United Cricket Board, freely admitted to a potential cricketing nightmare if South Africa did not play in the best-of-three finals, but rain saved him when Sri Lanka were well placed to win the final qualifying game.

So to the first day-night final at Newlands on Tuesday 10 January 1995. Pakistan were odds-on favourite of 4-7 for the match and 1-2 for the best-of-three finals. Anyone suspecting that Salim had a betting interest in the game was provided with plenty of apparent evidence.

The toss first. South Africa traditionally perform better in one-day cricket when they bat first and field second – unless conditions are such that it would be folly to do that. The reasons are twofold: firstly, they do not chase a target well, because their workmanlike batsmen lack a class performer, and are much happier batting first when there is no pressure about reaching a finite score. Secondly, their strength is in bowling and fielding, allied to an unquenchable resilience that enables them to defend moderate looking totals with an outstanding success ratio.

Therefore, all other things being equal, which they were at Newlands, the opposition captain is better off batting first – for the two reasons that South Africa's bowling and fielding is robbed of a finite target to defend, and their batsmen are then put in a situation they like least.

Basic tactics. Obvious tactics – except that when Salim called correctly (to the obvious dismay of Cronje as seen on the televised recording of the toss), the Pakistan captain announced that his side would *field*. The question was put to him by SABC's commentator Trevor Quirk, 'Why have you done that, Salim?'

Salim answered: 'Because we chase well and I think that is the best way to beat South Africa.'

The game followed a predictable pattern, with South Africa pegged back by the regular loss of wickets, but their middle-lower order took them to 215, with three late run-outs depriving them of a dozen or so more runs. The pitch was good, and that sort of total does not win more matches than it loses.

Particularly when Aamir Sohail hit nine fours from his first 23 balls, and fast bowler Steven Jack was plundered for 29 off his first two overs. The 50 came up in eight overs, and Sohail reached his sixth 50 in eight innings out of 65 from 41 balls.

The hundred came up in the 22nd over with only two wickets down and, if the Bombay bookmakers were betting on what they thought was a 'straight' match, they would have bet about 1-10 on Pakistan scoring 116 from 28 overs with eight wickets in hand. Those odds mean that the batting side would win the match five times out of six, although, realistically, any side would be disappointed to lose one in ten. The Bombay syndicate decided not to answer the telephones for an hour, so the Dubai syndicate's plan to back South Africa heavily was successfully countered.

Twelve overs later, Pakistan were 133 for seven with the top order dismissed in reckless fashion, and the target now 82 from 16 overs with only tail-end batsmen left.

Reckless? Of the seven wickets, three were run-out, including Salim, and two batsmen were caught in the deep when, needlessly, they slogged wildly when the match situation cried out for a period of consolidation. The two batsmen were Ijaz Ahmed and Basit Ali, but even their wild dismissals were no more culpable than those of Sohail and Rashid Lateef.

To be run out in that sort of match situation is bad enough, but to take on the world's best fielder in Jonty Rhodes for impossibly tight singles was cricket madness. The mutterings started, particularly among South African bookmakers who, for the first time in their history, were allowed by government legislation to bet on cricket. Naturally they were swamped by patriotic wagers, and they were not best pleased, not just with the result, but more by the manner of it.

They adjusted the odds a touch for the second game, two days later at New Wanderers in Johannesburg. The newspapers were naturally full of praise for the way South Africa had won a match which seemed lost, but they expressed caution about the second game. They forecast a Pakistan backlash which would square the series and take it to a decider in Centurion Park. And, they said, Salim would have learned his lesson about the toss and would not make the same mistake again.

By toss-up time at 1.45pm on Thursday 12 January 1995 in Johannesburg, two other things had happened which must have removed any unlikely remaining doubts in the mind of Malik about what to do if he won the toss. The local weather forecast said there was a 40 per cent chance of rain, and a poll among his players showed an overwhelming wish to bat first if Pakistan won the toss.

In England, the side batting second is greatly favoured in a rain-interrupted match. For example, side 'A' scores 200 in 40 overs and then rain restricts side 'B' to 20 overs. They need 100 with all wickets in hand. Clearly not equitable, but the TCCB are reluctant to seek an alternative formula, following the farcical situation at Sydney in the

1992 World Cup semi-final between England and South Africa. Rain fell towards the end of the match, and when the players came out again, an improbable, but perfectly possible target of 21 in 13 balls became 21 off one ball.

As the injured party, the South African authorities decided to look for a fairer method of recalculation, but the one they adopted for the quadrangular series only served to swing the balance too far the other way. For instance, in the final qualifying match in Port Elizabeth to decide Pakistan's opponents in the final, South Africa scored 237 for eight in their 50 overs, and Sri Lanka were still in the game needing 163 in 28 overs when there were two stoppages for rain.

On resumption, the target was 184 from 34 overs, which meant that 163 in 28 overs had now become 110 from 12, with the considerable difference between that formula and the English one now emphasised. In England a score of 237 in 50 overs gives a run-rate of 4.74 runs per over, A side only batting for 34 overs in reply would thus need 34 x 4.74 = 161. Then came a second stoppage and when the players came back, Sri Lanka's new target was 83 from 5.3 overs. Impossible, but the lesson was there for all captains to learn. Bat first when rain threatens.

The same four people assembled in the middle for the toss. An anxious Hansie Cronje, Salim, match referee Peter Burge and SABC's Trevor Quirk. Salim won again, and a distraught Cronje put his head in his hands in despair.

Quirk pointed the microphone at Salim and asked what he thought was a rhetorical question. 'Another correct call, Salim. What are you going to do?'

'*We will field first*.' There was a perfect double-take from the disbelieving Cronje, who thought he was hearing things. Quirk gulped, but ploughed on. 'But why? You fielded first at Newlands and lost.'

'Yes,' replied Salim, 'but we batted badly, and I still believe we can chase anything successfully.'

'But there is rain forecast, and surely that means you will be at a big disadvantage.'

Salim: 'I am not bothered about the weather forecast. You cannot plan a game around the weather. I am sure my decision is the right one.'

It seems that Salim returned to a dressing room that was just as incredulous about their captain's decision as was Cronje. Part of the pre-match team talk concerned the toss, and there are several estimates of the strength of opinion to bat first – with the most conservative head count giving a maximum of three Pakistan players who did not mind fielding first.

The game was a one-sided mismatch. Mike Rindel, promoted to open the innings with Gary Kirsten, scored 105 off 139 balls out of a South African record first-wicket partnership of 190 in 38 overs. Waqar and Wasim were hit for 104 from 19 overs between them, and Cronje's 37 from 36 balls drove the important final nails into the Pakistan team's suicide coffin. A total of 266 wins most 50-over matches, even on a good pitch with a fast outfield.

Aamir Sohail might have received an unlucky lbw decision in a marvellous opening spell of three wickets in 11 balls by De Villiers. Donald followed up with three more in 12 balls – Inzamam, Salim and Rashid Lateef – and at 42 for six, the game was won and lost. Their second successive collapse meant they had been bowled out twice in 48 hours in 75.2 overs.

Was Malik's second successive toss blunder the act of a stubborn man? The rumour-mongers had a field day, and they were growing in number. The all-conquering Pakistan side of December was now a thing of bits and pieces. Wasim had arrived, and Waqar was about to go. The side had lost through appalling misdirection from the top. Was Malik that bad a captain, or was he driven by another force?

The inaugural Test match between the two countries would settle some, if not all of the questions. Things happen quickly in the helter-skelter of one-day cricket, but in a five-day Test, surely Pakistan would offer sterner resistance? Again, Pakistan were favourites, although their selection was so curious and unpredicted that one of their team was unable to bowl for the first thirty-six minutes of the first session of play, because he was not on the ground when the Pakistan team took the field.

Aamir Nazir had flown to Johannesburg from London that morning, but was declared to play despite a fourteen-hour flight and the fact he could not be on the ground for the start of the match. It was hardly a shock when he left the field with cramp after bowling seven overs. A shambolic bowling and fielding performance by the touring side enabled South Africa to recover from 59 for three and 168 for five to 460, with De Villiers scoring a career best 66 at number 10.

Unusually in a Test match, the home total of 460 came at four runs per over, with extras contributing 64, including 36 no-balls. Accusers will say that Wasim bowled over half of those although, as umpire Mervyn Kitchen knew from past experience, Wasim Akram always 'lives on the line' and only ever deals in inches with his front foot.

Pakistan did not avoid the follow-on target, being bowled out for 230 in 65.5 overs with several injudicious off-side flashes and hooks punished by De Villiers, who took six for 81. Because he was carrying a few niggles and Donald was playing in his first first-class match since the Oval Test six months previously, Cronje did not enforce the follow-on, thus giving Pakistan a chance of drawing the match, if they batted better in their second innings.

They did not, and compounded a second profligate display of out-cricket in which another 32 extras were conceded, to take the Pakistan match aggregate to 96, seven fewer than the record of 103 conceded by West Indies against Pakistan at Bridgetown in February 1977.

The declaration left Pakistan to score 490 to win but, more realistically, five sessions to bat out for a draw on a good pitch, against a four-man attack in which De Villiers was struggling and Donald ring-rusty. The South African crowds – 28,000 on the fourth day when Pakistan began their second innings – had given the tourists a generous welcome, but were perplexed by a lacklustre display which gave every impression that the players concerned were demob happy.

If the first three and a half days had disappointed a cricket-starved public who were delighted to welcome Pakistan to the country for the inaugural Test match, the next two sessions were pathetic.

Seven wickets fell, with Saeed Anwar, Asif Mujtaba and Ijaz Ahmed out hooking, and Moin Khan driving airily into the covers. Aamir Sohail and Salim were out to good deliveries to the heroic De Villiers, but the stroke played by Salim to his first ball off Donald ranked among the worst of the match.

Salim took guard, with the score then three runs for two wickets, to face Donald, who had just induced Anwar to mis-hook to fine leg. The match situation was dire, and the previous wicket had fallen to a reckless stroke. So what did Salim do? Off a full length delivery just outside off stump, he aimed a wildly ambitious square cut on the up and edged a catch to wicket-keeper David Richardson...only for the roars to die away as umpire Cyril Mitchley called and signalled no-ball.

Salim did not profit. A single took him to the other end whereupon he was lbw to a lovely delivery from De Villiers. That was 5 for three, but Mujtaba and Inzamam resisted for 41 overs with the sort of application which should have been the order of the day for everyone.

McMillan broke the partnership and the innings plunged into freefall. Like his brother-in-law before him, Ijaz came to the wicket because of a mis-hook, and promptly did the same.

After finishing my television commentary stint, I walked out of the ground and was stopped at least half a dozen times by bewildered spectators who wanted an explanation for what they had just seen. I could not offer one which made cricketing sense.

It was the same on the final morning, when the last rites took forty-five minutes to complete. Several members, old enough to have watched pre-war Test cricket, said they had never seen such bad cricket at that level. How could anyone argue? Only Inzamam of the first seven applied himself and Salim's misery continued.

Including the two one-day internationals, Pakistan were dismissed in four successive innings in 210.4 overs, all within eleven days and all on blameless pitches. The prosecution case against Malik will thus point to three defeats, all of them as the bookmakers' favourites. Nothing had yet been heard about grumbles from Bombay, but they were only two weeks away.

A dispirited and bickering party flew to Harare and into the biggest shock of the tour. Zimbabwe were priced at 40-1 against beating Pakistan. Silly odds? Zimbabwe had not won a Test match in eleven attempts since their first against India in October 1992. They broke that duck in the most emphatic way, beating the beleaguered Pakistan side in Harare by an innings and 64 runs, the biggest 'first win' by any of the Test playing countries.

The basis for the win was laid by the Flower brothers. Andy joined Grant with the score 42 for three, and their magnificent fourth wicket partnership of 269 beat the previous best by brothers, 264 by the Chappells against New Zealand at Wellington in March 1974. Wasim, again without Waqar, was relatively innocuous and Pakistan could only try to save the game, facing a first innings total of 544 for four from 165 overs.

They fought for over four sessions against hostile bowling from Heath Streak, well supported by brilliant catching and fielding. The first five wickets of the second innings fell for 35, and only Inzamam threatened to take the game into the fifth day. With an injured shoulder, he scored 65 to add to his 71 in the first innings, and he was the only Pakistan batsman to stand firm while the foundations tumbled around him, as he did in the second innings of the Johannesburg Test.

The *Racing Post* in England reported that the Bombay book-makers were refusing to pay on the result, with a twist in the tail concerning the previous Test against South Africa. Their chief feature writer, Dominic Chapman, wrote this on Valentine's Day 1995 about the massacre in Johannesburg three weeks earlier:

'Last month's one-off Johannesburg Test between South Africa and Pakistan stirred up a row between punters and bookies. It is understood that a big betting syndicate, made up of expatriates based in Dubai, had backed Pakistan with Indian bookmakers, although there was also plenty of money for South Africa. When the tourists were easily beaten, the punters cried foul and refused to pay up, claiming that the match was suspicious. The illegal Indian layers responded to the result and the subsequent row by voiding all bets on the Test.'

Because the Bombay syndicate did not answer their telephones, the Dubai syndicate refused to pay. The Bombay bookmakers then voided all bets.

What a remarkable situation, and one which could only happen with illegal betting. Punters can also refuse to pay in England, but the inevitable black-balling means a damaged reputation which makes it almost impossible to open a new, legitimate account. Yet the Dubai syndicate were reported as suspecting a reverse 'sting', namely one of which they were unaware as opposed to the many they have instigated. They refused to pay to leave the Bombay bookmakers with a completely one-sided book, so they voided all bets to deny genuine backers of South Africa their rightful winnings, and the other sort which, according to the prosecution case, included Salim, or his paymaster connections.

It was during the tour of Zimbabwe that the Warne and May allegations were made public, the only saving grace for Salim being that by then, Pakistan had squared the series before they won the deciding Test in Harare after asking for that second affirmation of the oath on the Koran from his players. Cynics would say two things: 'He would do that, wouldn't he?' and also point out that, if there was the slightest truth in the stories, Salim dare not run the slightest risk of being seen as less than squeaky clean.

To sum up the case for the prosecution: Salim made two toss decisions in the one-day finals in Cape Town and Johannesburg that baffled everyone, including his own players. Whatever cricketing reason he advanced in the first game, was certainly rendered further invalid by the threat of rain in the second match. He sought the views of his players and then ignored them.

In the five-day Test against South Africa, he sanctioned the selection of a four-man attack including a debutant who, when the coin went up, had just stepped off the plane following a fourteen-hour flight. He presided over a second innings batting display that was guilty of surrendering over half the wickets in irresponsible fashion. Crushing defeats in Test matches are usually because of one side having the worst of conditions, or being on the receiving end of a string of brilliant performances. South Africa played well, but not well enough to register the biggest win in their history, by 324 runs with nearly a day to spare.

Of all the rash, give-away strokes played by his batsmen, none was worse than the first ball slash by Salim. That, together with the subsequent puffs of smoke from Bombay and Dubai, and the revelations about the two oaths on the Koran, forms most of the case for the prosecution. Tenuous? Circumstantial and based upon rumour? Slender? Yes, to all of those descriptions, but does that necessarily mean that Salim was not guilty of anything financially improper?

CHAPTER 12

Case for the defence

Salim could point to the results of the two qualifying one-day games against South Africa in the quadrangular tournament to explain his stubborn insistence that Pakistan's best chance of winning the trophy was to bat second in the finals. The first game was played at the New Wanderers on 10 December 1994 and South Africa won by seven wickets. Pakistan scored 214 after a collapse in which they lost their last seven wickets for 49 runs when they looked on course for a total of 250 at least.

That could have convinced Salim that his batsmen needed a fixed total to concentrate their minds. Such a thought would have been confirmed in Durban a week later when Pakistan won in spectacular fashion by eight wickets with 15 overs to spare. Good bowling, particularly by Waqar, restricted the home side to 206 for eight in 50 overs, and then Ijaz hit a brilliant unbeaten 114 and shared an unbroken partnership for the third wicket with Salim of 136, the last 41 coming in three overs.

In the first of the finals at Newlands, Pakistan were miles ahead on points, until one mad hour presented the game to South Africa. The key run-out was that of Malik himself, who was the victim of a brilliant piece of fielding by Gary Kirsten and the closest possible decision by the third umpire, thanks to the Panaeye technology. He ran his bat in along the ground, but the freeze-frame showed that while the toe of the bat was over the line in the air, the grounded bottom edge was only on the line. He was out by 1-50th of a second, but that was enough. As for the other run-outs to Jonty Rhodes, Salim could claim that when the red mist falls on a team, it blinds everyone and cricket commonsense goes out of the window.

And the wild slogs of Rashid Lateef and Basit Ali? That is the way that, usually, Pakistan react to danger. Old hands like Javed Miandad have a more innate streak of caution, but the naturally volatile character of the modern young Pakistan cricketer precludes a head-down approach when it is needed. They play 'blaze-away cricket' which can win games which look lost, and vice versa. Pakistan's approach is uninhibited. They wear their hearts on their sleeves, and they charm and infuriate because of their unpredictability.

If Salim still believed that he was better off batting second, notwithstanding the twin tactical advantage South Africa would thus enjoy, it was logical to back his judgement to the hilt in the second final in Johannesburg. Regarding the 40 per cent chance of rain, an optimist might claim that there was a 60 per cent of none, so the odds were in his favour. For the record, a brief light shower fell during the Pakistan innings, but the players did not have to leave the field. As for ignoring the views of his players, Salim would not be the first captain to seek such views and then ignore them.

Strong captains such as Mike Brearley and Mike Gatting believe that such consultation benefits everyone, but the final decision belongs to them. Regarding the one-sided nature of the second final, that often happens in one-day cricket when one side has posted a big total. The side batting second has to attack from the start, and the loss of early wickets can end the game as a contest. Aamir Sohail believes he hit the ball from which he was given out lbw, but Lady Luck has a perverse way of hiding her best cards from the side that needs them most.

Salim's defence for the five-day Test match is not so strong. The selection of a bowler still at the airport when the sides were announced, is difficult to understand. A one-off Test match can be a spur to a side, or a nothing match to a side that gets motivated most in a series of three or five matches. For South Africa, it completed a round of full Tests against the major countries in the three and a half year period since their re-entry into official international cricket.

For Pakistan, it came at the end of a tour of eight weeks in which they unexpectedly lost to South Africa in the quadrangular tournament. And for Salim, if the evidence of Warne and May is to be believed, the Johannesburg Test came only four months after his alleged approach to the Australian spinners. Conversely, no news is often good news, and he might not have known that the incident was about to go public. As a captain, he knew he had come under fire, both in South Africa and Pakistan, for his side's sudden fall from playing grace.

The final match of a tour is often a poor one for the visiting side. West Indies and Australia lost at the Oval in 1991 and 1993. So did South Africa in 1994, and they did it in even more embarrassing fashion than did Pakistan in Johannesburg. Nobody pointed the finger at South Africa in England, in fact nobody has ever pointed the finger at any side following an unexpected heavy defeat in England, because there the big bookmaking firms, all legal, keep a close watch on the pattern of all sporting bets.

Big money is wagered on cricket, but rarely all on one side, especially if it is the outsider of two runners. Salim must have known about the rumbles following the two one-day defeats, and his state of mind can hardly have been conducive to concentrating on a one-off Test match.

He can point to a two-man attack, Wasim and Aqib Javed, supported only by two untried youngsters, with his senior bowler well below top form and fitness. Wasim had joined the party only in early January, following treatment for injury, and it was asking a great deal, even for a bowling genius, to click into top gear straightaway. He looked overweight, and operated mostly off a short run.

He has always had a problem with no-balls, although to bowl over twenty in one innings, as he did against South Africa, was excessive even for him, and indicated that he was out of sorts and that his rhythm was erratic. Umpire Mervyn Kitchen has umpired Wasim a lot and knows that he has to watch the front line like a hawk. Some bowlers resent being called and make a pointed show of examining the footprint evidence as though they might get the call revoked. West Indies bowler Ian Bishop did this virtually every time he was called in England in 1995 – all to no avail. In fact it can be counterproductive with a prickly umpire who, even subconsciously, can be affected by a bowler's attitude and rule against him in a 50-50 situation.

Wasim has never been a bowler like that, certainly not with Kitchen who has worked out his own method of dealing with a front-foot problem that, with Wasim, is a peculiar one. Wasim bowls his left arm pace from, mostly, over the wicket and two things prevent Kitchen from getting a clear view of the position of the front foot when the ball is released. A part of Wasim's action involving the trailing left leg gets in the line of vision, and Wasim runs through his action, as compared with a 'body-rocker' such as Allan Donald or Devon Malcolm.

Wasim is like Malcolm Marshall used to be – there is hardly a check in his running stride as the ball is delivered, whereas with most other bowlers they jump on to the back foot to wind up a body action, and then thump the front foot down hard across the front crease. Wasim, on the contrary, sprints in and through the delivery stride in a whirl of pitter-patter steps.

Since Kitchen recognised Wasim's problem in the early 1990s, he spoke to the Pakistan bowler and they agreed the following procedure. Before he bowls, Wasim puts his foot across the front line, with a part of the heel behind the line. Kitchen then scratches a lateral line, parallel with the crease and across the line of Wasim's toe. He can see that and once Wasim's toe breaks that extra line, Kitchen knows he has over-stepped and calls him.

When Bob Willis had a no-ball problem in the famous Headingley Test of 1981 against Australia, his captain, Brearley, told him to forget it and just run in and bowl, which he did with the spectacular reward of a match-winning eight wickets for 43. Wasim and his captains work to the same theory, in the belief that the bowler is more effective if he clears his mind of the problems of varying his run to avoid being called. Frustration can bubble over when a bowler takes a 'wicket' with a no-ball, but that price is unavoidable if the bowler benefits overall.

Wasim did not in the Johannesburg Test, and Salim had nowhere to go when his strike bowler could not break through. Once a fielding captain loses control, he usually loses the match, although the perfectly trustworthy batting pitch gave his side ample opportunity to save the game.

That they did not and were rushed out twice in 135.2 overs could be explained by the fact that his batsmen not only did not alter their approach, but could not. When they were bounced, they accepted the challenge. When the ball was slanted across the left-handers, they went for the gaps left by Cronje's attacking field placings. The domino effect in cricket is common, as Salim's defence counsel might argue in the Johannesburg Test.

When a side can only play for a draw, it needs a good start to convince the rest of the side that they can fight their way towards safety to prevent repetition of a draw. Conversely, the effect of an early wicket or two can run through a dressing room, particularly if the wickets are the result of rash strokes. In the first innings, Pakistan were 44 for three and 5 for three in the second innings, and only three batsmen played an innings of note.

In the second innings, Inzamam scored 95, while Wasim's 41 in the first innings looked as though it might help his side to avoid the follow-on, coming after Salim's 99. Another bull point for the defence. It would have been his third hundred in successive Tests, to follow his 237 in Lahore and 143 in Karachi against Australia. When he slashed one from Donald to Clive Eksteen in the gully, it was his second 99 for Pakistan. Only five other batsmen have done that, including current Test captains Michael Atherton and Richie Richardson.

The follow-on was academic because of Cronje's decision to nurse his pace attack, and Malik can argue that his bowlers did well to force South Africa to extend their second innings to 80 overs. By restricting the home batsmen to just over three runs per over, compared with nearly four in the first innings, Pakistan thus reduced the batting time left for them to negotiate and so increased their chances of drawing the match.

They knew they had to survive the first new ball, but found the challenge of deliveries outside off stump and bouncers too tempting to refuse. It looked bad. It was bad, but it was not necessarily sinister.

Nor was the Test against Zimbabwe in Harare. Only the bookmakers in Bombay and the betting syndicate in Dubai know whether, after the match, they spoke out of knowledge or pocket. Umpire Kitchen, who had moved north from Johannesburg with the Pakistanis, stood in both games. He makes two significant points about the Harare game.

'I can't remember when the ball beat the bat and went so close to the stumps so often as happened when Zimbabwe made their 544 for four. Aqib was especially unlucky, and I remember him turning to me and asking if it was his fault, or was he bowling all right? Of course he was, but the luck was with the batsmen, and a lot of it. Also, when Pakistan batted, I have never seen such brilliant fielding and catching. You get a couple of great catches in a match sometimes, but this time there were half a dozen.'

The conspiracy theory suggests that, once the bookmakers had been stung at odds of 40-1, the Pakistan team could get down to business and win the series and point to that first Test as a one-off which has happened regularly ever since David was about the same odds against Goliath.

To sum up the case for the defence, Salim would claim there were sound reasons for giving the toss away twice to Cronje, and that because 'cricket is a funny game', that explains a succession of poor performances which brought four thrashings in four weeks, including two by 324 runs and an innings and 64 runs in the long-awaited inaugural Tests in southern Africa.

He can point to the absence of Waqar and the palpable lack of match fitness of Wasim. He can say that his tour was not the first to fall apart, either because of poor performances or because of differences off the field. For every winner there is a loser... and so on.

Tenuous? Yes. Convincing? Not entirely, but neither is the proof of any betting coup in South Africa or Zimbabwe. Which leaves the other piece of evidence.

That is the statement from Warne and May. The fact that their claims were not substantiated does not necessarily mean they are not true. The reason given for not complying with Salim's request for the two bowlers to travel to Pakistan is a reasonable one. Until someone has been approached with a bribe and refused it, he cannot know what his fears might be about the consequences of his decision.

Whether fears are real or imaginary, they are just as upsetting for the person in question. If Warne and May believe they would be in physical danger if they visit Pakistan again, that view must be respected.

Which left one avenue for Salim to explore if he wanted to establish his innocence beyond doubt. He could have cross-examined Warne and May in Australia, but he refused, as did his Board on procedural grounds which, surely, in the wider interests of the good name of cricket worldwide, should have been ignored. They stood firm on what they saw as an inviolable principle. The alleged bribery offence, committed by Salim, took place in Pakistan and, therefore, the hearing must be held in that country. Arif Abbasi quoted an adapted Islamic saying thus: 'The mountain does not go to Moses.'

The case for the defence would also point out, however, that it was not for Salim to prove his innocence, but for the accusers to establish his guilt. A man is innocent until proven guilty, after all.

The background to Salim's selection for the tour of Australia is a maze of wheelings and dealings which, even for Pakistan, is unique in the limit to which it pushes brinkmanship. Starting in March:

1. Salim is suspended, then reinstated but not considered for international selection.
2. Among the reasons given by the Board were the 'evidence of betting and bribery' and 'other incidents involving discipline on the tour of southern Africa'. Salim threatens litigation.

3. Moin Khan is appointed to lead the side to Sharjah for the Champions Cup. He develops chicken-pox and Saeed Anwar takes over.
4. Pakistan are heavily beaten and Rameez Raja is the next appointed captain for the home series against Sri Lanka and a second trip to Sharjah in October, finishing a few days before the squad flies into Australia on 23 October 1995.
5. Pakistan lose the series to Sri Lanka – their first home defeat in fifteen years, and only their third in thirty-five years.
6. Pakistan do not qualify for the Sharjah final, and Aamir Sohail reportedly refuses to play in the last two matches, because he was so disenchanted with the captaincy of Rameez, although he claims an injury. Rameez said, 'I wanted Aamir to play, but if an individual says he has an injury, we have to trust and believe him.'
7. A three-man committee was appointed to analyse the defeats in the home series against Sri Lanka and also the side's poor showing in Sharjah. This met on Wednesday 18 October, three days before the squad was picked for Australia and, in turn, the selectors met forty-eight hours before the players flew to Perth.
8. A week before the squad was selected, and with Salim looking certain to be omitted, the first puffs of smoke signalling a recall began to emerge from Karachi.

Arif Abbasi, the man who was reported to have said privately that Salim's international career was over, now whistled a different tune. He outlined a 'process which was under way and could clear Salim within days'. The process was the appointment of a former Pakistan Attorney-General, Fakruddin Ebrahim. A man of impeccable qualifications, he had served as a Supreme Court judge, Chief Justice of the Sind High Court and Governor of the Sind Province.

Abbasi then revealed that Australia had refused, for a second time, a request for Warne and May to attend the hearing in Pakistan. He said that Australia 'had kindly made a counter-offer of every possible assistance if Pakistan wished to send the inquiry to Australia'. The mountain and Moses were then brought into the argument – and argument it now was.

Abbasi said: 'If the inquiry officer's findings are such that there is insufficient evidence of any wrongdoing, then it could be expected he would be making clear recommendations to the executive council, and I cannot see the selectors ignoring someone of Salim's ability for too long. It could all happen in the next couple of days.'

The puffs of smoke were now plume-like, and surely would not have appeared without a strong card-mark from Ebrahim. How else could Abbasi have put forward such strong views unless he knew that, in the continued refusal by Warne and May to fly to Pakistan, the case would be deemed to have collapsed for lack of evidence?

Abbasi revealed that 'within the two previous weeks' letters were sent to the Australian Cricket Board and the ICC at the behest of the inquiry officer. The two main points in the letters were the four and a half month delay in the allegations being made, despite the fact that Alan Crompton, Chairman of the ACB, was in Pakistan for part of the tour, and the fact that the burden of proof rested with the accuser 'and that requires more than four little letters'.

A third point was that natural justice demanded equal opportunity. 'We want to examine the issue threadbare. The matter will have to be resolved, and our justice system is also based on the English system, which is similar to that in Australia. That means this cannot be left in limbo. *You cannot sweep a human being under the carpet.*'

Abbasi then turned on the ICC. 'The ICC had the audacity to entertain the allegation instead of throwing it out. I requested from them the opportunity to cross-examine and was told this was not possible. Mr Ebrahim cannot go trundling off to Australia.'

The former Attorney-General was, apparently, not impressed by the affidavits. He told Abbasi, 'I don't see anything here. Can you obtain more information?'

The statements came thick and fast before the verdict. Abbasi's next utterance concerned the signed statements lodged by the Australian players and whether, as the ACB considered, they were 'private and confidential'.

'I don't think I'll have anything to hide, and I will advise the executive council not to hide anything. I don't see a reason for cloak and daggers. Once the decision is out it is common knowledge, and I don't see why somebody should be unnecessarily protected or otherwise.'

Abbasi also queried why his Board had not received a copy of the tour report from Australia's tour manager Colin Egar, or from match referee John Reid. 'Those reports should have been here a long time ago and, because most people would assume that neither gave any mention of any wrong doing, it makes the case against Salim very dicey.'

The hint that the charges made by Warne and May would be made public took only a couple of days to implement. While the Pakistani players were in the air – minus Salim who was still obtaining his visa – the inquiry officer, Ebrahim, explained the reasons behind his decision to dismiss the allegations.

The charge was that Salim telephoned Warne on the evening before the final day of the Karachi Test when Pakistan were 155 for three, needing 314 for an improbable win. Warne went to Salim's hotel room, and said in his statement that he was told that he and Tim May were the key bowlers for Australia and 'that Pakistan could not afford to lose because our pride is at stake'.

Warne's statement continued: 'Malik then said he could have US$200,000 in my room in half an hour. I couldn't believe what I'd heard and said, "You're kidding". I asked if he was serious and he said he was.'

Judge Ebrahim then quoted further from the Warne statement. 'Shane goes on to say that either that night or the next morning he told Salim to f*** off and forget it. I think that the promise to pay the money to the Australians "within half an hour" was an unbelievable story.

'It's ridiculous. Nobody pays money of that amount before the event. According to Shane, US$200,000 was to be paid to the players if they lost the first Test. Tim May said that that amount would be paid to each one of them. And he was a room mate. The story just did not click.'

Ebrahim also repeated that Salim had the right to cross-examine his accusers. 'These allegations have not been substantiated and, in its totality, it is a story of no consequence. I could not place any reliance on the statements. I also questioned Salim as to why the Australian cricketers would level such a damning accusation at him. All he could say was "that it was a conspiracy to humiliate Pakistani cricketers and to demoralise its most successful captain".'

Ebrahim's nine-page findings also picked out the ACB's refusal to send their players to Pakistan as 'inadequate and irresponsible'. He also cited coach Bobby Simpson for failing to notify the Pakistan Board, and finally blunderbussed everyone involved from the ACB to the ICC.

'It would appear from the ICC's letter dated 12 February 1995 that Mr Graham Halbish, Chief Executive of the ACB, Mr Alan Crompton, Chairman of the ACB, and Colin Egar, the team manager, wanted to speak to the ICC off the record about various issues of alleged attempted bribery that had unfortunately now become public, with the aim of leaving the ICC to deal with the matter discreetly and behind the screen.'

Plenty of billowing smoke, but not a spark of fire for the judge to act upon.

The Australian Board had a chance to play a dead bat stroke or go for a match-winning six. Chief Executive Graham Halbish chose not to pick his bat up out of the block-hole. 'Regarding our players flying to Pakistan, they have nothing to add to the statements and therefore there is no need for them to go. It is an internal Pakistan matter. Current relations between the two countries are very cordial.'

He then said his country was acting in the game's best interests when it brought the bribery allegations to the attention of ICC. 'Pakistan can go ahead and choose who they like to play this season in Australia, and we don't believe it's going to have any impact at all on the coming summer.'

Sydney journalist Phil Wilkins found reality to be different. Near retirement from the regular treadmill of reporting Test cricket, he believed he might even take a back seat for the three Tests against Pakistan. Not only did the *Herald* squash that idea as soon as Salim was included in the touring party, they insisted that Wilkins fly to Perth to meet the Pakistanis, and he would travel with them for the next six weeks. Quite a way to ease yourself into gradual retirement.

The way was thus cleared swiftly for Salim to return to a side which was now in even greater disarray than when he was banned seven months earlier. Even as late as the day before the selectors picked the squad, the prevailing opinion among Pakistani journalists was that his immediate return would be too big an embarrassment, and that his term of exile should end in time for the World Cup in February, played on his home soil.

The news broke to an incredulous cricketing world on Saturday morning 21 October 1995, although no captain and vice-captain was announced that day. The squad of, more or less, Pakistan's best players were back together, but how best to shuffle a pack which already included six players who had captained the side in two disastrous years?

The answer was to revert to the first of the six, Wasim Akram, and make Aamir Sohail his number two – appointed within a few days of refusing to play under captain number five, Rameez. The possibilities of internal trouble were endless. Nearly half the party had rebelled against Wasim's first brief reign, including Waqar. At one stage, the two great fast bowlers were reduced to passing messages to each other on the field through a third party.

Then how would the deposed Rameez react at being returned to the ranks? And what about Salim's relationship with, in particular, Rashid Lateef and Basit Ali against whom he had issued writs because of their reported statements about his involvement in betting?

The reaction in Australia varied from the disbelieving, to the cynical to the 'forgive-and-forget' thoughts of former Somerset batsman Peter Roebuck.

He said, 'It has not been a glorious affair. Cricket did not want to be hurt, so it ran away. Now the matter must end, and in good grace. Once Australia refused to send its players as witnesses, the outcome was inevitable. Written words are a poor substitute for the truth plainly told and sustained against cross-examination. *Australian cricket lacked the will to tell its side of the story.*

'Nor is it appropriate to question the rigour with which the matter was pursued in Pakistan. A noted jurist was appointed and his judgement cannot be taken lightly.'

Roebuck believed that ICC deserved censure. 'Here was a matter demanding immediate action from the game's ruling body. Nothing less than the bona fides of international cricket was at stake. There was talk of gambling and drugs and stockbrokers and hot money. It was pretty ripe stuff, yet the ICC did not set up its own commission of inquiry.'

Roebuck then posed the questions the whole of cricket wants answering. 'Had bribes been offered? Was bribery widespread? Had any bribes been accepted? These were issues which demanded vigorous international investigation. Instead it was left to Pakistan to consider their own affairs. Their inquiry found Malik innocent of all charges, and that verdict must be accepted.'

The ACB changed tack once Ebrahim's findings were made public, two days after their bland statement that Pakistan could pick who they liked. Now they loaded both barrels and let fly.

'The ACB has always sought to have the matter of bribery allegations resulting from the 1994 tour of Pakistan dealt with in the appropriate way. The ACB referred these matters to the ICC in London well before the story was broken publicly by the media. We have never sought to put forward the Board's case or the players' case through the press. It is others that have chosen to do that.

'Now that the Pakistan Cricket Board has seen fit to produce not just the statement of Judge Ebrahim's reasons, but also the statements made by the three Australian players, the ACB feels it has no alternative than to say something.

1. Allegations that the ACB only acted four months after the event are completely untrue. The ICC was made aware of ACB's concerns on no less than three occasions prior to the story breaking in the media.
2. We have continually declined to send the players to Pakistan because, as we have maintained all along, the players have nothing whatsoever to add to what is their legally-sworn statements.
3. With respect to the judge's findings, we have no idea how the inquiry was conducted or what evidence in totality was considered, other than a perusal of the players' sworn statements. The Board stands behind its players and believes those statements are correct.
4. While the Board understands Judge Ebrahim was not convinced beyond reasonable doubt, because he did not have the opportunity to verify the Australia players' sworn statements personally, the invitation was extended to the judge to visit Australia to do so.

'The ACB finds most regrettable the innuendo that has appeared in the press that the statements were concocted and the players are liars. *The ACB rejects that suggestion outright. What possible reason could our players have had to concoct such allegations?*'

The third player, Mark Waugh, signed his sworn statement regarding a separate alleged approach on the eve of a one-day international in Rawalpindi. He also identified Salim who, he claimed, offered US$200,000 to be divided between 'four or five Australian players if you play poorly tomorrow'. Waugh then claimed that Salim said the Australians 'could bat slowly and not bowl well – a few full tosses and long hops'.

Waugh insisted the meeting and conversation took place. 'This is what happened. It was head-to-head at a function.' Australia lost the game, despite Waugh hitting 121 from 134 deliveries. His captain Mark Taylor said: 'I don't think anyone is lying.' Coach Bobby Simpson said the matter should have been dealt with by the London-based ICC. 'The fairest way would have been for the ICC to have a hearing on neutral territory.'

They didn't, and so the three-match series began in the most tense atmosphere in modern times. The Australian press speculated about the possible repercussions of what they saw as the unwarranted insensitivity of the Pakistan authorities in picking Salim.

Every possible consequence of the Judge's findings, his comments and those of the Pakistan Board and Salim were examined closely. At first, Arif Abbasi's defence was to attack, and he fuelled the flames by using the word 'crooked' in referring to some of the Australians whose reaction to the astonishing events was never in danger of being understated.

Salim was asked why, as he claimed, the allegations from Warne, May and Waugh were concocted. His answers were inventive even if, as in the case of Waugh, not true.

He claimed that Waugh was 'probably upset because I forced him out of the overseas position with Essex'. An interesting theory, but slightly weakened by the fact that Salim went to Essex only because Waugh could not return in 1991 because of international commitments. As for Warne, Salim blithely claimed that 'he made it all up because he could not take my wicket once in the series'.

The Australian players were angry and bewildered. Dennis Lillee wrote that the Australian Board would be crazy to allow any of the three cricketers to travel to Pakistan for the World Cup, because their safety could not be guaranteed – the same point considered by the authorities when they refused to allow the trio to travel to Pakistan for the hearing.

Richie Benaud, as usual, pursued a different line. 'The problem for Australia is that their Cricket Board took their eyes off the ball when they didn't recognise that the World Cup in 1996 was certain to play a massive part in any decisions taken in 1995 on the betting and bribery allegations.

'The Australian Cricket Board has not been on target because they have this endearing, but very old-fashioned habit of thinking and reacting as they believe other people will think and react.'

Benaud expanded his lateral theme thus. 'In captaincy and administration you need to keep two overs ahead of the play otherwise you will be swamped, or even shafted if the opposition happens to be very experienced and professional in damage limitation.

'The ACB handballed the problem on to the ICC and let them get on with it as best they could. The ICC then smartly handballed it on to Pakistan and let them get on with it as best they could. Both the

ACB and the ICC were happy to be rid of the matter. The betting allegations had surfaced in September 1994 in Sri Lanka and then again in Johannesburg and Zimbabwe. The alleged bribery was publicised in early 1995.

'However, the handballing, and in effect inaction from both bodies, created a climate beautifully organised for anyone with a quick mind and an ability to draw up a page with a line down the middle.

'On the left was a rather extensive list of what needed to be done in the face of allegations and rumours which put Pakistan cricket in poor light. On the right were two words: World Cup. There are two lessons for the ACB in this.

'Taking your eye off the ball on the field or in the corridors of power can be, if not fatal, certainly very painful.

'And, they need some clear thinking now, and not least of that needs to be in the area of player-administrator relationships which will have been severely bent, though not yet terminally broken by what happened to Shane Warne, Tim May and Mark Waugh.' A relationship which, by all accounts, was strained to breaking point after the Test against South Africa in Cape Town in March 1994.

Graham Halbish and Alan Crompton watched a famous Australian win at Newlands, but infuriated the players by not only not going to congratulate them in the dressing room, but flying out of Cape Town without seeing them at all after the match.

Allan Border was captain then, but it was his successor, Mark Taylor, who probably avoided any further trouble in the series in November 1995, by ensuring that, in the words of Benaud, the eyes of his players were focused on the ball.

Press speculation said that Malik would be subjected to all sorts of verbal abuse when he batted, so Taylor let it be known that his players would take the opposite option, and not say a word to the alleged briber. He would therefore bat in silence.

Warne received counselling in the run-up to the three-match series, as did May who administered his own bit of instant justice in Adelaide in the mid-November fixture between Pakistan and South Australia. He had Salim – referred to as 'the rat' in the published text of May's affidavit – stumped on the charge and was immediately swamped by the congratulations of his colleagues.

And so to Brisbane for the first Test, which Australia won by an innings and 126 thanks to Warne taking 11 for 77. It seems he would have traded ten of the wickets for the eleventh – Salim, who was caught off the fourth ball he received from the bowler 'who could not take my wicket once in Pakistan'.

Warne was forthright and overjoyed at the post-match press conference. 'It shows you there is justice in the game. I really enjoyed that wicket for obvious reasons. I set myself two targets before this match – you can probably work them both out.'

The most tell-tale incident came after the match, when players from both sides lined up to shake hands, except for Salim. Said Warne, 'Yes, there's still bad blood between us, but I don't care if he doesn't want to shake hands. There's a very good spirit between the rest of them and us.'

That defeat, quickly followed by another at Hobart, which settled the series 2–0, brought this attack from Imran back in Lahore.

'Pakistan's cricket has declined into a shambles. The organisation of cricket in this country is a shambles. I feel sorry for Wasim Akram, because our game will be in ruins if we are thrashed by Australia. The side is riddled with individual cliques. The talent has been squandered and there has been this constant squabbling over the captaincy and other issues.

'After the last World Cup, the players got greedy. They became very materialistic. There is no structure in the first-class game, no one owns or maintains the grounds and matches are not arranged properly.'

Deposed coach and former Test captain Mushtaq Mohammad echoed those views. 'The Pakistan Board is the most disorganised organisation I have ever known. Everything is done haphazardly. They just do things on the spur of the moment without planning.'

So, the tour of Australia came and went, with no further outward bleeding from the gaping wound. The ICC undoubtedly fought shy of taking the lead it could and should have done – possibly because of legal advice but, more probably, because it would have divided the ruling body into east–west lines of entrenchment. The reconstituted ICC has not altered the fundamental mistrust of England, Australia and New Zealand by the subcontinental countries. The divide is deeper than cricket, enveloping politics, religion and culture.

It is a simmering divide that last erupted at the special meeting to award the 1996 World Cup, with favourites England pushed back four years at an acrimonious meeting. Had the bribery allegations occurred between, for instance, England and Australia, the matter would surely not have dragged on for nearly eight months after the allegations were made, and those allegations would not have taken four months to surface.

The Pakistan tour of Australia was played between two sides whose authorities had let them down. Neither the cricket Boards of Australia nor Pakistan wanted to get their hands dirty. They should have been pushed into more incisive action by the ICC. *The game was brought into disrepute by someone – either the players of one side or another, or their two respective authorities, or the ICC.*

Yet the game of pass-the-parcel indulged in by the three parties – players, domestic and international authorities – left the issue dangling in mid-air. That benefited nobody, including Salim.

The editor of *Wisden*, Matthew Engel, passed this judgement. 'The ICC has proved to be very bad at dealing with the issues that confront the game. They should take a more activist view of their jurisdiction.'

It is no coincidence that the majority of rumours about betting and bribery in cricket come from India and Pakistan, simply because the bookmakers concerned operate on an illegal basis, in order to avoid a swingeing government tax. Bookmaking of any sort is not allowed in Pakistan, although it takes place openly at race meetings. I attended one in Lahore during England's 1984 tour there, and was soon pointed towards the chalk-men and, to use Richie Benaud's Australian euphemism, the 'satchel-swingers'.

The odds were penally cramped to yield a profit of around 50 per cent of stakes, compared with the mutually acceptable and more normal return of around a quarter of that. It was fun, but no place for business. Unlike the Karachi Stock Exchange which is a smaller version of the nerve centre of much of the betting on cricket in India, which is handled in Bombay.

Indian horseracing is centralised, unlike Britain with its many and varied courses all over the country, but cricket has outstripped all other sports for sheer volume of business. It is because of weight of money that the wagering can only become legal if the government lightens the tax load. At the moment it is such that it would kill off bookmaking anywhere in the world. For instance, in 1995 there was a 21 per cent tax on bets – nearly *three times* the levy in Britain – and 40 per cent on winnings above 2500 rupees (about £50).

Small wonder that bookmakers and punters alike have a huge interest in ensuring that the bigger bets are undeclared. Sums of

£10,000 are common, and amounts of double, triple and quadruple that are frequently placed and do not have the bookmakers running for cover.

The link between horseracing and cricket has a Gulf connection. Bombay became the betting capital of the subcontinent once Prime Minister Narashima Rao introduced a radical programme of liberalisation to the Indian economy which engendered so much spare cash that investment in stocks and shares was switched to gambling on racing and cricket.

Bets are placed in Bombay from racecourses in Dubai, Abu Dhabi and, most significantly of all, from Sharjah. Once that cricket centre was established as a regular venue for Indian and Pakistan cricketers – some of whom have had benefit matches played there for them – it was inevitable that televised, one-day cricket would become a live medium for massive gambling.

Cricket journalists are pestered by telephone for any scrap of information that could enable the caller to be one step ahead of the game. Ayaz Memon of the Bombay afternoon daily *Mid-Day* told Amit Roy of the *Sunday Telegraph* that he received many calls when he toured abroad with India. 'I am not sure if they were punters or bookmakers. The Bombay connection is that many bookmakers have emerged from the Bombay Stock Exchange, which is a hotbed of corruption. It is quite clear that syndicates run the betting. The game is being seriously undermined, especially when respected names are tossed into the controversy. The largest cricket audiences are here, and the largest sponsorship money, but once people lose trust, you can't have sport.'

He is right, which is why baseball in the United States has never been the same since the greatest sports scandal of that time took place in 1919 when Chicago White Sox players threw the World Series to make a gambling killing. The players concerned included the legendary 'Shoeless' Joe Jackson, and when they were banned, it provoked one of the most famous quotes in sport. A tearful young White Sox supporter stood in front of Jackson and sobbed, 'Say it ain't so, Joe, say it ain't so.' But it was.

Until the illegal bookmakers in Bombay are lured into legitimacy by a governmental change of heart about its ridiculous betting tax system, the subcontinent will continue to be dogged by gambling troubles which besmirch cricket in that part of the world.

Unlike Britain, where the authorities in cricket and betting have combined to ensure that any betting is clean, legal and above suspicion. The reaction of everyone in Britain was interesting when the Malik stories broke in February 1995, together with a much less substantive claim by Allan Border that Mushtaq Mohammad had told him there was £500,000 on offer if Australia threw the fifth Test against England at Edgbaston in 1993.

Mushtaq said the conversation was a joke, but Tim Zoehrer did not. Australia's reserve wicket-keeper said that he was asked by Mushtaq if he could talk to Border. If true, the alleged conversation was not a casual one, and therefore more unlikely to be a joke.

William Hill's organisation issued this statement from spokesman David Brown. 'If there was an abnormal betting pattern, alarm bells would ring. I am perfectly happy with the integrity of cricket in this country. The public is not going to be taken in by unsubstantiated rumours. I have been compiling odds for eight years and I cannot remember any match where we have worried about it being bona fide.'

Rivals Ladbrokes agreed, with spokesman Ian Wassell saying: 'There is no reason to doubt the integrity of cricket in this country. And there is no reason to doubt that we will be betting on all the matches in the next World Cup in February and March 1996.' As they did.

John Wright of Coral did not believe the rumours about Salim and Pakistan. 'We are talking about the World Cup holders and, as far as we are concerned, the last competition in Australia was straight.'

The Ladbrokes view carries most weight, because they have betting shops on most of the first-class county ground headquarters, although they do have the safety valve of only betting before the game and at scheduled intervals, not ball-by-ball as do the Bombay bookmakers.

There is one dissenting voice, perhaps significantly, the newest entrant into cricket betting. Wilf Rosseff of the H Backhouse firm says: 'The market is growing, but these sort of rumours are discouraging. People don't like even a whiff of something crooked, and I would be careful about taking large bets on matches involving Pakistan. For instance, supposing they were playing Zimbabwe who were 4–1 and somebody wanted a £2000 bet. Unless he was a regular customer, I would refuse.'

The 'Big Three' have other safeguards, including refusing to accept single bets on Sunday league matches, thus following soccer who, after the Kay-Swan scandal in the 1960s, also refused to allow single bets on football league matches. They also pick and choose which Sunday matches they will price up towards the end of the season, when those sides out of contention rest key players.

These safeguards form part of the reason for cricket's low place in the league of betting on other sports than racing. Soccer leads the way with 70 per cent, well ahead of second placed golf (11 per cent), with cricket a mere 3 per cent.

Coral have an average turnover for a Lord's Test against Australia or the West Indies – the biggest showpiece games played in England – of around £50,000, which is small change compared with the sub-continent, where that amount is often staked on a one-day game.

The former Derbyshire captain Kim Barnett is a keen punter and racing enthusiast. 'To fix a match, you would have to have corruption on a massive scale. I do not believe these people would put big money down unless they were absolutely certain that the match would go their way. The captain cannot make it happen on his own, nor can a star player, because anyone can pop up in a one-day game with a performance that turns a game. Everybody would have to make a concerted effort to throw a game.'

The cry of 'fix' is seldom heard in English county cricket and, when it is, it has nothing to do with betting.

As with charges of betting on the opposition or bribery, theories are often formed to fit a peculiar set of facts over a weekend of cricket, when two sides are accused of doing a deal to enable one side to win one match and lose the other. The two most suspicious looking games concern Warwickshire against Nottinghamshire in 1981, and Lancashire against Essex in 1991, with both matches taking place late in August when the county championships and Sunday league titles approach their climax.

Warwickshire won the John Player League competition in 1980 and made a strong bid to retain their title in 1981. They played Nottinghamshire in a three-day county championship match, starting on a Saturday, with the 40-over match played on the next day. Nottinghamshire, led by Clive Rice, had not won the championship since 1929, and their only top-three placing since then was the previous year in 1980 when they finished third behind Middlesex and Worcestershire.

Warwickshire had a good batting day on the Saturday, scoring 331 for nine declared, with the game then suspended until Monday. Everything straightforward so far, even when Nottinghamshire rested three players for the John Player match, including Richard Hadlee. The New Zealand Test player was crucial to their championship title hopes, and it made sense to rest him.

Derek Randall and 'Basher' Hassan put on 188 for the first wicket, and Nottinghamshire were on course for a minimum total of 250. Their innings closed at 221 for three in slightly odd circumstances, in that young players like P G Wood, M A Fell and Paul Johnson batted in the closing overs, while an experienced striker of the ball like Rice dropped down the order and did not bat at all.

Warwickshire won easily by six wickets with 23 balls to spare. Again, Rice took a back seat by bowling only four overs – a curious tactic in the absence of Hadlee – and occasional bowler Hassan bowled four overs for 33 runs. In a first-class career at Trent Bridge of twenty years, he took six wickets at an average of 67 apiece – and that included a career best three for 33.

The odd whiff of a deal circulated that evening in the members' bar at Edgbaston. As I left the ground after filing my match report for the *Birmingham Post*, two members approached me separately to tell me that a deal had been done and that Nottinghamshire would win the championship match on a quid pro quo basis.

I dismissed the suggestion, because Warwickshire's first day total of 331 for nine seemed to preclude any chance of a result, other than by a third-day declaration. Any over-generous target would immediately attract the attention and displeasure of Sussex and Somerset, who were the other chief title contenders.

The Nottinghamshire innings started in normal fashion on Monday morning, but the first seventy-five minutes play, during which Bob Willis, Willie Hogg and Gladstone Small bowled their only overs of the innings (20 between them), was the only part of the day which made sense. Willis was the Warwickshire captain and, once he rotated his new-ball trio for seventy-five minutes, he switched on to automatic pilot in the most astonishing fashion.

He brought on the Indian left-arm spinner, Dilip Doshi, and South African all-rounder Anton Ferreira, and did not make another bowling change until Nottinghamshire declared at 303 for nine in the 75th over. Ferreira was hit for 121 from 28 overs, and Doshi for 94 from 26.3. They picked up seven wickets between them, but for two bowlers to concede, on average, four runs an over while 215 runs were scored, poses a question about the captaincy tactics that has no obvious answer.

The use of 'joke' bowling in three-day cricket was a common occurrence at the time, and perhaps the agreement was that Nottinghamshire would be ushered to maximum batting points as quickly as possible, in order to give Warwickshire time enough to set up a run-chase on the Tuesday afternoon.

If that was Plan A, it was never implemented. The ease with which Randall scored 117 before and after lunch against the gentle seam and spin of Ferreira and Doshi, gave no clue about the carnage that was to follow. When Hadlee produced a ferocious lifter from nowhere to Dennis Amiss at throat height, it raised a question about the decision by Willis not to bowl himself or his other two main pace bowlers.

If there was that amount of life in the pitch, would not Warwickshire have been better trying to bowl Nottinghamshire out? That question was soon forgotten as more searching ones were posed. Hadlee's figures of 9–6–8–3 precipitated an ignominious collapse in which the first five wickets went for 19 runs, and the home side was bundled out for 49 in 33.2 overs.

The crowd was incensed, but worse was to follow. Nottinghamshire needed 78 but, with only a handful of overs left to bowl, it looked certain that the game would go into the third day. On the same lively pitch on which the Warwickshire batsmen had found so much trouble, the Nottinghamshire second innings got off to such a flying start that the extra half hour was claimed, *and the 78 runs were scored in 8.1 overs.*

Paul Todd hit an unbeaten 52, with Hogg and Doshi each conceding 17 runs from the only over they bowled. The entire day's play defied either belief or analysis, and brought this comment from team manager David Brown in the club's annual report. He wrote about the club's first ever wooden spoon, 17th place in the championship: 'I feel I should say that in my opinion the side only once lost direction and fell apart – against Nottinghamshire.'

But why? When a side is trying to avoid finishing bottom of the table, and they are playing a team at the top, the situation is ripe for exploitation by setting the most difficult task possible. This is a legitimate match tactic and also pays cognisance to the principle that the sides in contention expect nothing easy, neither for themselves nor for their rivals from other opposition.

Yet Willis ignored that principle by allowing Ferreira and Doshi to bowl unchanged for 54.3 overs in the Nottinghamshire first innings. The pitch offered assistance to Hadlee & Co, yet Willis was unaware of it until his side batted or, if he was, he chose to do nothing about it.

Is there an innocent explanation? Probably, just as there might be about the events of the Sabbath. Why did Rice not give his side the best chance of capitalising on an opening partnership of 188, by batting himself higher than three youngsters in the final few overs? And why did he split his own eight-over ration with Hassan, who hardly ever bowled?

And why was I assured by two Warwickshire members – independent of each other – on Sunday evening that they had heard from players in the bar that a deal had been done?

If only there were sound cricketing reasons to explain the events of the two days.

As also applies to a match ten years later, at Old Trafford in August between Lancashire and Essex. The scenario was the same – Essex were close to the Britannic Assurance county championship title and Lancashire badly needed a win in the Refuge Assurance league game on the Sunday. An additional factor, more sinister than anything that was said about the Warwickshire match, was the admission by Don Topley, published in a national tabloid newspaper after he had left the first-class game, and denied by Essex after an internal inquiry, that a deal had been done which gave the three-day match to Essex, and the Sunday match to Lancashire.

The remarkable similarity to the Warwickshire match was that the three-day championship match at Old Trafford came to the allegedly contrived conclusion on the Monday following the Sunday league match, although this time the game started on the Friday and so Monday was the final day.

The first two days were rain-ruined and 76 overs were lost, which partly explains the two exchanged declarations on the second day. Only partly because, as with Warwickshire against Nottinghamshire, Lancashire's lower position in the table – they finished eighth – gave them the perfect opportunity to drive a hard bargain. The sort where the title-chasing side can risk defeat in pursuit of victory, safe in the knowledge that their conquerors were not title contenders.

Lancashire were 175 for five at the end of the first day, but batted on in the shortened second day to reach 246. An earlier declaration would have left Essex a longer chase on the third day but, dare one say it, would have denied the visitors the two other bowling bonus points they obtained on the second day. Essex declared at 150 for three, and then helped Lancashire to a second innings declaration on the third day at 173 for two.

Gary Yates, in as nightwatchman, scored the second first-class hundred of his career, thanks to ten overs of help-yourself bowling from Nasser Hussain and Nick Knight – not a first-class wicket between them then, and only three by the end of the 1995 season.

Wisden terms the declaration 'a generous one of 270 from a minimum of 67 overs', and with Knight hitting a maiden championship hundred in his fourth match and Salim Malik hitting 70 after John Stephenson had opened with 85, Essex won by eight wickets.

Essex thus took 21 points and went to the top of the table, but what about the previous day, when Lancashire were equally in desperate need of a win? It was the final round of matches and a win could have given them the title if Nottinghamshire lost their last match at home to Derbyshire. They did not, and Lancashire finished two points adrift as runners-up for the second successive year.

Essex left out Neil Foster and Salim from the championship match, in which Wasim Akram was not playing, although he did play in the Sunday match. Lancashire played a full hand of seamers with Paul Allott replacing Yates, but Essex played two slow-left-arm spinners, John Childs and newcomer Guy Lovell.

Lancashire won the toss, fielded first and restricted Essex to 169 for six from 40 overs, with that total only achieved thanks to an unbroken seventh-wicket partnership of 78 between Derek Pringle and the confessor-to-be, Topley. He was also his side's most successful bowler with figures of 7–1–29–3, so either he was not in on the secret at the time, or he paced his all-round contribution to perfection, as Lancashire won by five wickets with five balls to spare.

Another hole in the evidence of a rigged weekend is that Salim's absence on Sunday came the day after he had retired hurt, one of two batsmen to be hit on the hand from a pitch which was awkward at one end. Mendis was the other.

A 40-over match can be thrown in more ways than one. Odd features of the Warwickshire–Nottinghamshire match included the minor role played by Rice and the curious decision to bowl Hassan. Just as effective a tactic – and more difficult to pin down – is the setting of the wrong fields to enable batsmen to score more easily.

Cases proven? Of course not but, as long as cricket is played, suspicions will exist if things happen between two sides on an apparent exchange basis, which cannot be explained in a cricketing sense.

If such an arrangement is ever made, it clearly does not come under the same banner as betting, but it does under the muckier one of bribery. Remember *Chambers*? '*A bribe is something offered to influence the judgement unduly or corrupt the conduct.*'

Such a deal would cheat the public, the other sides involved in the competitions concerned and, most important of all, the game of cricket.

Until there is a court case, firm conclusions are impossible, but educated guesses can still be made. To the question, 'Are some matches fixed?' there are two answers.

On the subcontinent? Probably.

In England? Possibly.

W C Fields had a maxim which, in betting parlance, is rock solid. 'Never give a sucker an even break.' In cricket, it is difficult for would-be tricksters *not* to give the innocent suckers an even break, because 22 players are involved, not to mention two umpires and many other variables.

The Authorities

CHAPTER 13

Umpires and match referees

Sir Colin Cowdrey was the driving force behind the introduction of the concept of match referees, and he was prompted by what he, together with many others, saw as an alarming fall in standards of on-field behaviour.

'It became a gradually increasing clamour of the 1980s, and followed the World Series cricket organised by Kerry Packer in 1977/78. There was probably no deliberate attempt to erode behavioural standards, but it was an inevitable consequence of full scale aggression under floodlights. The cricket played offered great theatre, but helped to cast aside the courtesies of the game as I knew them.

'I remember my son Christopher went to Australia about the same time on a Whitbread scholarship, and he told me that the same sort of confrontational attitudes had spread quickly into their grade and league cricket. He didn't mind it, in fact I think he quite enjoyed it, but it did not seem acceptable to me. Such a speedy change took the wrong sort of behaviour to the nth degree. The spirit of the game was bound to suffer, and it did.

'It had always been important to me that the spirit, as well as the letter of the law, is observed, because that is what makes cricket different from other sports such as soccer and tennis, among others. I played Test cricket that was just as hard and competitive as the modern game, but I like to think that sheer nastiness was a rarity then.'

Cowdrey had the difficult task of trying to sell a behavioural concept to the modern player, who was mostly unaware of the object of the exercise. Australian and South African domestic cricket has always been more overtly competitive and aggressive than county cricket in England, mainly because of the lesser amount of first-class cricket played in those countries.

A story from a tour of South Africa by a Derrick Robins party in 1972/73 illustrates the point perfectly. The side was captained by David Brown with John Murray as vice-captain. It was a goodwill tour, but the English county players were less than enchanted by the appeal-for-everything attitude of the home players. Catches were claimed that were not, batsmen stood when they knew they were caught behind, and so on.

It was the only way they had ever played the game. First-class matches numbered about half a dozen in the season, so a poor decision was more upsetting than to a county cricketer, who would play in twenty-five games or more in a season and was brought up to accept that rough and smooth decisions would balance out.

On the eve of the Robins game at Kingsmead against Natal, Barry Richards met Brown and Murray to see how the tour was going. They told Richards that they would be far happier if the games were played in the same spirit as county cricket was at that time, twenty-five years ago. Richards had then had a couple of years with Hampshire and understood their point of view. He said he would talk to his players and try to ensure that 'the English approach' be adopted for the match. It seems that the idea of a batsman walking just because he had hit it, and a bowler not appealing for lbw because he knew it was missing the stumps had never occurred to them. They protested that the more they appealed or stood there, the more chance of getting away with something, and the opposition always did it, so why shouldn't they?

With great reluctance, the Natal players agreed to give this new form of cricket a trial, only for the *d'etente cordiale* to last for one ball – the first ball of the match. It was bowled by Pat Trimborne, a hyper-aggressive cricketer who had found particular difficulty in understanding the pre-match talk from Richards. The batsman was Middlesex's Clive Radley, normally a 'walker' when he knew he was out. He played forward and the ball went off something to forward short leg who rolled over and came up to claim the catch.

As the Natal fielders had promised not to claim 'on the bounce', fielder and bowler expected Radley to go...except he was not convinced that he had hit it, so he stood his ground. The local umpire, aware of the gentlemen's agreement about walking, ruled in Radley's favour.

The verbal balloon went up. A disgusted short leg threw the ball from a sedentary position back to Trimble. He tried to flick the ball from foot to hand but missed and Radley, who never missed anything, nipped through for the overthrow.

Whatever insult was not immediately added to injury then came from the bowler's umpire, who did not signal a leg-bye. Peacemaker Richards, at slip, drew his attention to the scoreboard, pointing out that it must be wrong because Radley was credited with the run. The square-leg umpire heard the alarm bells and tried to signal to his colleague the fact he had disallowed the catch but had awarded a run. Too late.

'I gave the run because he hit it.'

'But you gave him not out because he did not hit it.'

'That's right.'

A deathly hush, and then Richards, the innocent party whose motives were spotless, was warned not to interfere, otherwise he would be punished. Collapse of the peace treaty, and normal shouting service was resumed.

There are contrasting views of the ethos about walking or waiting to be given out. The walkers have accepted, albeit reluctantly, the opposite standpoint, always providing that the non-walkers accepted the odd bad decision against them, as part of the price to pay for being given in when out.

Conversely, some walkers were criticised for only walking when the decision was obvious, or when the state of the game lessened the importance of their dismissal. A third view, much more difficult to understand, was that an umpire's authority was usurped by a batsman surrendering his wicket before the umpire had ruled on an appeal, as happened in Cape Town in the New Year Test between South Africa and England in 1965. Before batsman Ken Barrington gave himself out to a catch behind, bowler Fred Titmus and slip fielder Peter Parfitt were convinced that opener Eddie Barlow was out caught before he reached 50. The subsequent aggravation was such that only captain M J K Smith applauded when Barlow reached a hundred, but the other ten fielders clapped in sarcastic fashion when he had added 100 runs to his score when he was given not out.

That sort of incident was commonplace, even thirty years ago, but not so the unusual dismissal of Barrington on the third day, with the same umpire involved. Peter Pollock found the edge and wicket-keeper Dennis Lindsay took the catch. Barrington turned to watch the ball into the gloves and started to walk off, only to see the not-out shake of the head from the umpire.

Barrington checked his first stride, stood for a few seconds while he thought it out, and then went, to the amazement of the home fielders, the press box and most of the crowd. The Barlow incident had filled the back pages after the first day, and such was the suspicion of Barrington's motives that tour manager, Donald Carr, felt obliged to call a press conference to explain to the doubting South African journalists that Barrington was *not* trying to show up the umpire.

The two stories illustrate the gulf between the two schools, and it is a fact that most of the troubles involving sledging and dissent stem from incidents in which the fielding side are convinced that a batsman has got away with something. The carpers conveniently forget that, given the same situation of trying to con the umpire, the majority would do the same.

So do the old-fashioned standards espoused by Cowdrey have any place in the modern game? Of course they do, as evidenced by this story from Richie Benaud, a typically hard-nosed Australian, but one who combined acceptable aggression with the innate sense of sportsmanship that Cowdrey felt was dissipated by Packer cricket.

Benaud recalls: 'My father came to watch me play when I was still in my teens, and he saw me turn my back on an umpire when there was an appeal when I was batting. I did it because I knew I wasn't out, but I got a fearful shellacking from him. He told me it was just not on to do that, because it showed everyone that I thought the umpire was wrong if he gave me out. I never forgot that lesson.'

Cowdrey traces the reversal of the insidious trend thus: 'I was out of the game in the 1980s, but I was told how the umpires were coming under increasing pressure. Even the strongest of our English umpires felt it, but all they were trying to do was to do their thing and prevent the game going downhill. Someone like David Constant felt it keenly, and eventually he withdrew from the Test panel when he was at the age and stage of his career to have continued for several years at least.'

Constant agrees: 'I was first appointed to the county list when I was 27 in 1969, and I stood in my first Test in 1971 at Headingley when England played Pakistan and won by 25 runs. My next game was two weeks later at Lord's with India. That was the game in which John Snow collided with Sunil Gavaskar and was dropped from the next Test at Old Trafford as a disciplinary measure.

'I did 36 Tests in all as well as 29 one-day internationals, but in the end I decided I had had enough, and it was not worth carrying on. I always did my job to the best of my ability, and I must have got most things right to get so many Tests, but the attitude of players changed so much, it took a lot of pleasure out of the game.

'The Pakistanis first turned criticism into an objection when they asked the TCCB not to let me stand in their Tests in 1987, because of decisions and incidents at Lord's and Headingley in 1982. Kenny Palmer was also objected to, but our Board stood by us both and gave us two Tests each that summer.'

Wisden said, 'Among the less salutary moments of the tour was Pakistan's grievance over the selection of D J Constant and K E Palmer to the Test match panel, and the TCCB's subsequent refusal to replace them, was allowed into the public domain.'

That was penned by Graeme Wright, then Editor of *Wisden*, whose notes in the 1988 edition were swingeing in their criticism of the Pakistan management for their expressed criticism of Constant.

'A leak from the Pakistan management made public the TCCB's decision not to accede to Pakistan's request to remove umpires D J Constant and K E Palmer from the Test panel. Mr Constant had officiated in the Headingley Test of 1982, after which Imran was critical of the umpiring, claiming that errors had cost his side the match and so the series. Pakistan's request in 1987 was not the first time that a visiting side had requested Mr Constant's omission from the Test match list. In 1982, India, who came to England ahead of Pakistan, requested that he be replaced. This might have been a retaliatory measure following complaints by England about umpiring standards in India during the previous winter. It was also thought that the Indians had been unhappy with Mr Constant's umpiring during the final Test of the 1979 series. *Whatever the reason behind the Indians' request in 1982, the TCCB complied with it, although paying the umpire his match fee.*

'Last year (1987), not only was the Pakistan request turned down on the grounds of prejudice, but A C Smith, the new Chief Executive of the TCCB, read a statement from the first-class umpires in support of their colleagues on the Test match panel. Mr Constant officiated at Lord's and he and Mr Palmer stood at the Oval in the final Test. At both venues, the Pakistan manager, Mr Haseeb Hassan, was publicly critical of Mr Constant, *at one time describing him as "a disgraceful person".'*

So, in the summer of 1982, Constant was pilloried by both touring teams from the subcontinent, and this was a material factor behind his premature retirement from the Test panel in 1988. By then he had also been criticised by New Zealand and Australia. The controversial Headingley Test between England and Pakistan in 1982 was his twenty-fourth, and his thirty-sixth and final five-day match was at Lord's between England and Sri Lanka six years later.

In part justification of Pakistan's stand, it must be said that, of all the major Test playing countries, they have campaigned longest and hardest for so-called 'independent' umpires. They maintain that, at a stroke, it would remove from the minds of players the suspicion that umpires showed home bias.

As for the criticism of Constant during the second half of his seventeen years as a Test umpire, there are two views. The overseas teams either assumed he was 'a homer' or a bad umpire. The only comment about the former theory is that England players have long held the view that English umpires have tended to favour overseas teams in tight decisions, simply because of their fear of being accused of showing home bias.

Both are convoluted arguments with no supporting evidence. As for the idea that he was a bad umpire, the fact that the TCCB appointed him to stand in 36 Tests in 18 years means either their judgement was poor, or they were satisfied that he had the ability to control a Test match as well as and better than most of his colleagues.

When Constant informed the Board in 1988 that he wanted to go, they asked him to make sure it was a considered decision and not one taken in haste. He was not 50, but at the peak of a profession where top umpires could still be appointed for Test matches when they were more than ten years older. He was fit, young and vastly experienced, yet he wanted to go.

Constant: 'I talked it over with my wife, telling her all the problems of being challenged, and she put it into perspective by telling me I should only do it if I enjoyed it. I didn't, so I stopped.'

That is the ultimate comment on the modern game and says more about current players than about any hurt pride of the man in question. It goes to the heart of the role of the umpire. Namely, *an umpire is never more right than when he is wrong*. Once that principle is no longer sacrosanct, anarchy is not far away, and Cowdrey made one of his biggest ever contributions to the future of cricket when his persistence about match referees and international umpires finally carried the day.

'My predecessor, Field Marshal The Lord Bramall, nominated me as President of the MCC and told me that he thought we were losing control over the lead players. The captains in my time used to be more responsible for the conduct of their players, and now there was a widening rift between the authorities and the players, just as had happened in other sports.

'I knew he was right and felt that the great priority was to hold the line on discipline on the field. If we could do that, the rest was more likely to fall into place, but how best to do it? I was appointed at the July annual meeting of the ICC at Lord's in 1989, and was charged with travelling to each country that winter to prepare a structure for approval at the 1990 meeting. At the 1989 meeting, Australia and England outlined their own codes of conduct and they provided the basis of what I was looking for.

'I sat in each country's board meeting to explain our common aim, and they all were conscious of growing player power. That had developed since Packer and was mainly because of strong captains such as Imran and Clive Lloyd who wanted to push as hard as possible for what their players wanted. The drive was for more money, which in turn increased the importance of winning and losing.

'The 1980s were littered with instances of players and authority getting at odds, yet nobody had the executive clout to sort things out. I honestly think that a match referee would have defused the Bodyline tour in 1932/33. He would surely have stepped in before it escalated to a degree where cables were flying to and fro, involving governments as well as cricket.

'It was a classic case of a strong captain in Douglas Jardine being too much for the manager, "Plum" Warner, to deal with on such a big issue.'

There are other instances, notably when Trevor Bailey bowled leg theory in preventing the Australians from winning the fourth Test at Headingley, and thus keep the series all square and enable England to win back the Ashes for the first time since the Bodyline series.

Australia needed 177 runs in 115 minutes against only four England bowlers, Alec Bedser, Bailey, Jim Laker and Tony Lock. Bedser and Lock opened the bowling, but Australia batted so well that victory seemed theirs...until Bailey came on to fire it down legside in six overs which cost only nine runs. The other three bowlers went for 130 runs from 27 overs and Australia ended 30 runs short, so the Bailey ploy was the difference between an England defeat and a draw.

The Australian captain, Lindsay Hassett, was upset at what he saw as tactics which were unsporting and certainly not within the spirit of the game, but did not make a big fuss.

Cowdrey trod a careful path. 'After seeing various codes of conduct, I realised that on their own, they were not enough. They needed an enforcer, but first we had to get the idea of a match referee accepted. The umpires were not sold on the idea, because they thought they would be usurped, so we had to explain that the referee would be there to back them up and act swiftly when necessary. How many times in the past have we seen disputes between countries drag on and on, whereas prompt on-the-spot action would solve that problem?

'We also had to consider how best to avoid cutting across the authority of the chief executive in question, because he represented the ground authority. That is why we decided that all statements about sanctions and penalties must come through him. It was a learning curve for everyone, and we got considerable help from Lord Griffiths, then President of MCC. He played for Cambridge and Glamorgan and was a scratch golfer who was a past president of the Royal & Ancient, so he had a great feel for what we were trying to do, and his legal background meant he could take a judge's position. He helped us work within the freedoms of the law, and knew that the idea was not for the referee to get up front all the time, but to solve disputes on behalf of the authorities. That done, he should then give a verdict and keep out of the limelight by leaving the rest to the chief executive in question.'

Any lingering doubts about the necessity for the referee were swept away by the infamous Test match in Trinidad between West Indies and England in March 1990, where West Indies shamelessly wasted time to save the Test, with England vainly trying the same deplorable tactic in the following Test in Barbados.

In Port of Spain England needed 151 to win and were 73 for one at lunch. Rain then took two hours out of the day, but 78 from a scheduled 30 overs should have produced a result. Instead, acting captain Desmond Haynes orchestrated a go-slow so successful that, despite play continuing for an hour after the scheduled close, only 17 overs were bowled before the rapidly failing light made conditions dangerous with England then 120 for five, needing 31 from what should have been another 13 overs.

It was cynical and went against every principle of sport, yet neither the umpires, nor the ground authorities, had power under the regulations to impose a penalty. Even had the West Indies been punished, it would not have recompensed England for being prevented from obtaining a 2–0 lead in the series with two Tests to follow.

The umpires were only empowered to warn the fielding side and then report Haynes at the next interval to the ground authorities. By which time, the game was over and drawn. England protests were muted, which explains why they duplicated the tactics to try to save the Barbados Test which followed two weeks later.

England were unsuccessful under the captaincy of Allan Lamb, mainly because they tried to slow things down over a much longer period throughout the fourth day. An over rate of 11 per hour still forced Viv Richards to delay his declaration until half an hour before the close of play, but England lost in the final 15 overs of the match next day.

Those two Tests gave Cowdrey the ammunition he needed. 'What they showed was that home Boards naturally wanted to win and so were not the best people to uphold standards. A match referee could tell them to relax and keep out of it. He would make his decision and that would be that.'

Which means that a match referee would severely punish time-wasting, although that would not hand the time back to the batting side if bad light was a factor. Nevertheless, the referee has the power to suspend, and the first captain to be penalised in this manner will probably be the last.

Cowdrey found plenty of support for the concept from leading administrators such as Alan Smith from England, Graham Dowling from New Zealand, David Richards from Australia and Steve Camacho from the West Indies. He was determined to make full use of his then unique four-year period in the chair of ICC, and chipped away at the resistance until it disappeared.

He saw the major issues troubling the modern game as those involving dissent, slow over rates, sledging and intimidatory, short-pitched bowling and, of course, ball tampering. What a comment on the modern game and its players that their behaviour – or rather misbehaviour – should force the hand of authority to add another level of control to that of the umpire.

Critics of the match referee concept claim, with every justification, that the laws and playing regulations gave full authority to the umpires in matters of indiscipline. True, but there were two problems. Many international umpires did not have sufficient confidence to clamp down on behavioural misdemeanours, and those that did found that the process of dealing with reports was a painfully lengthy one. Another point in favour of the introduction of an independent enforcer was the fact that touring managements seldom dealt with their erring players in a strong way.

Punishments rarely fitted the crimes, and the players bulldozed their way through the 1980s regardless of the damage caused to the reputation of a game which, together with golf and snooker, offered to the public all that was best in sport. The spirit of the game – again that phrase which Cowdrey was so keen to preserve – was of paramount importance, even if it meant authority by enforceable litigation rather than persuasion.

The meeting which endorsed his proposal was an historic one in many ways. It was a special meeting of the ICC in Melbourne on the 9 and 10 January 1991, and the first to be held away from Lord's. It was agreed that independent match referees would be appointed for Test matches and one-day internationals to enforce the forthcoming Code of Conduct and to oversee the imposition of fines for slow over rates. The meeting also approved, in principle, independent umpires from a third country standing in all international matches. There were, however, too many existing problems for the plan to be implemented that same year.

Costs were an estimated £500,000, so the innovation was impractical without sponsorship, and Australia in particular believed that their umpires would not be willing to participate because of the difficulty of taking time off from their regular winter employment.

Nevertheless, Cowdrey was happy that the first step had been taken. The new over-rate system was devised because of the problems highlighted the previous year in the series between West Indies and England. To try to prevent a repetition, a minimum of 90 overs per day was stipulated but, typically, authority fudged it when it came to the small print. It was decided that, following a break for innings, the time remaining before the scheduled close of play would be divided by four and that would be the new minimum ration.

The only reason advanced by opponents to a 90-over day, regardless of who bowled them, was the fatuous one that it was unfair for a side fielding second to have to make up any shortfall by the side bowling first. There are two unanswerable counterpoints which still took a further four years to make a sufficient impact on the disbelievers.

1. The public were being short-changed.
2. Usually on the fourth day, but it could be any time that suited, a side trying to save a match which they could not win, could take overs out of a game that could not be replaced. Here are three examples, one of which affected the result of a Test match. England forced New Zealand to continue their second innings at Lord's in 1994 until well after tea by bowling their overs so slowly that, when the declaration finally came, the re-calculation rule meant that only 82 overs were bowled in the day. As the England ninth wicket pair had to survive for half an hour the next day, the importance of the missing overs cannot be over-emphasised.

Only three months earlier, England suffered another fourth-day robbery from the West Indies in Barbados. England finally won after tea on the final day, but a match aggregate of overs of 393.2 shows the dilatory over rate of the home side. Each session should produce 30 overs, so the game lost 27 overs, or 21 if two for each innings break are allowed. The tactical use of the re-calculation rule was obvious on the fourth day, when England received only just over 50 overs in the four hours before tea.

Similarly in Cape Town two weeks earlier. South Africa took seven overs out of the fourth day which ended with Australia well on top with the home side tottering at 100 for six. They collapsed from 94 for two in the final half hour, and Australia were thus robbed of another seven overs to finish the job. South Africa prolonged the match next day for nearly two sessions.

The second innovative experiment was to limit short-pitched deliveries to one per over to each batsman. The West Indies were, predictably, against such a change, but the decline in the amount of spin bowling in Test cricket was too marked to allow to continue unchecked. Not only that, but the amount of short-pitched bowling frequently overstepped the intimidatory mark. Again, the umpires must bear responsibility for the ugly trend.

They rarely stepped in to warn a bowler for the over-use of a bouncer or 'throat ball', and when they did, the fuss made by the fielding captain discouraged other umpires from firm action. A typical example was when Dickie Bird warned Malcolm Marshall for intimidatory bowling against Ian Botham at Edgbaston in 1984.

It was a toss-up who was most surprised, Marshall or Botham who clearly fancied taking the bowler on. There was no toss-up about which cricketer was most offended – it was the West Indies captain, Clive Lloyd. He raced from slip to remonstrate with Bird – probably from sheer shock at having one of his four fast bowlers called into question. That was the same Lloyd who defended his bowlers on Black Saturday at Old Trafford in 1976 when, for the last hour of the day, John Edrich and Brian Close were subjected to the most brutal assault seen in England since the war.

Umpires Bill Alley and Lloyd Budd said not a word, and Lloyd answered criticism about the bowling of Andy Roberts, Michael Holding and Wayne Daniel by saying he was quite happy to leave it to the umpires. They had not intervened, so it was all right.

There was one note of black humour in the hour that convinced Edrich, at the end of the match, that he was sick of being made an Aunt Sally with no protection from umpires, and he announced his retirement from Test cricket. A shocked England dressing room watched in silence as the two veteran left-handers – 84 for two in combined age – were battered without mercy in poor light.

Edrich looked up at the balcony once and saw it was empty, so he guessed they were sorting out who would be the reluctant nightwatchman. There were not many volunteers and he thinks it was Alan Knott but, somehow, they survived. Back in the dressing room, Close and Edrich relaxed in contrasting ways. Within seconds Close was naked, except for a jockstrap, a cigarette and a bottle of beer. Edrich sat in a corner, quiet and contemplative.

The Middlesex seamer, Mike Selvey, made his debut in that Test and, having been startled by the last hour of play, he was even more surprised to hear a sudden high-pitched cackle from the hitherto speechless Edrich.

Selvey: 'I thought he had cracked under the strain, but he had just caught a glimpse of the scoreboard through the open dressing-room balcony door.

'Close looked at him and asked him what he was laughing at. Edrich pointed at the board and said, "Closey, it's you. After all that in the last hour *you are one not out.*"'

Clive Lloyd pioneered the four-man pace attack after his multi-talented side was thrashed 5–1 in Australia earlier that year, when Dennis Lillee and Jeff Thompson took 56 wickets between them. The West Indies captain learned a lesson which was eventually to prove a costly one for the rest of cricket – hence the eventual limitation of short-pitched bowling.

A big argument against one bouncer per over per batsman was that it took away the element of surprise from the bowler. If he bowled a bouncer in the first five balls of the over, the batsman knew he would not receive another. That argument won the day four years later when the experiment was modified to allow a bowler the same number of short-pitched deliveries per over – two – but they could be bowled to anyone. Namely, if a batsman got one, he might still get another.

The Melbourne meeting in January 1991 established the ICC's determination, under the diplomatic but firm influence of Cowdrey, to put into place a framework to reverse the unsavoury trends of the previous years, and the annual meeting at Lord's in July of that year was a momentous one. South Africa was readmitted, and that decision also had much to do with Cowdrey.

Often referred to as indecisive, the first ICC Chairman to hold office over four years accomplished as much for the game in that period as he did as one of the most elegant batsmen of his time.

The meeting accepted the official introduction of the new Code of Conduct, as well as the terms of reference of the match referees, whose duties would start later that year in Australia for their series against India. Of the Code of Conduct, Cowdrey says, 'I remember writing the first paragraph, which I honestly thought was the most important of the eight. It said: "The captains are responsible at all times for ensuring that play is conducted within the spirit of the game as well as within the Laws." I attach so much importance to that codicil, because if that is carried out, none of the other rules come into play. Also, I thought that if we highlighted the spirit of the game, it would be beneficial as a commercial tool regarding sponsorship etc to show that we wanted to preserve cricket as a different game from other sports, most of whom had even greater discipline troubles.'

The brief of the referee was difficult to define. Cowdrey knew he had to allay fears of everyone – players, umpires, and home authorities – and the carefully drawn-up terms of reference were worded to avoid the more obvious objections.

The next step was to choose the right sort of person to pioneer the implementation of a concept that would cause many ripples in its first few years of existence. Cowdrey and Secretary John Stephenson were the original selectors of the first referees. 'John and I picked them, but we had three problems. We needed former Test cricketers whose records would make them credible with players, because we wanted the referee to lay down the guidelines before a Test.

'The second quality we looked for was the ability to fit in easily with the home authorities in their committee and lunch rooms. It sounds trivial, but we were looking for people who had been ambassadors for the game, on and off the field, and would now carry the same command of respect into the demands of a Test match. I stressed to them that they must not drink at lunch times for obvious reasons. Also, they must not miss a ball of play, so I expected self-discipline.

'The cost was another problem, although all countries decided to fund the visit of a referee themselves. Some referees were housed privately to save money, but it did not take long for them to be put on the same basis as players regarding flights and hotels. I was criticised about my early choices – Mike Smith, Peter May, Raman Subba Row and Donald Carr – as being part of the old boy network, but I needed to have men I knew, could trust and were available. The last point was a problem, because not everyone was in a position to take a month or two off without payment. They did receive a daily expense allowance, but the trips were not profitable for them, other than the chance to travel and become involved again with Test cricket.

'I picked them for the first year or so, and then each country was asked to put up three or four likely candidates. We used a lot of men in the first two or three years, but the idea was always to work to a much shorter list comprising perhaps half a dozen of the better, stronger referees, who would then do it more or less on a full-time basis, as happens in tennis. Again, the problem is availability because some of the best referees are still young enough to be involved, actively, in other projects, but I think the whole system is much more solidly based after the first five years.

'They have had their ups and downs, but that was inevitable. The biggest difference is that the job started more as a political exercise, but now there is a much greater day-to-day involvement with the umpires. That is how it should be, because we want consistency in interpretation of issues and that will only be achieved by getting to know each other.'

Cowdrey is right. I saw the first referees in South Africa in 1992/93 for the series against India – Clive Lloyd and M J K Smith shared the tour – and I saw Peter Burge operate two years later in the same country for the series against New Zealand and the quadrangular series involving Pakistan and Sri Lanka.

There was a considerable difference in 1994 in their duties and how they carried them out. I stayed at the same hotel in Johannesburg as the officials and often was allowed a lift with them to the New Wanderers ground at 8.45am each morning of the Test match. Burge, a large amiable Australian, supervised the three umpires in benevolent fashion, and spent most of each day with the third umpire.

On arrival at the ground, he would accompany them to the middle to see that the pitch preparation was done properly, and would rarely leave them before the start of play. He would wait to see them in at each interval, and always maintained a line of communication with the press and television when it came to a recalculation of overs, or on any other relevant information.

Doing television commentary for SABC, it was often necessary to ask for an interpretation of a playing condition, and we always knew where to find Burge. He made it a hands-on job in the nicest possible way, and it is no coincidence that he is regarded as among the strongest and fairest referees. On the other hand the match referee set-up, as with any other system, is only as good as the people who operate it, and there have been some glaring weaknesses as different men have been tried and discarded.

The first appointees were Peter May and Mike Smith, who made history by sharing the duties for Australia's home Test series against India in December 1991 and January 1992. It was also the first series in which the restriction on short-pitched bowling applied, but the only intervention from the referee was when M J K Smith warned the Indian management of its responsibilities when manager Ranbir Singh Mahendra revealed, halfway through the second Test, that he had objected to an Australian umpire. Cricket manager Abbas Ali Baig, a former Indian Test batsman, escaped censure when, commenting on what he saw as a disparity in lbw decisions given against both sides, he said, 'Perhaps there are changes in the lbw law of which we have not been made aware.'

India lost 14 wickets to lbw appeals, and Australia seven, with India losing 90 wickets in the five-match series, compared with 76 by Australia. The umpire objected to was L J King, who refused to give Dean Jones out following an incident in which the ball was trapped between glove and thigh. Wicket-keeper Kiran More tried to secure the ball and claim a catch but Jones knocked the ball away and survived appeals for handling the ball and obstructing the field.

The next thirteen months were to test the referee system to the limit, and it was found sadly wanting. Conrad Hunte, Deryck Murray,

M J K Smith and Donald Carr all had difficult situations with which to deal and chose not to take strong action; Clive Lloyd was frustrated by lack of televisual evidence when one player was accused of striking another; and Carr's careful approach to a second misdemeanour by a Test captain in two months, was to lead to the same referee's action against two Australian players in March 1994 in Johannesburg being considered inadequate by the Australian Cricket Board, who immediately increased the fines imposed from 10 per cent to 100 per cent of the match fee.

The first series in 1992 to run into serious referee trouble was that between England and Pakistan. The events at Old Trafford and Headingley have already been chronicled, and it cannot have helped the two sides that four referees shared the English summer.

Australian Bob Cowper officiated for the first two Texaco one-day internationals and the first two Cornhill Test matches. He acted in curious fashion at Lord's where he allowed Pakistan to escape a potentially heavy over-rate fine because they bowled 24 no-balls, and he said that the time taken for a new batsman to reach the middle from the dressing room was more than at any other ground because of the distance involved. He did not make the obvious counterpoint during the first Test at Edgbaston, where the distance between the dressing room door and the outfield is approximately ten yards.

Hunte was the unlucky man, because he was called in at short notice to deputise for the original appointee, Walcott, on the fourth and fifth days, when it was discovered that those days clashed with the ICC's annual meeting at Lord's. As both dates were known more than twelve months in advance, Walcott should never have started a match he could not finish. Which is why the wrong sort of history was made, certainly as far as umpire Roy Palmer was concerned.

Perhaps Hunte was reluctant to crack down without referral to Walcott and Cowdrey at Lord's, but the action taken – or rather not taken – undoubtedly led to the subsequent acrimony at Headingley and then at Lord's in the Texaco one-day international.

The English summer thus ended with large question marks about the system, and much attention was focused on two series in particular in November and December of that year and in January 1993. The four-match series between South Africa and India was not expected to be a difficult one for Lloyd and Smith, but that between Australia and West Indies was always likely to be too combustible for comfort.

Raman Subba Row and Donald Carr shared the series, with Carr taking over for the last three Tests. In the first Test at Brisbane, Allan Border was cited for dissent when in the field and was fined half his match fee. He was so incensed at being reported for what he believed was acceptable talk to umpire Steve Randell, that he refused to attend the hearing. It is believed that Subba Row considered imposing the first suspension since the introduction of the Code of Conduct, but was dissuaded from such a swingeing penalty by Cowdrey.

Border's defence against the dissent charge was that he made nothing more than a 'cheeky remark' to the umpire about the lack of lbw decisions, particularly against Richie Richardson who Border said was 'using his pad more often than his bat as his main line of defence'.

The Australian captain had no defence for not attending the hearing. 'I regret that. It was poor form on my part and offensive. I deserved the AUS$2000 fine, and was probably lucky I didn't get a game or two suspension as well. I concede that we need to preserve the spirit of cricket, and I appreciate how important to that end a good relationship is between umpires and players, but it is equally important that we don't turn the umpires into some sort of protected species.'

Which explains, but does not justify, the gesture made by Border which led to his second citing of the series – this time for the more serious offence detailed in the Code's 1(c); 'Players or officials shall not use crude or abusive language, nor make offensive gestures.'

Umpire Colin Timmins annoyed Border by no-balling debutante fast bowler Jo Angel for too much short-pitched bowling, and the Australian captain promptly gestured his annoyance with a wave of the left hand. It was a gesture which, according to Border, said 'Given the amount of short-pitched balls the West Indies have been allowed to bowl at us during the summer without an umpire stepping in, that is the most ridiculous call of all time.'

It must have been quite an expressive wave to say all that. Border defends himself thus: 'I didn't kick the ground. I didn't wave my fist – I made a cynical gesture that I doubt any member of the public could have seen.' That is a doubtful argument, particularly as it was unlikely that the eagle-eyed television cameras would not highlight the incident.

The straight-talking Border did not accept without protest the censure of referee Carr. 'I told him that what he was telling me about my gesture is that that gets me at this hearing, but what about the West

Indies? Is it okay for them to appeal for a catch behind the wicket and all rush up to the umpire in an intimidating fashion, and when they don't get the decision, fall down on the ground or just stand there with their hands on their hips staring in disbelief? How is it that none of them are in here for obvious dissent? Is the Code of Conduct for the protection of the umpires, or protection of the game?'

An answer to that is that it is there for the mutual protection of everyone. Whether Carr was swayed by the argument or not, he chose to reprimand Border severely, and also did the same to Merv Hughes, despite it being his second dissent offence of the series and that he had been fined for the first, and warned about his future conduct. This happened in the Brisbane Test in which Border did not attend the hearing, and Hughes was fined 10 per cent of his match fee by Subba Row for dissent and abusive language to an umpire.

That 'future conduct' warning given to Border and Hughes in Brisbane was now in the present in Perth, but only earned the two players another warning which was to be ignored by Hughes in the next match in which he played and Carr refereed, thirteen months later in Johannesburg against South Africa. That match produced several incidents from Hughes and one from Shane Warne which seemed to make for an open-and-shut case.

Hughes blustered his way through the game, glaring and talking to batsmen if he was hit for four or had an appeal turned down. His attitude was certainly more predictable than that of Warne, who left umpires David Shepherd and Barry Lambson with no alternative but to report the player. Perhaps frustrated because of his late entry into the Australian attack – he did not bowl in the first 40 overs of each South African innings despite the 100 coming up twice with only two wickets lost – Warne was at boiling point in his first over of the second innings when he bowled opener Andrew Hudson for 60.

He immediately chased down the pitch shouting volleys of abuse, and but for wicket-keeper Ian Healy intercepting his colleague as he headed towards the departing batsman, a physical clash looked likely.

A worse case of misbehaviour it would be difficult to imagine, but Carr only deducted 10 per cent of Warne's match fee of AUS$4000. Incredibly, he treated Hughes in the same way. 'Incredibly', because it was Hughes's third offence in fifteen months, two of which were dealt with by Carr, with both transgressions following warnings given about his future conduct.

Although it was Warne's first offence, the television evidence of his complete loss of control was so damning, that even the travelling Australian media was in uproar about the light penalties imposed. As for Hughes, the wrist-slap 10 per cent fine meant that, in fifteen months, Hughes had been fined a total of AUS$800 for three offences out of match fees in fifteen Tests of AUS$60,000.

The Australian Board moved swiftly and in an unprecedented manner. They ignored Carr's verdict and invoked their own code of conduct to fine both players their entire match fee – a surcharge tax of 90 per cent which, more than anything said or written, indicted the match referee for an inadequate response to one of the worst behavioural incidents involving Warne, and another transgression by a persistent offender, Hughes.

A surreal postscript was that Carr fined South African Jonty Rhodes 10 per cent of his match fee for breaking the regulation about advertising logos on the straps of his pads.

The most severe punishment meted out by Carr was in January 1993 when he fined Desmond Haynes 50 per cent of his fee in a World Series one-day international in Brisbane for 'dissent at the umpire's decision' when he was given out on appeal for a catch at the wicket by Healy off Paul Reiffel.

The other major series in 1992/93 was between South Africa and India, with the referee becoming involved in, firstly, a one-day international at St George's Park, Port Elizabeth on 9 December 1992, and then the five-day Test match on the same ground which started seventeen days later. Clive Lloyd officiated in the first match and M J K Smith did duty in the second.

The background to Peter Kirsten being fined 50 per cent of his match fee for 'showing dissent when he was run-out and also for the use of offensive language' is interesting. Two days earlier, he was batting in the closing overs of the one-day international in Cape Town and, according to Kapil Dev, was warned three times for backing up too enthusiastically at the non-striker's end.

The claimed warnings had no effect. Kirsten came in at number three, and was soon run out by Kapil, who ran in to bowl and held on to the ball as Kirsten backed up too far. No warning, but clearly a plan of action, with Kapil receiving congratulations from unsurprised colleagues. Kirsten's angry reaction was understandable, but it was inevitable that Lloyd would fine him. The incident led to the most controversial point of a tour that was publicised as being one of 'friendship', and was generally free from acrimony.

Kirsten's partner was skipper Kepler Wessels, and he was visibly upset about the circumstances surrounding the dismissal. Later in the over, he took two runs after hitting the ball wide of mid-on and, in turning for the second, his bat came into contact with Kapil's shins. Down went the Indian bowler. On came the Indian physiotherapist who was quick to inform the press box that Wessels had apparently rapped Kapil's legs with his bat as a retaliatory gesture.

The travelling media forced an inquiry which, otherwise, might not have happened, but Lloyd could only decide that the act was unproven. He sought television evidence, but the cameras had followed the ball and missed the clash, and Kapil refused to claim that it was a deliberate act by Wessels.

A postscript to the incident highlights the responsibility sportsmen have to young spectators. The fifth one-day international was played in Bloemfontein six days later and, on the eve of the game, both teams attended a dinner with all the under-13 schoolboys who were taking part in the longstanding Permlaser cricket week.

The boys – well over 100 of them – all had miniature bats on which they eagerly obtained autographs, and Peter Kirsten was approached by one youngster who left South Africa's oldest batsman shaking his head. I asked him about the conversation.

Kirsten: 'He said that he had watched Kapil run me out on television, and he now knew how easy it was, *because he had already done it that week in an Under-13 game*. I don't know whether to laugh or cry.'

Clive Lloyd certainly did not duck any issue, and did well in an incident in the Johannesburg Test in which umpire Steve Bucknor did not refer a run-out appeal to the third umpire, although the replay showed that Jonty Rhodes was out. Lloyd had a quiet word with the Jamaican and then brought him to a press conference to admit an error of judgement. It was the best way to defuse a difficult situation.

Which cannot be said about the course of action taken by M J K Smith during the third Test match in Port Elizabeth. David Shepherd was the 'independent' umpire, but operating under the considerable handicap of not flying from England until three days before the start of the Boxing Day Test. He had not stood in the middle since the end of the English season over three months earlier, and there was the problem of acclimatising from mid-winter to high-summer temperatures in the mid-80s.

The immense physical strain was lessened by the experimental system of rotation tried by South Africa for one season. They used three umpires, with Shepherd standing for days one, two, four and five, accompanied by a local umpire on alternate days. Shepherd's day in the pavilion – not really a rest because he became the third umpire with all the concentration involved to deal with replays – was the pivotal day of a tense match. It meant that, for the only time in the game, Rudi Koeıtzen and Wilf Diedricks stood together, and was the day when the game boiled over.

South Africa progressed from 163 for three to 275, thanks to 135 from Hansie Cronje, and India recovered from 31 for six to 71 for six after Allan Donald and Brett Schultz created havoc among the top order. The trouble started when India were fielding with wicket-keeper More the centre of shows of dissent after appeals were refused. The home batsmen allege that abuse and sledging was non-stop, but the umpires did not report anyone to the referee.

When India batted, Mohammad Azharuddin and Sachin Tendulkar were given out to catches by wicket-keeper Richardson, with both batsmen shown to be not out on television replays. The Indian captain left the crease in resigned fashion, but the shocked Tendulkar showed dissent and left the field in tears. Non-striker Ravi Shastri hurled his bat to the ground when Tendulkar was given out, but still Smith chose to do nothing.

Questioned later, he said that his brief was to act upon reports from the umpires, and there were none. This begs the important question of why he did not encourage them to report unseemly incidents which were highlighted on television, and were clearly visible to spectators.

He quoted ICC Code of Conduct 2(b) to explain his lack of action: 'The referee shall liaise with the appointed umpires, but not in any way to interfere with their appointed role.'

Smith should have recognised that he was dealing with two inexperienced home umpires who should have been encouraged to make a strong stand against the worst sort of on-going dissent which soured the day. Even more important, the booklet from which Smith quoted includes these two sentences:

'The referee must not interfere with the traditional role of the umpires, but should urge them to be decisive in upholding the Law.'

'A referee always has the right to investigate any incident whether or not it is the subject of a report.'

That is the bottom line, and one which gives a referee the unlimited power to investigate anything he has seen, even if the umpires refuse to report it after he has spoken to them. Smith was reluctant to be seen to usurp the umpires' authority, and perhaps understandably so with the system only in its infancy. It might even be argued that the early Tests supervised by Smith and other referees pinpointed weaknesses, most of which have now been eradicated. Another view would repeat that the men who operate the system are at least as important as the system itself.

The third day in the Port Elizabeth Test provided at least three incidents which should have been investigated, but were not. It seemed anomalous when, on the fourth and final day, Manoj Prabhakar was given out to another catch by Richardson and, as he left the crease, his gestures showed he did not think he had hit the ball. It was the mildest of the offences committed in the match, yet he was reported and Smith docked him 10 per cent of his match fee – about £20. This is not to say Prabhakar should not have been fined, but rather that he should not have been the only one.

Aqib Javed was the first international cricketer to be fined, being docked 50 per cent of his match fee at Old Trafford in July 1992. He was also the first cricketer to be suspended, when Peter Burge ruled him out of a one-day international in Auckland on 30 December 1992, two days after an obscene outburst against umpire Brian Aldridge in Napier.

Andrew Jones gave a lobbed, gloved slip catch off a short-pitched delivery from Aqib. Aldridge called no-ball because, as television replays showed, the ball was above shoulder height. Aqib swore, Aldridge reported and a 75-minute hearing was attended by Ramiz Raja, fielding nearby, and Martin Crowe, the non-striker.

Crowe said Aqib called Aldridge 'an effing cheat', a comment which the player claimed was made in talking to himself. Crowe said, 'It was a funny thing to call yourself,' and Burge bounced Aqib out of the next match.

Including Aqib's first fine at Old Trafford, referees have dealt with forty-two reported offences up to and including the end of the English 1995 season. The breakdown makes interesting reading (see table on pages 218–21). The first five cricketers to be fined, reprimanded or suspended were Pakistanis, with the quintet disciplined between July and December 1992. Since then, they only provide three further entries on the list of thirty-seven more miscreants. Australia head the list with ten, followed by India, South Africa and New Zealand, who each provide five.

Bottom – or top – of the list is Sri Lanka with only one wrongdoer, Arjuna Ranatunga, followed by England with three. Michael Atherton was the first English cricketer to be fined, when he was found guilty of dissent over his lbw dismissal in the Oval Test against South Africa in 1994. Phil Tufnell was fined 30 per cent of his match fee in Melbourne on 13 December 1994 on a charge of 'bringing the game into disrepute by an aggressive gesture after having an appeal turned down. The other player was, ironically, Chris Lewis, who was reprimanded by John Reid at Adelaide in January 1995 for 'gesturing Craig McDermott to the pavilion four times after dismissing him'. Ironic, because the constant criticism levelled at Lewis is his apparent lack of aggressiveness.

Of the forty-two offences, twenty-seven produced fines, there was one suspension plus a fine – Nayan Mongia for India against Australia in Sharjah in April 1994, and one suspension, Aqib Javed for Pakistan against New Zealand in Auckland in December 1992. Most of the offences concerned unbecoming conduct, dissent, intimidation and crude language, with the following eight points comprising the Code of Conduct.

1. The captains are responsible at all times for ensuring that play is conducted within the spirit of the game as well as within the Laws.
2. Players and team officials shall not at any time engage in conduct unbecoming to an international player or team official which could bring them or the game into disrepute.
3. Players and team officials must at all times accept the umpire's decision. Players must not show dissent at the decision.
4. Players and team officials shall not intimidate, assault or attempt to intimidate or assault an umpire, another player or a spectator.
5. Players and team officials shall not use crude or abusive language (known as 'sledging') nor make any offensive gestures.
6. Players and team officials shall not use or in any way be concerned in the use of distribution of illegal drugs.
7. Players and team officials shall not disclose or comment upon any alleged breach of the Code or upon any Hearing report or decision arising from such breach.
8. Players and team officials shall not make any public

pronouncement or media comment which is detrimental either to the game in general, or to a particular tour in which they are involved, or about any tour between other countries which is taking place, or to relations between the Boards of the competing teams.

Only one man has been found guilty of contravening three sections – Salim Malik against Zimbabwe in Harare in February 1995, when he accused umpire Ian Robinson of interfering with the ball by wetting it. He was also given a two-Test ban, suspended until 31 October 1995. As he was shortly to be suspended by his own Board, it was irrelevant, and also exposed a loophole in the punishment system. Such a suspended sentence should apply only to Tests for which the player concerned is available.

Malik is one of four men penalised because they were captain in the relevant match – Ken Rutherford was one in a one-day international against Pakistan in East London in December 1994. Rutherford, as captain, queried a point of law in the wrong way, just as Malik accused Robinson of ball tampering when he was captain. Also penalised was Allan Border for his first offence at Brisbane when, as captain, he made a remark to umpire Randell. Also, Javed Miandad was reprimanded for failing to control Aqib at Old Trafford in July 1992. To that, referee Hunte might have noted that Javed also failed to keep control of most of his team, including himself.

Other curios from the collated list included Rashid Lateef – still the only substitute to be fined – and Peter Kirsten, the first man to be fined for separate dissent offences in the same match in Adelaide in January 1994.

Kirsten and Hughes are the only two cricketers to fall foul of the referee three times, with the South African committing three separate offences. He swore when Kapil Dev held on to the ball and ran him out. He showed dissent following a colleague's lbw dismissal and later offended in the same way when he was also given out lbw.

Intikhab was the only official cited, at Old Trafford in 1992, and Brian Lara is the only batsman to be given a suspended fine for showing dissent when he was given out stumped in Goa against India in October 1994.

It is always fun to pick a side with a common denominator. The gloom of a rainy day is often lightened by the players picking a Fat XI to play an Ugly XI, or Smokers v Non-Smokers, Happy v Grumpy, etc. So how about a Whingers XI to play a team of Quibblers drawn from the list of transgressors?

WHINGERS XI	QUIBBLERS XI
M. Atherton	A. Jones
D. Haynes	A. Sohail
B. Lara	P. Kirsten
Javed Miandad	A. Ranatunga
Salim Malik	V. Kambli
A. Border	K. Rutherford
D. Richardson (w.k.)	R. Lateef (w.k.)
C. Lewis	D. Nash
S. Warne	F. de Villiers
M. Hughes	Aqib Javed
C. Ambrose	P. Tufnell

The 12th man duties would be shared by David Houghton, Jo Angel and Manoj Prabhakar, and John Reid and Peter Burge combine forces to referee what would not be a silent game. As for the two umpires, even Dickie Bird and David Shepherd would be taxed to keep on top of things, but they have no serious challengers when it comes to a quiet but firm upholding of law and order.

Without National Grid, there would probably be no international panel of umpires, nor would the list of match referees have been slimmed down from its original ad hoc composition to the current smaller, but more effective group of strong enforcers of the Code of Conduct.

National Grid signed a contract worth £1.1 million with the ICC for the period 1 February 1994 to 31 March 1997. This money was placed at the disposal of the international governing body to fund the cost of the panel, and the costs of the match referees. Chief Executive of the ICC, David Richards, explains who pays for what.

'Regarding umpires, we pay Business Class return air fares, plus their match fee which is the same as they earn in a home Test, plus a supplementary fee which varies from £200 to £500. Because there is quite a difference between the fees paid to English umpires in England and umpires from other countries, the supplement is paid on a reverse sliding scale. The Englishmen will be topped up by the minimum of £200, and the lowest paid from abroad will get an extra £500. We also pay the umpires £50 a day on non-match days. The internal flights and hotels are paid for by the host country, because they would be in for those expenses anyway for a home umpire. We also ask a country to accommodate any wish of an umpire to travel well ahead of the game if he wants time to acclimatise. It does not arise much during the English winter, because all the other countries are playing cricket and the umpires only need a few days before they stand in another country. But English umpires appointed to stand from December onwards really need at least one game before they officiate in a Test.

'The United Cricket Board of South Africa is particularly good in this respect, and other countries are now beginning to appreciate what they need to do to get the best out of the system.

'We pay for the match referees' return international trip as well as hotels, internal flights and a fee of £100 per day while they are in the country.'

Former England and Kent captain Mike Denness works for a consultancy firm KBMD Public Relations, and he first discussed with Cowdrey in early 1992 the idea of an international panel of umpires being sponsored. 'I told Colin that we had little chance of raising the sort of money he was after – something like £500,000 – but I had met John Hatch of National Grid on a supporters' tour of New Zealand.

'We pursued the idea and eventually formulated a pilot scheme in October 1992 for the Indian tour of Zimbabwe and South Africa. We only dealt with the five-day Tests, and were sufficiently encouraged to press on in 1993 when we made four significant strides.

'National Grid extended the pilot scheme by sponsoring Dickie Bird and Raman Subba Row to officiate during the West Indies Tests against Pakistan in Barbados and Antigua in April 1993. They then went further, by sponsoring the home summer against Australia, including the three Texaco one-day internationals, and finished a great summer by sponsoring the inaugural ICC Test match umpires' conference held at the company's headquarters in Coventry.

'Colin attended the meeting, and there was a terrific exchange of views which concentrated on consistency of interpretation of the Laws and regulations. All nine Test match countries were represented and it was a great success.'

Richards endorses that. 'It was a terrific boost for their self-esteem. For the first time they could see that they were influencing events and they responded magnificently. I am all in favour of such get-togethers and the aim is to extend it to captains and referees. It makes sense for consistency in all departments of international cricket, and regular conferences can only improve the understanding of problems all the way round.

'We held a second umpires' conference, also at Coventry, in August 1995, and it was astonishing to see how the level of self-confidence had gone up. They believed in themselves, to such an extent that it was actually put forward that we drop the three-year experiment of limiting bouncers to two per over and go back to Law 42.8. They felt more confident of implementing the Law because they knew they would be backed by the referee. I know several countries need convincing of that, because it was the fact that the Law was not being enforced that led to a limit being introduced.

'That is just one example of the progress made in a couple of years and, as I am a person who believes that the fewer regulations the better, I know we are on the right lines.'

The 1993 umpires' conference cleared the decks for the first proper exchange of views among men who had to cope with a game that was becoming increasingly difficult to control. Denness said, 'John Hatch chaired the meeting at the request of Colin, and every relevant topic got an airing, including television replays. Everything started to bubble up to what would best suit umpires all round, and we were left with one thing to do, which came about in December of that year, 1993.'

The final step was the biggest one of all. It brought about the formation of the international panel, with a numerical base of four from England and two from each of the other eight countries. There are contrasting views about a system which is not automatically based upon merit.

The argument is that Test matches need the best umpires, and it is unlikely that umpires from the lesser experienced countries would be ranked in the top dozen or so from around the world. A counter-argument makes two points. The umpires from such countries – B C Cooray and K T Francis from Sri Lanka, and Ian Robinson and Kantilal Kanjee from Zimbabwe are examples – can only gain experience one way, and also they act as role models in their own country. By making two positions on the panel open to each country, the theory is that it will encourage and nourish a stronger grass-roots growth of new umpires in that country.

A stronger argument is that, as with selection of teams in modern times, the best team is picked for a match, almost regardless of the future. Therefore, the modern Test match needs the best officials to control it, and the panel should be reduced in numbers to increase the overall quality.

That presupposes a more uniform system of marking and assessment of the umpires than the arbitrary one used in 1995, when the captain's written marks and comments could be influenced unduly by one or two decisions which might have gone against one side. Richards is working towards a data-based system which will include marks and comments from captains and referees, and can be analysed to give a more objective assessment of an umpire's performance.

For instance, there are easy matches, in which an umpire might not be asked anything difficult, and hard matches in which he is bombarded with marginal decisions. If he makes a proven mistake – much harder to establish, whatever television armchair critics might think – why did it happen?

Whenever I do television commentary and have to talk about a decision that looks palpably wrong, I try to work out why the umpire decided as he did, even if I do not agree with the reason. Most of the arguments revolve around lbws, and if a plumb-looking one is refused, I try to suggest, over the slow motion replays, whether the umpire thought there was contact between bat and ball, or did he think the ball had struck the pad outside the line of off stump with a stroke played; or did it pitch outside leg stump, or would it either have gone over the stumps or missed the leg stump?

On only two occasions have I been unable to second guess why the umpire gave a batsman not out, and I do not detail the two incidents to criticise the two umpires concerned, Ian Robinson and Dickie Bird, but simply to point out that everyone makes mistakes, commentators included.

I was on air at Kingsmead in December 1994 when, on the final morning of a tense Test match between South Africa and New Zealand, home batsman John Commins got in a dreadful tangle against a near half-volley bowled by Danny Morrison. The latter delivers from close to the stumps and a complete misjudgement of footwork by Commins found his front foot a few inches across and forward as the straight ball hit him on the lower shin on middle-and-off. Clearly, Robinson was doubtful about something, but the more times I saw the replay the less idea I had of what it was.

Somebody in the commentary box, off microphone, offered the suggestion 'perhaps the ball was going *under* the stumps'.

The second decision was the one which occasioned more debate, verbal and written, than any I can remember, concerning Dickie Bird in the 1995 NatWest final at Lord's. Anil Kumble bowled to Dermot Reeve who, typically, tried to improvise an unorthodox sweep to a straight on, full length delivery which hit him on the inside of a bent back leg, on the line of middle stump and only a foot or so in front of that stump. An appeal for lbw was turned down by Bird.

It was suggested that the ball flicked the front pad on the way through, but that would not have negated the appeal, because the only part of Reeve's front left leg that could have been hit was bent for the sweep stroke, and was clearly inside the line of off stump.

The Richards database would presumably make an allowance for the occasional mental block, always assuming that it remained 'occasional'.

The appointment of umpires and referees is a complicated exercise. Between September 1995 and January 1996, the month before the last World Cup, eighteen Test matches were played around the world, and Richards and his Chairman, Clyde Walcott, juggled their lists to cover every game with an overseas umpire and a referee. Within reason, they try to spread the load evenly but, certainly as far as the referees are concerned, they are moving towards a single-figure personnel.

Richards said, 'We ask each country to nominate three or four possible referees, but only if they measure up to the standard we want. It wouldn't be fair to anyone if all nine countries nominated three, because they would not all get appointed. We try to ensure that there is no possible clash between a host country and the referee we are thinking of.'

What about the umpires?

'That is different. We don't consult about them, because we work from the assumption that any umpire on the twenty-strong panel is good enough to stand in Test cricket anywhere. It would be counter-productive if we conducted the equivalent of a popularity poll, and would certainly lead to undercurrents.'

An example of that policy was the decision to appoint Australian Daryll Hair for the Johannesburg Test between South Africa and England in November 1995. Hair was the controversial centre of matches involving both countries in Australia in 1994 and 1995.

Wisden records that 'Kirsten had an animated conversation with Hair after three of his colleagues, Andrew Hudson, Brian McMillan and David Richardson, were given out lbw'. He was fined 25 per cent of his match fee, followed by a further 40 per cent when he was given out in the same way in the second innings.

England were not impressed when Hair did not refer a run-out decision to the third umpire although, as with Steve Bucknor in Johannesburg in 1992, the replay showed that the batsman was out, although given in.

The principle invoked by Richards must still be the correct one. Like bad law, the umpires' panel must be changed in a proper manner. The odds are that, by the end of the 20th century, the international panel will number no more than a dozen, and the list of referees half that number. The choice of referees for the 1996 World Cup was significant. Clive Lloyd, Raman Subba Row and John Reid were the three appointed by the ICC, with two from each home country to do duty.

National Grid's sponsorship has enabled the ICC to improve their control of Test cricket at a time when Cowdrey feared for the future. His foresight, born from a love of the game and the spirit in which it is played, deserved the support engendered by the Denness contact with National Grid.

They had more than one reason for sinking so much money into cricket. John Hatch's love of the game was a factor but, as a non-executive director, he only had limited clout. The marketing people had to be convinced, and they agreed because of the company's considerable overseas interests, particularly in the cricket-playing countries. Also, they have a marketing policy in Britain of encouraging private competition among what they term as 'other players in the game'.

The cricketing analogy applied, and the £1.1 million deal was struck.

CHAPTER 14

Whitherwards authority?

By midway through the 1990s, Pakistan had upset the ICC, England, Australia, New Zealand, West Indies and Zimbabwe on various issues, including allegations of ball tampering, bribery and sledging. Of the aforementioned five countries, only Australia did not make any allegations of ball tampering, but their accusations of bribery against Salim Malik were just as devastating and damaging.

Each country was frightened off by the lawyers, and so was the ICC when it came to ball tampering. The various incidents, charges and counter-charges have been detailed earlier, with the Pakistan cricketers and authorities mostly escaping punitive action. David Houghton of Zimbabwe willingly invoked a fine from match referee Jackie Hendriks in February 1995 by publicly denouncing the Pakistani cricketers for racist sledging to which he took great exception.

Seldom, if ever, has a Test captain led his country through such a troubled short period of time as Salim, yet he fell foul of the referee once only when, in bizarre fashion, he accused umpire Ian Robinson of ball tampering.

Why is Pakistan cricket so frequently in the eye of a storm? Why are they accused of so much, but convicted of so little? Are they, as the records suggest, innocent of all charges levelled at them? And if they have been guilty on occasions, why was no action taken?

In most walks of life, the example set at the top is reflected at other levels, and the Pakistan administration must shoulder the blame for perceived behavioural and disciplinary lapses which make the wrong sort of headlines in most of their Test matches and one-day internationals.

No other cricket country is bedevilled with such instability and, until the administration is trusted at home and abroad, the players will continue to charm and annoy with a switchback level of cricket which is either brilliant or awful, but seldom boring. Moreover, it is no good their cricket officials claiming that the world is against them, because their style of administration is akin to that of a boxer leading with his chin against a big puncher.

The events leading up to the start of their tour of Australia in October and November 1995 are a typical example of a topsy-turvy firing and hiring of players and officials which was bewildering, even to people who were familiar with Pakistan cricket's ability to surprise and shock.

If English and other international cricketers and administrators were asked to pick a shortlist of past and present Pakistan cricketers who were trustworthy and commanded universal respect, Majid Khan would figure in most lists, like Javed Burki, a cousin of Imran, whom he preceded to Oxbridge and the captaincy of Pakistan.

Majid was hero-worshipped by Imran, six years his junior...until Majid was dropped by his Pathan first cousin on the tour of England in 1982. The two have not spoken since, not even when Pakistan won the World Cup ten years later. Majid became a selector after Imran retired and was then appointed manager of the second trip to Sharjah, with Mushtaq Mohammad, the third coach of the year following Intikhab and Khalid Ibadulla.

Neither manager nor coach was to survive Pakistan's third successive humiliation since the suspension of Salim in March. Majid had this to say of his removal from the party to tour Australia. *'I made a grave error of judgement in associating myself with this Board. I have been obstructed, harassed, maligned and insulted in the press.'*

When a man of Majid's standing and innate dignity feels the need to comment thus, the rest of the cricket world must believe that most of their criticism is well founded. He subsequently announced his resignation from the 1996 World Cup technical committee, and blamed the Pakistan Board's chief executive, Arif Abbasi, for the team's recent dismal displays against Sri Lanka.

Abbasi does not emerge with much credit from the turbulent happenings of 1995. It is said that he pressurised both umpires, Khizar Hyatt and England's Nigel Plews, in the pivotal second Test in Faisalabad in September 1995 between Pakistan and Sri Lanka. The issue concerned the amount of time spent off the field by Inzamam-ul-Haq, following a blow to the head while batting. The playing conditions did not make the matter crystal clear, but Abbasi virtually insisted on a ruling which allowed Inzamam to bat earlier than he otherwise would have done on the final day.

Batting at number four, Inzamam scored 26 but Pakistan still suffered a first-ever home defeat by Sri Lanka, when they were bowled out for 209 and lost the match by 42 runs.

Pakistan have one defence against the rest of the world, graphically explained by Imran. 'Pakistan cricketers are treated somewhat like Islam in the West. Most of the time, such images are depicted of terrorists, fanaticism, veiled women and so on. Similarly, our cricketers are looked upon as an undisciplined, unruly mob who pressurise umpires, cheat, doctor cricket balls, whinge about umpiring decisions and are generally unsporting. Consequently, English umpires make mistakes, but Pakistan umpires cheat.'

Whatever the explanation, the gulf between Pakistan and most other members of the ICC is wider now than it has ever been. Until a stable administration is in place, and one which is prepared to grasp one or two nettles, the rest of cricket continues to suffer. Meanwhile Pakistan's own cricketers play under the handicap of not trusting their own officials.

England, Australia and New Zealand have all disciplined leading cricketers in 1994/95 – Atherton, Hughes, Warne and Nash, Fleming and Hart. Yet all three authorities backed off when it came to substantiating charges against Pakistan.

Pakistan cricket has much to offer the game, but not until its own authority faces up to its responsibilities in a more consistent manner.

The English authorities are no different from other Boards when it comes to making a decision which runs the slightest risk of being challenged legally. The Test & County Cricket Board, the cricket authority formed in 1967 to administer the first-class game in England, was due to be replaced by the new English Cricket Board in 1996, which is comprised of all levels of cricket in Britain. The reason for the change was, primarily, a financial one, with the carrot of government grants too tempting to refuse.

To be fair, the TCCB has a more difficult boat to row than any other country, for two reasons. Firstly, it administers the largest professional game in the world, with around 400 contracted cricketers spread among the eighteen first-class county clubs. Secondly, Britain is a member of the EEC, and is thus subject to the Treaty of Rome. This stipulates a free movement of labour, and

English cricket is well aware of the wafer-thin tightrope it treads regarding rules of registration. Soccer has already felt the full might of a European Court ruling concerning transfers, and many sports in Britain have approached the Minister of Sport to see if the Maastricht Treaty can be renegotiated to allow for a reasonable restraint on players moving from one club to another.

The Cricketers' Association has always tried to work with the TCCB in maintaining a compromise between free movement and a reasonable restriction, but the Board is heading for the legal buffers unless it does away with its present system of categorising all cricketers in two lists – known as List 1 and List 2.

These lists are completed by clubs towards the end of each English season, with any cricketer who is offered a new contract being placed on List 1. This is meant to deny other clubs the chance of trying to sign him, while the players on List 2 are free to move anywhere without restriction.

The praiseworthy aim of List 1 is to preserve stability in a structure which only comprises 18 counties. Players on List 1 do change clubs but, in order to prevent two or three counties cornering the best talent, no club can sign more than one contested cricketer in a year, and no more than two in five years. The system is being diluted gradually, with the odd cricketer now moving from List 1 to List 2 on appeal, but the first cricketer to challenge in court would probably win.

Cricket has tried to move with the times, ever since the TCCB and the Cricketers' Association were formed within months of each other in 1967. Since then, cricketers have found it gradually more easy to move, as should have been the case from a starting point which was legally unsustainable.

Prior to 1967, any cricketer wanting to change clubs against the wishes of his own club had to miss a complete season while he qualified – examples include Tom Graveney, M J K Smith and Peter Richardson, all of them England cricketers who were forced to sit out one year.

Contested moves then allowed cricketers like Bob Willis, Bob Cottam, Roy Virgin and Imran Khan to move on a deferred registration which usually reduced their waiting time to half a season, although the resistance to Imran's move from Worcestershire to Sussex meant he could not play until 1 August 1977.

The first total botch up by the TCCB of a request for special registration occurred in 1980, and concerned the controversial move from Lancashire to Derbyshire of Barry Wood. A combination of circumstances in January and early February meant that Lancashire withdrew an offer for that year after trying to reach agreement for several weeks. Feelings ran high because, in 1979, his benefit realised £62,000, and the moral high ground was taken by the Board's Registration Sub-Committee under the chairmanship of Dennis Silk.

He believed that the precedent of a cricketer leaving immediately after a successful benefit was a dangerous one. From a purely ethical point of view, he was right, but the law is not based upon ethics. With Lancashire having withdrawn their offer, the way seemed clear for Derbyshire to sign Wood – except Lancashire's then chairman, the fiery Cedric Rhoades, went out of his way to try to block the move as 'not being in the best interest of county cricket'.

I sat on the Registration Sub-Committee and was amazed when Silk led the committee into refusing the Derbyshire application. It was not granted on a deferred basis – as in the Willis case – but was simply refused. That left Wood with only the county of his birth to play for but, as that was Yorkshire whose policy then was rigidly against employing cricketers from other counties, Wood was effectively put out of cricket for the whole of the 1980 season.

He sought and obtained backing for what was only natural justice from his fellow professionals at the Annual General Meeting at Edgbaston before the start of the season. The point was made forcibly to him that although many players did not agree with the move, he should not be denied the right to work. The Board, under the chairmanship of George Mann, refused to agree to his move, and the Association used precious funds to employ a lawyer to fight his case. Coincidentally, that man was the late Peter Bromage, who was to become Chairman of the Board's Disciplinary Sub-Committee and a leading Rugby Football Union official.

The Board finally bowed to the inevitable and Wood was allowed to play for Derbyshire from 1 June onwards. The costs were over £6,000 which, perhaps naively on the part of the Association, were not made part of the final deal, and the Board refused to pay, despite its intransigence which could never be justified legally.

No subsequent special registration has been so challenged, but the ice is becoming ever thinner.

On the disciplinary front, the TCCB's record is a chequered one. In the last fifteen years it has alternated between trying to hang top cricketers such as Ian Botham and Allan Lamb, and slapping wrists for disciplinary offences reported by umpires, some of whom then became reluctant to take strong action because of what they perceived to be a lack of support.

The English first-class umpires are in the same stranglehold grip of the authorities as were the county cricketers twenty years ago, before the Association started to loosen the chains. The umpires have a representative body but, although negotiations take place annually on pay and working conditions, it is still, effectively, a take it or leave it situation.

The majority thus settle for a quiet life. 'Don't quote me. I don't want to get involved. No, I don't agree with a lot, but what can I do?' I must have heard that sort of comment more than a dozen times in writing this book. Don Oslear is correct when he pinpoints the weakness in a system of appointing umpires to the Test panel, that seems to penalise the strong umpire who is unafraid to take whatever action he deems necessary.

Oslear says, 'I thought that strong umpires are required to officiate at top level, but not any more. John Hampshire, Ken Palmer and John Holder all took action in home international games about ball tampering in 1991 and 1992. None of them lasted long on the Test panel, with Holder going the very next year. Add to them Alan Whitehead, who was dropped after standing his ground in a Test at Trent Bridge where he clashed with Ian Botham, and David Constant, who became so fed up with the antics of touring sides that he voluntarily stepped down.

'That is not to suggest that the present panel are not good umpires, but I cannot believe that of the above five, not one is considered among our best umpires. I also do not agree with the selection method of that panel, which is not based entirely on marks at county level. Again, I can see that different qualities are needed to control a five-day Test compared to county level cricket, but surely those marks tell a story about an umpire's ability and consistency.

'I still do not know who picks the Test panel. It should be the Appointment of Umpires Sub-Committee which includes an Umpires' representative, normally the chairman. *But he has to leave the room when that item is discussed.*'

Oslear has put forward a powerful case against the English authorities, including his detailing of officially reported cases of ball tampering which were never punished until the derisory £1000 fine levied on Surrey CCC in 1992.

The Board's big mistake was not in fining Allan Lamb £5000 for talking about an offence for which Surrey were fined £1000 for doing repeatedly after a warning. The two fines appear to be incompatible – Lamb's was even reduced on appeal. The mistake lay in trying to deal with both offences on the same day, because after the Lamb hearing, the Surrey charge was delegated to a Summary Panel from the full Disciplinary Sub-Committee, and they had limited powers.

A shortage of time should not mean rushing through a serious case using the wrong procedure. Lamb knowingly broke his contract with the TCCB regarding the making of unauthorised public pronouncements, but he pleaded guilty to that, with his legal advisers pleasantly surprised that he was not charged with something more serious, such as bringing the game into disrepute.

Despite his plea of guilty, the hearing occupied most of the morning of 23 September 1992 and, with several committee members unable or unwilling to stay all day, the Surrey hearing was delegated to the Summary Panel. The £1000 fine they imposed was the maximum allowed under the summary procedure, but the error was in allowing the most serious case on record of ball tampering by one club to be examined by a body with such restricted powers.

The Test & County Cricket Board has never grasped the nettle of ball tampering, despite making public and private noises about their determination to stamp it out. In the presence of senior officers Alan Smith and Tony Brown, the Disciplinary Sub-Committee's action against Surrey was woefully weak. If they really did want to be shown to be determined to take strong action, they should have ensured that the case was heard at the highest level.

The strangest financial penalty imposed for a disciplinary offence was the £750 imposed on the chairman of the Derbyshire County Cricket Club, Chris Middleton, in 1991. He says: 'I believe I was the first "amateur" in cricket to be fined. I stress 'amateur', because in my eight years as chairman of Derbyshire, I never claimed one penny of expenses from the club. When I represented them at Lord's, I claimed expenses off the Board, but never from Derbyshire. Yet I got a fine which rendered me speechless – not easy to do – and I immediately resigned from the Discipline Sub-Committee, of which body I was a member for several years.

'Ironic isn't it? I must have been the first member of that committee to be accused of making derogatory remarks about another representative of the Board. It happened when the England team manager, Micky Stewart, came to Derby to coach Devon Malcolm between the first and second Tests. I didn't mind that, because it seems that he had contacted the club on the Friday before he worked with Devon next day.

'What wound me up was that the story was splashed all over a Sunday newspaper referring to Devon as a dunce. I was very cross and as we had a home Sunday league match, I went round to the press box and gave them a field day. It wasn't a matter of club v country, rather the way that the whole thing was handled which made it look as though Stewart had descended upon Derbyshire to give Devon some instruction which our coaches had neglected.

'So I was fined by the committee which was chaired by Peter Bromage, and included Alan Moss from Middlesex, Eddie Slinger from Lancashire, and Donald Rich from Hampshire. They asked me to apologise and I refused, telling them that I stood by every word, because things were handled clumsily.

'That further disenchanted me with the Ted Dexter regime, because I never forgot how he was appointed to chair the first England committee. We were told at the December board meeting in 1988 about the concept of the new body and then, the following month, we had a special meeting at the Oval to consider our position regarding South Africa's readmission to the ICC.

'At the end of the meeting, the chairman, Raman Subba Row, told us that he thought he had exactly the right man for the new chairmanship. It was Dexter, but he impressed on us so emphatically the need for absolute secrecy, that I never told a soul, not even my wife. No decision was expected until the March board meeting, so imagine my surprise when, well before that meeting, I saw Dexter on television being announced as the new chairman of the England committee. As a county chairman, I feel we should have been consulted, even if only on a rubber-stamp basis, and I know other chairmen felt the same way.

'The same sort of thing happened when Keith Fletcher was appointed, and we were told that he had to have a five-year contract, otherwise he would not leave Essex. Overall, the Board's Executive committee did a good job, but there were too many times when they took decisions, or tried to take them, which needed discussion. That was my main criticism.'

Middleton's point was well made when the time came for Dexter to go. Middleton, together with several chairmen of a like mind, blocked the intention of Alan Smith and his Executive to appoint

M J K Smith as the next chairman of the England committee. Duncan Fearnley of Worcestershire was another man who felt things were being rushed in September 1993, and the intended announcement of Smith was deferred, pending the findings of a working party set up to look at alternative candidates, and to review the position of the England committee system.

Fearnley and David Acfield played a big part in drawing up a list of suitable candidates, with Raymond Illingworth and Smith the final two candidates to be voted upon at the spring board meeting in 1994. The rest, as they say, is history. Illingworth's appointment, and the way it was made, signalled the first breakthrough in an effort to break up what was perceived by many to be the perpetuation of the Oxbridge influence which first prompted the formation of the TCCB to weaken the MCC's previous stranglehold on the English game.

As for Oslear's conviction that he was denied a final year on the first-class list in his 65th year, the Board's defence that the quality of the new applicants was the determining factor in a discretionary situation has one flaw which was too big for Oslear to ignore.

Oslear: 'When the Appointment of Umpires Sub-Committee met after the 1991 season to appoint for 1992, the list of new applicants was headed with their name and age at 1.1.92.

'That proves what I have always maintained – namely that the determining age for all umpires was at 1 January. Therefore, when the same sub-committee met the following year on 5 October 1992, they would have had a list of new applicants with the age given at 1.1.93. I had just been replaced as chairman by Roy Kerslake, but he did not attend that meeting.

'John Harris did attend, together with other captains including Mark Nicholas, Kim Barnett and Mike Gatting as well as Phil Sharpe. I know I was awarded a two-year contract for 1993 and 1994, when my 65th birthday fell a few weeks before the start of that season. The members of that panel then had a letter from the Board saying that, as a mistake had been made regarding my age, the two-year contract would be reduced to one. I know they stuffed me.'

As shown by the extracts of letters from Alan Smith and Tony Brown to Oslear, a nuisance to them had been removed by moving the goalposts. That view is held by the majority of Oslear's former colleagues, most of whom are also disenchanted with the lack of positive support they have received from the Board in recent years.

I spoke to thirteen first-class umpires, and not one believed that a report about a player or a pitch would be acted upon in a firm way. The commonly held view is that it is not worth the time and trouble taken to compile a report when, as happened in 1995 with one specific case of reported foul language by an England Test cricketer, the subsequent umpires' reports were not even acknowledged.

The wish for anonymity by the umpires reflects the fear, under which they work, of damaging their prospects if they go public on any controversial matter.

David Constant and John Holder are two fearless umpires who believe that, since they first umpired in county cricket, the game has become much more difficult to control. They both make the same points. 'Players now orchestrate appeals on the basis that the more they shout, the more likely they are to force an error from the umpire. Behaviour is worse. Catches are claimed that are not. Gestures and language have deteriorated in the last ten years.'

Holder has umpired for thirteen years and says, 'The game has degenerated alarmingly in terms of acceptance of decisions and general behaviour. The right spirit is not there any more, which is a shame because we are all in the same game, trying to earn a living and give the public something to watch.'

Holder was understandably reluctant to name the worst sides but, on a happier note, he picked out Yorkshire and Nottinghamshire as two exemplary teams. 'I have never had any trouble with their captains, from David Bairstow to Phil Carrick, Martyn Moxon especially and now David Byas. All good blokes who ensured that their cricketers played the game in the right way. Just as Nottinghamshire's Clive Rice and Tim Robinson did. Clive would not tolerate anything wrong, and neither did Tim. It makes such a difference, because if an umpire is not put under constant shouting pressure of the wrong sort, he is more likely to do a better job. Cricket should be played hard, but fair. Too much, nowadays, is confrontational and that benefits nobody.'

The recent decline in standards of on-field behaviour is deplored by many, cricketers and ex-cricketers alike. Mark Nicholas, in the first of his sixteen years as a Hampshire player in 1980, remembers joining a well-seasoned side full of good pros. 'Players like Gordon Greenidge, Paul Terry, David Turner and Bobby Parks were good blokes and we never had any trouble on the field with umpires or opposing sides. There was fun to be had in playing county cricket, and that is what has disappeared in the last few years. Not only that, but

I have never heard as much mindless noise on the field as in the last few years. It all comes from what the players see as a necessary effort to impress the manager. We never had a manager as such at Hampshire, because I have always believed that you sink or swim with the strength or otherwise of your captain.

'What sense does it make for fielders to yell "well bowled" when a ball thuds into the wicket-keeper's gloves but the batsman has left it because it is two feet wide of off stump? As for sledging, I have never had any problem with direct remarks to me.

'I don't put all the blame on the players, because some of them don't know any better. I really blame the captains. The umpires become affected as well. Most players now seem to work on the theory that the more they appeal, the more likely they are to force a mistake.

'The understanding and responsibility to the game is nil. Players don't even understand the phrase any more, and all because of the extreme pressure to win. It is no coincidence that there were nine new captains in 1995, and only Kim Barnett, Mike Gatting and myself were long-standing skippers before that.'

Views full of regret, as are most of those of David Gower. 'When I started out in 1978, the competition on the field was just as stern as now, and there was the occasional individual conflict. But England and Australia would get together after the game and have a beer or two. Now, the bulk of the team seem to want to get away from the ground as quickly as possible.

'At county level, my main worry is more about playing standards. If there is a genuine level of competition in the four-day game then standards should improve, but attitudes and the technique of youngsters worries me. '

Bob Willis has a problem with match referees. 'I don't like them. If the umpires had done their job, there would be no need for them. Some of the referees have been weak anyway, and it is difficult to get consistency from them. As for the culture of the game, it has changed completely.'

Former captain of Gloucestershire and Durham, David Graveney agrees. The current secretary of the Professional Cricketers' Association is glad he is no longer playing a game he served well for twenty-three years.

'Sharp practice has increased enormously, and I reckon that umpiring is ten times more difficult than when I started in 1972. Take claimed catches for instance. In the old days, the batsman would ask the fielder and take his word. Nowadays, most batsmen just stand their ground and wait for the decision. There is clearly much more concerted appealing and general practices which I never tolerated when I was captain. I'm proud of the fact that my sides never caused trouble with umpires, and I'm also proud to be called an old-fashioned cricketer.

'Some sides are harder to play against than others. For instance, Essex were always hard work, and my dad, Ken, also says that they never missed a trick, even back in the late 1940s and 1950s. I just think that the stature of the player has gone down since the early 1980s, and it is partly because we seem to have a different sort of umpire coming on to the list. Characters like Bill Alley and Cec Pepper were hard men who used to control a game better than most. It wasn't a question of them reporting you. They would simply tell you to get on with the game and cut out the funny stuff.

'That is one difference. The other is that from the time in the mid-1980s when there were more applicants each year to get on the first-class list, umpires seemed to become more defensive. Conscious of the fact they were being marked by captains, they seemed reluctant to report – and that was about the time when they should have reported more because the game was getting out of hand.

'I also know they were and are bothered that they don't get proper backing from the centre. I attended many captains meetings and also served for some while on the Disciplinary Sub-Committee, and I am convinced a lot of the present trouble could have been avoided if the TCCB had been stronger then and rapped a few knuckles. It became a vicious circle.

'The Board got worried because of falling standards and told the umpires to crack down. The umpires were disinclined to do that because they believed they would not get proper support. Players sensed the new mood, and now exploit it to the hilt. Also, the stronger umpires seemed to be picked out – men like Don Oslear, John Holder and Alan Whitehead are three examples. They never backed off, yet got a reputation for being over-zealous just because they did their job as they saw it.

'As it happens, I thought Don could take the letter of the law to the extreme, but he chose to do things exactly by the book, and I have no problem with that. One example was at Worcester in 1991 in a Sunday league game. We scored 235 for four from our 40 overs, and we were always in control. We eventually won by 18 runs but, I remember two overs towards the end of the match, I was fielding at backward square leg as one of the four fielders permitted in the ring.

'There was no fine leg and I was "hiding" in the field, being the old man of the side. In the middle of the over in what was then a dead match, I strayed a foot or two outside the circle. I wasn't trying to take advantage and, even if I was, it didn't matter because the game was effectively over. Not only did Don call "no-ball", but he made a big thing of it. Now, it was the right decision, and I am not moaning about it, but it exemplifies Don's approach to the game which is purely black and white.

'Another reason for the decline in standards is the little social time the players now spend together. In my early days any misunderstandings on the field disappeared over a couple of beers, but now they just fester. I guarantee that someone like Dominic Cork who might think that another England player is a "funny bloke" will come back off tour and say, "He's not so bad. I just never knew him properly". That never happened in the first half of my career.'

And what about ball tampering? 'I have thought a great deal about this. What I found in the 1970s was that most sides had an expert seam-picker – you know, he could do it with one hand while you didn't even notice it. That art – and it was an art – disappeared when the pitches were covered and the seams of the balls became flatter, thus reducing the importance of a prominent seam. So as the movement off the seam disappeared, the concept of making the ball swing increased.

'This is where the introduction of overseas bowlers became a factor. They were brought up on grassless pitches off which the ball never moved, therefore they had to swing it. The concept of how to swing a ball became more important and this is how reverse swing came into our cricket.'

Is Graveney hopeful about the future? 'Of course I must be, but only if players realise the extent of their responsibilities to the public, and if the authorities face up to their responsibilities to the game in general, and the umpires in particular. Until they resolve that problem, the game will drift on. If the umpires are happy they will be backed unequivocally when they report, most of the problems will disappear.'

Epilogue

What many believed to be the biggest scandal in modern cricket erupted during the fourth Texaco one-day international between England and Pakistan at Lord's on 23 August 1992. The question of who might have acted to stem the resultant growing tide of suspicion in modern cricket is worth examining.

What was the umpires' role in all this? The two officials on the field, John Hampshire and Ken Palmer, have made it clear that during the lunch break they decided to change the ball under Law 42.5 (Changing the Condition of the Ball) and *not* Law 5 (Ball Becoming Unfit for Play).

And what of the actions of the TCCB? Their Chief Executive, Alan Smith, had no final influence on the post-match statement, which is the sole responsibility of the match referee, in this case Deryck Murray. Smith had wanted the statement to include that the ball was changed because of illegal treatment. The decision to omit this was Murray's.

As for the International Cricket Council, their representative, John Stephenson, resisted improper pressure from the Pakistan hierarchy to say that the ball was changed because it had gone out of shape.

What of match referee, Deryck Murray? He is seemingly much more open to criticism for whatever reason he declined to include in his statement the reason for changing the ball during the lunch interval – and this despite requests to do so from umpires Hampshire and Palmer. He made full use of the Code of Conduct clause which prohibits a referee from commenting on his decision, and which thus absolved him from his responsibility for changing the proposed original statement.

Several months after the Lord's match, Murray appeared on London Weekend Television's programme *The Devil's Advocate* and admitted that 'Yes, there were scuff and scratch marks on the ball changed at Lord's'. So if not under Law 42.5, this begs the question, under which other Law or playing condition *was* the ball changed, and why did Murray not say? (Surely not because he was afraid of implicating any one person, for in such a situation individuals do not even have to be named as long as the officials are satisfied that the fielding side has transgressed.)

The simple fact is that *the ball was changed because of a breach of Law 42.5*, as confirmed under oath in the High Court fifteen months later by Don Oslear, the third umpire at the Lord's match.

Deryck Murray knew that, but chose not to reveal the fact himself. If only he had done so at the time, then further suspicions might never have been aroused.

An examination of events chronicled in this book suggest that it is difficult to refute Don Oslear's belief that the English cricket authorities run for cover whenever an unpleasant issue arises. The treatment afforded his reports suggests a reluctance to be seen to be taking strong and incisive action, but by whom?

Cases of alleged ball tampering appear to frighten officialdom more than any other breaking of a cricketing law. Straightforward instances of indiscipline are a different matter, but the legal implications of accusing an alleged ball tamperer of cheating seem to be the greatest inhibitor of all.

For instance, the ICC were reportedly threatened by the Sri Lankan authorities with legal action if the charge of ball tampering against them in Australia, made by match referee Graham Dowling, was not withdrawn – and withdrawn it promptly was.

The authorities seem afraid to take action unless they can defend themselves in law, yet sport must never lose its powers of self-regulation. After all, most umpiring decisions are 'according to the opinion of the umpire'. If that opinion is given objectively – and surely a player or team who claimed otherwise would be even more vulnerable in law – then any case taken to court would have little chance of succeeding. Yet the world's authorities are becoming increasingly unwilling to re-establish the control they used to hold because of a fear of challenge.

The Test & County Cricket Board is about to be superceded by the English Cricket Board, but the multi-layered levels of administration make it difficult to pinpoint those individuals responsible for the apparently weak responses to incidents detailed within this book.

As far as his reports on alleged ball tampering are concerned, Oslear dealt with three Board officials in the main: Chief Executive Alan Smith, Administrative Secretary Tony Brown, and Cricket Secretary Tim Lamb. On matters of discipline, such as the Northamptonshire issue, all correspondence was with Smith and Brown, with the Executive Committee of the Board unlikely to have considered the matter. As Chief Executive, Smith could argue, with some justification, that to refer every umpire's report to that body would have been administratively impossible.

A senior officer, such as Smith, must judge the extent of his executive powers each time he has to use them. The same applies to Brown, under whose authority the umpires work on a day-to-day basis. Both Smith and Brown are responsible to committees, especially the Executive body. Neither man would have a vote, but their advice would be sought on all major issues. It is not impossible, but extremely unlikely, that such advice would be ignored, which leads to the conclusion that the lack of action taken about reported cases of ball tampering during a five-year period was certainly within their cognisance, and probably with their agreement.

Oslear's account of the attempts by the Board, through the aforementioned officials, to dissuade him from pursuing the incident at the Lord's Texaco one-day international in August 1992 is not in itself proof of inept or weak behaviour by the English authorities. Their reluctance to become involved publicly was likely to have been because of legal constraints. That argument, however, becomes much more tenuous in relation to Oslear's reports of alleged ball tampering in domestic cricket. Remember, he reported Surrey *three* times in thirty-one days in 1991 and nothing was done, which is remarkable considering Surrey were also reported for the same offence in 1990 in the game against Gloucestershire at Cheltenham – this time by umpires other than Oslear. Yet those four reports in twelve months brought nothing stronger from the Board than the letter, signed from Brown to Surrey, warning the club about the consequences of any further transgression.

Why no stronger action? And why no publication of the warning? Why should Surrey and their players have been afforded such privacy about matters of such public interest?

Why did the same Board officials say that no cases of ball tampering were made in 1993, when there were at least two recorded instances? The same umpire that reported Surrey in the Cheltenham game of 1990 – Chris Balderstone – also reported a similar transgression in the game between Northamptonshire and Surrey in July 1993. The second instance was when the Derbyshire club forwarded the balls used in the game against Lancashire a few days before the Benson and Hedges Cup Final.

Oslear has given chapter and verse of those instances, and I know of one other. John Holder and Merv Kitchen spoke to the England captain, Graham Gooch, at the Oval against the West Indies in 1991 about the state of the ball, which they believed had been tampered with. Their on-field conversation was reported to the late Peter Smith, then press officer for the TCCB, with a request that the incident be included in a statement he would make that Saturday evening about another incident involving Phil Tufnell.

Smith agreed, but no statement was made. It was blocked by somebody, presumably a senior Board official. I detailed the incident in my book *Jack in the Box*, which was a television diary of that series. When the book was published the following April 1992, the TCCB officially denied any knowledge of the incident when an extract was published in the *Daily Express*. They still maintain that position, despite the two umpires including the incident in their report, which Lord's must still have on file.

If only because of that cover-up, the TCCB stand accused of dodging the bullets when it comes to officially reported cases of ball tampering. It is an issue which seems to create fear at Lord's, otherwise strong and public action would have been taken about a problem they have insisted they are determined to eliminate.

Among others, umpires Oslear, Balderstone, Holder, Kitchen and Dudleston, by their signed reports, gave the TCCB's Smith, Brown and Lamb the chance to push their committees into action. The subsequent lack of action, other than a warning letter to Surrey and a derisory fine of £1000, points to a dereliction of duty by somebody. If Smith, Brown and Lamb are not guilty, their committees are – and those committees are made up of county club representatives.

Whether individually or collectively, the English cricket authorities have chosen to allow the problem of ball tampering to go unchecked by punitive action. Cricket has suffered as a result.

Appendix

ICC Code of conduct – Individual breaches

PLAYER	SERIES & MATCH
Aqib Javed	Eng v Pak, 3rd Test at Old Trafford, 2–7 July 1992
Javed Miandad	Eng v Pak, 3rd Test at Old Trafford, 2–7 July 1992
Intikhab Alam	Eng v Pak, 3rd Test at Old Trafford, 2–7 July 1992
Rashid Latif (emergency fieldsman)	Eng v Pak, 4th Test at Headingley, 23–27 July 1992
Aqib Javed	NZ v Pak, One-Day International at Napier, 28 Dec 1992
Peter Kirsten	SA v India, One-Day International at Port Elizabeth, 1992
Manoj Prabhakar	SA v India, Test at Port Elizabeth, 26–30 Dec 1992
Allan Border	Aus v WI, Test at Brisbane, 27 Nov–1 Dec 1992
Merv Hughes	Aus v WI, Test at Brisbane, 27 Nov–1 Dec 1992
Desmond Haynes	Aus v WI, World Series at Brisbane, 10 Jun 1993
Allan Border	Aus v WI, Test at Perth, 30 Jan–1 Feb 1993
Merv Hughes	Aus v WI, Test at Perth, 30 Jan–1 Feb 1993
Vinod Kambli	Sir Lanka v India, 2nd Test at Colombo, 27 Jul–1 Aug 1993
Andrew Jones	Aus v NZ, 1st Test at Perth, 12–16 Nov 1993
Peter Kirsten	Aus v SA, 3rd Test at Adelaide, 28 Jan–1 Feb 1994
Peter Kirsten	Aus v SA, 3rd Test at Adelaide, 28 Jan–1 Feb 1994
Merv Hughes	SA v Aus, 1st Test at Johannesburg, 4–8 March 1994
Shane Warne	SA v Aus, 1st Test at Johannesburg, 4–8 March 1994
Curtly Ambrose	WI v Eng, 4th Test at Barbados, 8–13 April 1994
Nayan Mongia	Aus v India, One-Day tournament in Sharjah, 20 April 1994
Dion Nash	Pak v NZ, One-Day tournament in Sharjah, 20 April 1994
Michael Atherton	Eng v SA, 3d Test at The Oval, 18–22 August 1994
Fanie de Villiers	Eng v SA, 3rd Test at The Oval, 18–22 August 1994
Jo Angel	Aus v Pak, 1st Test at Karachi 28 Sept–2 Oct 1994

(excluding over-rate fines) 1992–96

DETAILS OF INCIDENT/ACTION TAKEN	REFEREE
Violated Code 2 and 3. Fined 50% of match fee.	C C Hunte
Failed to keep control of Aqib Javed on field. Reprimand.	C C Hunte
Violated Code 8 by speaking to Press. Reprimand.	C C Hunte
Showed dissent at umpire's decision. Fined 40% of match fee. Breach of Code 3.	C L Walcott
Violated Code 2 and 3. Suspended from One Day International Auckland on 30 December.	P Burge
Showed dissent after he was run out. Also used offensive language. Fined 50% of match fee.	C H Lloyd
Showed dissent. Fined 10% of match fee.	M J K Smith
Violated Code 3 by showing dissent to umpire. Fined 50% of match fee.	R Subba Row
Violated Code 3 and 5 by showing dissent to umpire and abusive language to umpire. Fined 10% of match fee.	R Subba Row
Fined 50% of match fee and warned as to future conduct. Show of dissent at umpire's decision.	D B Carr
Severely reprimanded and warned as to future conduct following violations of Codes 3 and 5.	D B Carr
Severely reprimanded and warned as to future conduct following violations of Codes 3 and 5.	D B Carr
Dissent against his dismissal. Severe reprimand.	P Burge
Dissent against rejection of bat/pad catch. Severe reprimand.	S Venkat
Dissent against team mates' lbw decisions. Fined 25% of match fee.	J L Hendricks
Second offence in match. Dissent against his lbw decision. Fined a further 40% of match fee.	J L Hendricks
Verbal abuse of SA batsman. Fined 10% of match fee and severely reprimanded.	D Carr
Verbal abuse of SA batsman. Fined 10% match fee and severely reprimanded.	D Carr
Breach of Article 2 for knocking a stump out of ground after being bowled. Fined US$1500.	J R Reid
Dissent against catch not given. Fined US$750 and one match suspension.	A M Ebrahim
Breach of Codes 2 & 5. Fined US$350.	A M Ebrahim
Breach of Code 3 – showed dissent at umpire's decision re. lbw. Fined 50% of match fee.	P J Burge
Breach of Code 3 – showed dissent at umpire's decision re. caught behind appeal turned down. Fined 25% of match fee.	P J Burge
Dissent against rejection of caught behind appeal. Severe reprimand.	J R Reid

Guy Whittal	Zimb v Sri Lanka, 1st Test at Harare, 11–16 Oct 1994
Brian Lara	WI v NZ, One-Day International at Goa, India 26 Oct 1994
Phil Tufnell	Eng v Aus 'A', One-Day International at MCG, 13 Dec 1994
Arjuna Ranatunga	Sri Lanka v NZ, at East London, 18 Dec 1994
Ken Rutherford	NZ v Sri Lanka, at East London, 18 Dec 1994
Ken Rutherford	NZ v SA, 4th Test at Cape Town, 2–6 Jan 1995
David Richardson	SA v Pak, 1st One-Day Final at Newlands, 10 Jan 1995
Chris Lewis	Eng v Aus, 4th Test at Adelaide, 26–30 Jan 1995
David Houghton	Zimb v Pak, 2nd Test at Bulawayo, 7–12 Feb 1995
Salim Malik	Zimb v Pak, 3rd Test at Harare, 15–20 Feb 1995
Aamir Sohail	Zimb v Pak, 3rd Test at Harare 15–20 Feb 1995
Brian Strang	Zimb v Pak, 2nd One-Day Inmternational, Harare 25 Feb 1995
Greg Blewitt	Aus v India, One-Day International at Dunedin, 22 Feb 1995
Shane Warne	Aus v India, One-Day International at Dunedin, 22 Feb 1995
Kerry Walmsley	NZ v Sri Lanka, 1st Test at Napier, 10–15 March 1995
Aamir Nazir	India v Sri Lanka, Asia Cup ODI, Sharjah, 11 April 1995
Nayan Mongia	India v Sri Lanka Asia Cup ODI, Sharjah, 11 April 1995

Breach of Code 3 – showed dissent at umpire's decision after being given out caught behind. Fined 25% of match fee.	P van der Merwe
Breach of Code 3 – showed dissent after being given out stumped. Fined 50% of match fee, suspended for next match in triangular competition and severe reprimand.	R Subba Row
Breach of Codes 2 and 3 – bringing game into disrepute by throwing ball in aggressive manner after caught behind appeal turned down. Fined 30% of match fee.	J R Reid
Breach of Code 3 – showed dissent after being given out caught behind by indicating that the ball came off his pad. Fined 25% of match fee.	P J Burge
Breach of Code 4 – attempted to intimidate umpire by moving towards him with hands raised shouting 'that's out'. Fined 50% of match fee.	P J Burge
Breach of Codes 2 and 3 – clear dissent at umpire's decision after being given out lbw. Fined 75% of match fee + 2 match suspended sentence.	P J Burge
Violation of Code 2 – hit a stump out of ground after being given run out. Severe reprimand and 20% suspended match fee for remainder of series.	P J Burge
Breach of Codes 2 and 4 – after dismissing Craig McDermott he 'gestured' him to the pavilion 4 times.	J R Reid
Breach of Codes 3 and 8 – public comments made re umpires and conduct of Pakistan team on field. Fined 10% of match fee and reprimanded.	J L Hendricks
Breach of Codes 1, 2 and 4 – suggested that Ian Robinson, local umpire, had interfered with the ball during Zimbabwe's 1st innings. Fined 50% of match fee, 2 Test suspended suspension until 31 Dec 1995, and severely reprimanded.	J L Hendricks
Severe reprimand for similar comments as above about the same incident.	J L Hendricks
Pointed batsman to pavilion in contravention of Codes 2 and 5. Issued with caution.	J L Hendricks
Breach of ICC Regulation 7(c)(ii) – logo on wristband. Fined 15% of match fee.	P van der Merwe
Breach of ICC regulation 7(c)(ii) – logo on wristband. Fined 25% of match fee.	P van der Merwe
Breach of Code 2 – audible bad language on field of play. Reprimand.	B N Jarman
Breach of Code 5 – offensive gesture after dismissing S Jayasuriya. Severe reprimand.	C H Lloyd
Breach of Codes 3 & 4 – dissent and attempted intimidation of the umpire after appeal turned down. Find 10% of his match fee.	C H Lloyd

Index